Licensing in International Strategy

A Guide for Planning and Negotiations

FAROK J. CONTRACTOR

Q
Quorum Books
Westport, Connecticut • London, England

Library of Congress Cataloging in Publication Data

Contractor, Farok J.
  Licensing in international strategy.

  Bibliography: p.
  Includes index.
  1. Foreign licensing agreements—Cost effectiveness.
2. Technology transfer—Cost effectiveness. I. Title.
HF1429.C66   1985   658.1'8   84-22756
ISBN 0-89930-024-3 (lib. bdg.)

Library of Congress Catalog Card Number: 84-22756
ISBN: 0-89930-024-3

First published in 1985

Greenwood Press
A division of Congressional Information Service, Inc.
88 Post Road West
Westport, Connecticut 06881

Printed in the United States of America

The paper used in this book complies with the Permanent Paper Standard issued by the National
Information Standards Organization (Z39.48-1984).

10 9 8 7 6 5 4 3 2 1

Licensing in
International
Strategy

To Joan

Contents

Figures

Tables

Preface

My interest in technology transfer began when I was working for an Asian company. More than a fifth of the entire world's supply of hides and skins were potentially available in the region but most were either wasted or exported as raw hides to be processed into finished leathers in Europe, North America, and other consuming nations. It seemed natural to invest in a leather-finishing factory to add value to the product before it was exported.

As project manager I looked at two proposals. One was from a West German company offering to set up a complete turnkey plant, give operating manuals, and train our people for two months. The other alternative was for us to buy the machinery piece by piece ourselves. (The Germans had, after several requests, kindly provided us with a list of the equipment.) Adding up the total cost of the machinery bought individually by us, I was intrigued to find the total cost almost exactly half the West German offer. But the sum of the equipment is less than the whole of a production capability. We had no in-house expertise. I could not prudently recommend to higher management that we proceed on our own. On the other hand, the German offer now seemed unpalatably high after my calculations.

We eventually solved the dilemma elegantly, by forming a joint venture with a French firm, giving it the rights to market the leather in Europe; in return, they provided us with extensive production expertise and engineering assistance, "free of charge." There were several other benefits to this arrangement, such as the French firm providing us with fashion and marketing information we could not have obtained; these are not directly related to this book. This experience, however, was the beginning of my interest in the field of technology transfer. I later found that in every industry sector there could be enormous variations in the price of an international technology package involving a roughly similar end capability.

What could account for the variation in the international price of a technology? This was the question I addressed in my new life as an academic. One can find several explanatory factors such as the absorptive capacity of the technology-receiving firm and country, patent, and trademark coverage; territorial coverage; the life of an agreement; and so on. This search comprises my first book on international licensing, *International Technology Licensing: Compensation, Costs and Negotiation* (Lexington, Mass.: D. C. Heath & Co., 1981).

It became increasingly apparent to me that the price or value of a technology could not be divorced from the strategic context in which the industry, and specifically the licensor and licensee firm, operated. The even larger question was the role of a licensing program in the international operations of a company. This book is, in a sense, a continuation of the first. But instead of concentrating on the particular issue of pricing technology, it treats the broader matter of strategy and planning of a licensing program, alternative ways of organizing a department, how companies may choose between direct equity investment and pure licensing (or combinations thereof), how to plan for a coming negotiation with a licensee or joint venture partner, and so on.

This is a book not so much for the licensing specialist as for the corporate planner and strategy formulator, though I have attempted a balance of focus between the individual brush marks and the larger picture. There are, for instance, several detailed cases of licensing at the agreement and company level, as well as multicompany, cross-sectional samples, and analysis of aggregate data for the United States as a whole. The book concludes with a chapter on government regulation, its aims, and its limitations. But the bulk of the discussion is at the corporate level; much of the data were obtained directly from companies in the United States. And since the United States is overwhelmingly a seller or an exporter of technology to the rest of the world, the discussion does favor licensor considerations (though it is obvious that a prospective licensee may also learn a lot by inference or reversal).

I have tried to abstain from a philosophical predilection or bias of the kind one encounters in international forums when the subject of technology transfer is discussed. I do not subscribe, for instance, to the idea that technology is somehow a free good or that companies should part with their expertise for merely the incremental cost of transferring it to another firm. At the same time I believe many companies do themselves harm by being too hard-nosed in their zeal to retain technology within the firm or to share it only with majority-owned foreign affiliates. Several corporations whose policies formerly barred joint ventures and arm's-length licensing now allow these. The world has grown uncomfortably more complex in the last twenty years for the senior cadre of American executives who remember the pre-eminence of American commerce in the middle of this century, when the preferred and available method for expanding overseas was the 100 percent owned subsidiary.

Notwithstanding the current fashion to beat the breast about the international competitiveness of the United States, its eminence continues today in a great many industry sectors. If anything, there are more foreign firms eagerly seeking American technology today than ever before—but not on the old terms, that's the rub.

There are greater complexities and greater opportunities. Where a fully owned subsidiary would have been the automatic choice, today an American-based firm may find it expedient, even desirable, to link up with a local company as licensee or equity partner. Where a technology may have been safely licensed twenty years ago, today the licensing executive may have to worry about creating a global competitor later on. Not only are there today more prospective licensees (because companies even in the less-developed nations may have reached a level of competence in some industries where they can be independent licensees), but there are also more licensors. The British, the Germans, the French, and of course notoriously, the Japanese are now international sellers of technology. In short, what has emerged in the last decade is a global technology market, seen in the proliferation of licensing executive societies, consultants, brokers, fairs, and data banks. These are not yet very effective vehicles, but they are portents.

What is the role of licensing and contractual methods in this complex environment for international business? One of the significant themes of this book is that where a mere license may not make for an attractive enough return for a licensor, a larger contractual package, with the technology transfer as a centerpiece, often makes an attractive total. There is no getting around the fact that mere royalties of perhaps under 5 percent may not in some cases comprise adequate compensation for having passed on a valuable technology to a licensee. Instead of simply abandoning the idea of a license, as many companies regrettably do, formulating a more complex contract will often do the trick. For example, in the company I worked for, a pure licensing agreement could not be negotiated; later we thought of forming the marketing joint venture company to sell the finished leathers in Europe. The French were principally compensated by the opportunity to participate in the European sales company. In return, they provided technical, marketing, and fashion information which a royalty payment alone would not have covered—certainly not under the royalty ceiling laid down by the exporting country's government.

While the principal focus of this book remains licensing, it repeatedly alludes to the idea of using a license as a strategic wedge, of using the technology as the centerpiece around which other modes of business can be spun. Chapter 8 is specifically devoted to designing and negotiating hybrid arrangements that include a mix of licensing, equity investment, and international trade between licensor and licensee.

Textbooks on international business have been laggard in devoting enough space to these new forms. Traditional theory indicates three ways of getting a product into the hands of an overseas customer: (1) export the product to him, (2) manufacture in the country, or (3) license the technology and patent or trademark rights to a company in the territory, which will function as a licensee. Chapters 2 and 4 examine how a corporate strategist may choose between licensing and equity investment. Chapter 8, on the other hand, examines a situation where licensing, equity investment, and trade are combined into a single deal. Let us suppose a technology transfer is proposed, but mere royalties and licensee fees will not suffice to compensate the licensor. Adding to the technology transfer core, extra arrangements such as the licensor being given a small equity stake in the licensee firm or the licensor supplying a component to the licensee, will augment the value of the agreement sufficiently to make it acceptable to both parties. Little is known about the frequency with which such arrangements are used. Circumstantial evidence suggests they are growing in popularity in international business.

While written for the corporate planner or strategist, the tenor of the discussion is academic; the book is after all intended as a research monograph. It presents in Chapters 3, 6, and 7 statistical analysis of various data on licensing. The corporate reader may pass over the discussion of statistical results without losing the thread of the argument. Aggregate data for licensing income for the United States as a whole, broken down by country and industry, were obtained from publications of the U.S. Department of Commerce; additional detail was occasionally provided by them on request, for which I am grateful. I gathered corporate data on the licensing activity of forty-four firms directly by questionnaire and interview. I am thankful for their willingness to provide proprietary data often scattered in different parts of the firm. An international licensing program is best executed as a cooperative venture between the product division that "owns" the technology, the corporate headquarters licensing staff and patent attorneys, and the international division whose territorial and overseas strategy prerogatives will be affected by any agreement. Information sought for this research had to be collated from different parts of the same companies. As the reader will see in Chapter 6, it was not simply a matter of checking yes/no boxes. Many questions involved financial and operating data. I am grateful to the executives who took the trouble to gather the information. The Licensing Executives Society did not encourage this research; however, data from their 1982 technology transfer survey were used with permission, and this comprises the 241 company sample in Chapter 6. I am grateful to Mr. David Mugford of Schering-Plough Corporation for obtaining the Society's permission.

A few MBA students were lured away from their more lucrative pursuits to assist this effort. Dimitri Katsabekis and Joanne Wilkes helped in the data gathering and interviews. Gwo-Jeng Cherng is to be especially commended for his successful wrestlings with the balky and sprawling computer system at our university and for putting up with the innumerable data corrections, changes, and iterations—a surprisingly tall pile of printouts has built up in a corner of my office, all reduced finally to a mere seventy-odd tables and figures in this book.

Last, I must record the obligatory but so true debt to my family. My son's earliest memory will probably be that of his father hunched over a desk instead of playing ball or lounging on the deck—which is just as well I suppose. But the greater debt is to my wife Joan who with cheerful grace has accompanied me through career changes and migrations to distant lands. Since these experiences have inevitably seeped into this book to some extent, it is fitting that it be dedicated to her.

Licensing in International Strategy

1

Introduction:
Why Companies Engage in International Licensing

The foreign gross licensing income of U.S. companies exceeded $9 billion in 1984 and comprised a large and indispensable fraction of foreign profits. In strategy, licensing plays a variety of roles, ranging from being an incidental income source in some companies to the basic means of overseas expansion in others. Consider three examples: at the Chicago headquarters of a heavy agricultural and industrial equipment manufacturer, a corporate planner felt the place of licensing was quite minor. He described licensing income as "found money," implying that the company occasionally stumbles upon licensing opportunities abroad but does not actively seek them. A few miles away, however, at a consumer electronics company, licensing was described as the dominant, if not the only, viable international strategy. To their international manager, many global licensees dependent on their technical service, international brand name recognition, market network, and components provided a relatively low risk, steady income stream, not only from royalties but also from technical fees and margins on components supplied. This was seen as preferable to the risks and competition they would encounter in direct investments overseas in their industry. Besides, the company did not consider that it had sufficient managerial and financial resources to make equity investments in the large number of countries their product was sold in. Later, at one of Detroit's automobile makers, a patent attorney lamented his organization's neglect of salable technologies and overseas licensing opportunities. He believed the company could very easily generate a few million dollars of extra profits by taking an inventory of technical assets spread throughout the many divisions of the company. Indeed, every few years there would be drives to take stock of licensable technologies; but because the strategic focus was on producing automobiles on which revenues were so large, a few million dollars worth of extra profit opportunities were described as easily "falling between the cracks."

As these examples show, the strategy role and income contribution of licensing in international operations not only vary greatly from one firm to the next, but there is considerable room in many companies for generating extra income by formally organizing to market their technologies abroad. In the last five years, there is some evidence that this is being recognized. Licensing departments have been augmented in many companies. Perhaps more importantly, the inventorying of technical assets and the possibility of licensing as a foreign market entry method are increasingly factored into corporate strategy in a formal fashion. Externally, there is emerging an international technology market serviced by brokers, consultants, and technology data banks, as well as the conventional industry associations and licensing executives societies. Last, most observers agree that the international business environment has become somewhat more stringent for the traditional methods of expanding overseas, namely, equity investment or exporting, compared with the less-constrained post-war period which ended in the early 1970s. This makes licensing a more attractive alternative for companies like our consumer electronics manufacturer. For them, even if sufficient managerial and financial resources were available, in most nations the risk-adjusted present value of foreign equity investment might be lower than for licensing. Moreover, many of the countries they are represented in have turned slightly more protectionist, so that exporting is not a viable strategy, notwithstanding economies of scale derivable in a few large plants, from which the product can be shipped to several nations at a tolerable transportation cost.

Given the traditional and declared preference for direct equity investment as the desired method for entering overseas markets, at least in the larger and higher-technology U.S. firms, licensing already contributes a surprisingly large fraction of foreign income derived by American companies as a whole. For instance, in 1981 net licensing fees and royalties totaled about $7.3 billion compared with $9.5 billion in net foreign affiliate dividend income.[1] The place of licensing fees and royalties in total foreign income and its strategic role remain significant even after we account for the fact that a majority of licensing occurs between a U.S. company and its own foreign affiliates. While there are no accurate estimates on this issue, we have estimated in Chapter 3 that in 1981 about one-third of foreign licensing income was received from independent licensees and licensees in which the U.S. firm has less than a controlling interest, leaving two-thirds in net licensing income from majority foreign subsidiaries.[2]

In corporate strategy, licensing can thus be a complement and a substitute for direct equity investment. One may license an independent firm to earn royalties and technical fees. A company may also make its own equity affiliate a licensee, earning both dividends and licensing fees from it. In the foreign operations of U.S. firms, the latter, as we saw, is the more common pattern and the strategic considerations are quite different from licensing to arm's-length parties. In either case, the objective is to maximize the return on a technology from the nation or territory in question. When there is an equity stake, the repatriation of declared dividends of the foreign affiliate might appear to be sufficient means for extraction of a return to the parent firm until we realize how many constraints exist on this income channel. Licensing then provides not only an auxiliary channel but also has other important taxation and strategy ramifications. Royalties and fees may be set at the internal discretion of the multinational firm and not necessarily reflect the value of the technology transferred, as is more likely to be the case with arm's-length parties. The actual propensity of U.S. firms to use licensing agreements with affiliates as a transfer-pricing device is very much an open empirical question, especially now that more governments are moving toward disallowing the deductibility of royalties and technology fees paid by a company to its own parent.[3] However, G. Kopits did find a tax-induced bias in affiliate royalty determination.[4]

But even if the foreign tax treatment of royalties and dividends is, in effect, identical, there remain other important reasons for having a licensing agreement with one's affiliate. First, the U.S. Internal Revenue Service (IRS) often requires it, in part to tax the foreign fruits of R&D dollars originally spent in the United States. Tax law is not the purview of this book, but we may note in passing that under select conditions the repatriation of foreign income declared as royalties and licensing fees, if considered a return of capital, will attract a lower U.S. tax rate than dividends.[5] A second reason for earning both royalties and dividends from a foreign affiliate is the pragmatic matter of spreading the risk. The firm is better insulated against ordinary commercial, and the so-called political, risk. Since royalties are usually keyed to output, they are stable even when profits are zero, enabling some return from the business. Also, when day-to-day operations are in the hands of a local partner, royalties are much more easily audited and monitored than profits. Turning now to "political" risk, in the event of a foreign exchange crisis and controls on conversion of local currency, governments are likely to accord a somewhat higher priority to requests to repatriate royalties, as they are contractual commitments, than dividends, which may remain frozen. In the case of a nationalization or expropriation, there have been instances where the new owners, or the government, have offered to continue the licensing arrangement even when the equity of the enterprise has been taken over.

The main focus in this book, however, will be on licensing as a primary international strategy rather than as an adjunct or afterthought to an equity investment decision. Its principal focus will be on "licensing out," i.e., leasing or selling proprietary intangible assets for income, rather than "licensing in" or acquiring technology, which is a distinct strategy issue to be treated in a separate publication.

A BROADER STRATEGY ROLE FOR LICENSING

The way licensing is perceived determines its place in corporate strategy. We examine below different perspectives, ranging from its narrowest definition as the transfer of patents or trademarks, to its broadest role as the catalyst or core of a larger contractual package. The next section relates this to various economic theories of the international firm.

The Narrowest Definition: Transfer of Patent Rights and Trademarks

In the narrowest definition, a license is merely a permission given to another firm to engage in an activity otherwise legally forbidden to it. The concept flows from the fact that patents and trademarks are legally sanctioned monopolies or rights, proprietary to a company. These production and market rights are transferred to a licensee under an agreement for a consideration. A simple transfer of only a patent or a trademark to the licensee presumes, however, that the licensee is independently capable and merely awaits the conferral of the right to proceed on its own. Studies show that this is true only in a small minority of cases.[6] In an analysis of some 3,500 agreements registered at the European Economic Community (EEC) Commission's office in 1976, patents were included in 56 percent of them, together with "know-how" (which is unpatented but proprietary information in production, administration, and marketing) and other agreement provisions calling for training of licensee personnel or similar services. However, pure patent licenses were found in only a quarter of agreements and trademarks alone in only 4 percent.[7] Similarly, in my earlier study of 102 international agreements made by U.S.-based firms, patents were included in 63 percent, but were deemed crucial in only a tiny minority.[8] A 1982 survey of 259 companies by the Licensing Executives Society treated this question. Results shown in Table 1 support the view that, in an all-industry sense, while patents might well be part of many agreements, in a majority of cases know-how is of greater value to the licensee or technology recipient. Pure patent licensing occurs overall in about one of twenty agreements.[9] (In specific industries like pharmaceuticals or chemicals, however, patents assume greater importance. An industry breakdown, and other questions on international licensing treated by this survey are detailed in Chapter 6.)

A Broader Definition: The Transfer of Technology

The transfer of technology is the transfer of a capability in production, administration, or marketing. It includes (a) rights to the use of patented information and trademarks in certain territories abdicated by agreement in favor of the licensee; (b) information that is proprietory but not patented, commonly called know-how (this may take the form of specifications, models, drawings, manuals, forms, layouts, checklists, charts, computer programs and so on); and (c) services such as equipment installation, start-up, testing, training, recruitment, management development, etc. Most international licensing agreements, as we saw in Table 1, are in fact technology transfers in a fuller sense.

Licensors properly view the process as not merely the one-time act of transferring patent rights, but as a relationship with the other enterprise over time. Some agreements specifically provide for the transfer of new models, technical changes and updates, or more efficient procedures as long as the agreement remains valid, foreseeing the licensee's need for a continuing liaison with the

Table 1
The Content of Technology Transfers in International Licensing

The majority of your company's transfers involve:

	(#A) IN DEVELOPING COUNTRIES		IN INDUSTRIAL COUNTRIES	
	# of Companies	%[a]	# of Companies	%[a]
● Patent license/sale only	6	4.2	15	6.6
● Knowhow license/sale only	28	19.7	18	7.9
● Patent and knowhow license/sale only	67	47.2	150	66.0
● Trademark and knowhow license/sale only	24	16.9	27	11.9
● Manufacturing facility only	2	1.4	1	0.4
● Manufacturing facility and knowhow license/sale only	15	10.6	16	7.1
TOTAL OF RESPONSES[b]	142	100.0%	227	100.0%
NO AGREEMENTS IN THESE COUNTRIES[c]	117		32	
TOTAL COMPANIES RESPONDING	259		259	

Source: Technology Transfer Survey, Licensing Executive Society, 1982. The returns were analyzed by the author who takes responsibility for any errors in the above data or interpretation.

Notes:

a. The percentages refer only to companies that did respond to this question.

b. Of the total returns from 259 companies, 142 responded to this question as it related to their agreements in developing countries and 117 did not if they had no agreements in developing countries. Similarly 227 companies responded for agreements in industrial countries, with 32 companies having no agreements in this category of nations.

c. Responses on other questions suggest however that these two numbers (117 and 32 respectively) are slightly understated.

licensor firm. *Business International* relates instances in the early 1970s where East European firms, having purchased only patent rights from British companies, could not convert them into effective production and had to call back the technology suppliers for further assistance and training.[10] In general, my earlier study showed that the less developed or industrialized the country, the greater the incidence of attendant services that have to be provided to the licensee, as opposed to the mere patent or trademark right.[11] Formally, the statistical relationship is expressed in the regression equation

$$D_i = \beta_0 + \beta_1 G_i + \beta_2 H_i + \beta_3 J_i + \epsilon$$

D is the ratio of payments (made to U.S. licensors by licensees in country i, in the aggregate, in 1976) for intangible property rights alone over payments for both rights and attendant administrative, professional, and management services to accompany and facilitate the technology transfer. As hypothesized, this ratio for each country had (in a cross-sectional study of thirty-three nations) a positive relationship with G, the per capita GNP in 1975; with H the percentage of manufacturing in GDP; and with J the number of research scientists and engineers. The conclusion of the study is that there is a considerable variation in the technical absorptive capacity of nations. (The study also implied that in less-developed countries licensing may be a less effective method for technology transfer compared to equity investment which, by definition, calls for a greater, continuous commitment on the part of the technology supplier. Nevertheless, many countries prefer licensing, believing it to be cheaper for the nation compared to equity investment. Chapter 4 examines American companies' propensity to use licensing versus investment as a function of foreign country and industry characteristics).

The Broadest Perspective: Licensing as the Core of a Larger Contractual Package

Just as most international technology licensing agreements comprise considerably more than the conveyance of intellectual property rights to the licensee, the past decade has seen the growth of even more broadly defined contractual or "non-equity" agreements, where the technical license might constitute only the nucleus or catalyst of the whole arrangement.

These agreements are often tied to new projects. Their recent growth, particularly in developing countries, is at least partially attributable to the recycling of oil and commodity income through international banks and the general expansion of international credit.[12] For instance, while corporate direct investment in developing nations from seventeen leading Organization for Economic Cooperation and Development (OECD) countries (comprising its Development Assistance Committee) grew from $4.72 billion in 1973 to $12.74 billion in 1979, over the same interval net portfolio investment, mostly in private bank loans, grew from \$3.27 billion to \$23.45 billion. This does not include the considerable expansion of multilateral lending.[13] There are no data on what fraction of these loans have been project-specific. But there is no doubt of the increase in this category.

While typically including a technology license on which front-end fees and royalties are paid, a broader package might include any of the following elements: turnkey plant, supply of components to the licensee, contract assembly or production for third countries, guaranteed "off-take" or "buy-back" in lieu of cash, management service, marketing assistance, advertising support, and cross-licensing of technologies. An illuminating taxonomy is used by the French in describing agreements as "clef en main," "product en main," or "marché en main." The first is "key in hand" or turnkey, where the technology supplier's obligations cease after plant erection. In the second case, the technology supplier is required also to ensure effective production, through training or on-site personnel under a production management contract. In the "marché en main" or market-in-hand case, they are also required to market the product under a general management service agreement that renders marketing assistance or in the extreme by guaranteeing purchase of some fraction of output.

The use of a broader contractual package wrapped around a technology licensing core is one of the basic strategy recommendations of this book. Two of the principal objections to licensing can be overcome thereby, namely, inadequate compensation and the danger of possible loss of the technology and the creation of competition. Four important hypotheses or propositions are listed below. They will be treated more fully in later chapters.

The broader-based agreements are profitable where traditional licensing may not be. Let us return to the example of our Detroit-based automobile company. While their corporate strategy has neglected the licensing of their small process technologies (such as special paints, thermo-adhesion, or the use of microprocessors) despite a few million dollars' incremental profit opportunity, they do regard their agreements for license-cum-assembly of cars as important. The royalties themselves are rather modest, ranging in some countries to below a quarter of 1 percent of sales after a volume of a few thousand automobiles has been achieved by the licensee. The licensee, however, will buy considerable value in parts to be assembled. This is the substantial profit maker, especially in the early years before local component suppliers have been developed. Additionally, some or much of the assembly line equipment and dies are purchased from the licensor.

Control can be achieved without an equity position. There are several ways of wielding influence on the licensee. Among the common ones are leaving the licensee dependent for critical components, access to international markets, and future technical improvements. Of course, patents, when they exist, may be used, effectively, to restrict the licensee to a territory.[14] The use of a licensor's trademark in the foreign country will lock its consumers, and therefore the licensee, into its continued use, thereby enhancing the future leverage of the licensor when the agreement comes up for renewal. Trademarks, component supply, and technical improvements in new models have been essential elements in the successful licensing program of our U.S. consumer electronics manufacturer in more than twenty countries.

Undoubtedly, these have come under attack as "restrictive practices." Under current interpretation of U.S. antitrust law, territorial and field-of-use restrictions are not *per se* illegal for trademarks, patents, or even trade secrets.[15] Nor is purchasing components from the licensor as long as there is no prohibition of alternate procurement sources in the agreement. In less-developed countries (LDCs), such practices have been challenged, not so much in the courts, but *ex ante*, in newly enacted procedures for the registration of agreements, where the government may require modifications before the agreement is registered and has legal validity in the country.[16] This will be treated more fully in later chapters. Our electronics company has, however, grasped an essential fact: in most instances, the LDC licensee is more than willing to use their trade name, to buy their parts, and to introduce model changes because that makes for marketing success, especially in protectionist countries. Accordingly, in dealings with the government, the licensee's interests are allied with the licensor's, and whether written in the agreement or not, they will often seek to tie themselves in to these provisions.

In many nations licensing can be as profitable as direct investment. One often hears of the superiority of licensing on a return on investment (ROI) calculation.[17] The investment, or cost, incurred by licensors in transferring technology is far lower than a capital investment (though by no means negligible). Even if royalties and technical fees are usually smaller than dividends, the ROI figure is thus larger.[18] This is more true on an after-tax basis if, as we saw above, licensing returns incur effectively lower taxation as compared to dividends. But, of course, corporations are not so much in the business of seeking the highest ROIs as in seeking to maximize net present value (NPV) summed over all global markets or countries. Here it would appear that licensing, if it yields lower net cash flows, would be an inferior strategy. This book will argue, however, that there are many situations facing companies where a larger contractual package, carefully designed as to its short-term cash generation (and long-term consequences on the firm) can produce as attractive a NPV as a majority or fully owned subsidiary. Moreover, there are several good reasons to use a smaller discount factor in evaluating licensing proposals, such as its lower environmental, i.e., political and convertibility risk, as well as the inherently lower volatility or variance of royalties in contractual payments. There are several cases where the earnings of foreign affiliates of U.S. companies have not only been "smoothed out" by licensing income, but in a few years licensing has comprised the bulk of repatriated foreign income. For the U.S. economy as a whole this is illustrated vividly in the last economic downturn. The Commerce Department reported that in 1981 foreign affiliate dividends (net, after foreign withholding taxes) amounting to $9.5 billion, represented a decline of 12 percent from 1980. "Direct investment income,'' defined as affiliates' earnings plus interest on intra-company loans (net, after foreign withholding taxes on dividends and interest) declined by 14 percent.[19] In the manufacturing sector the decline in income was 26 percent. By contrast, net receipts of fees and royalties grew slightly to total $7.2 billion in 1981. (See Table 7 in Chapter 3.) In general, the more risk-averse the company, the more it will tend toward the licensing option, *ceteris paribus*; that is to say, all other things being equal.

Another perspective on licensing's contribution to global profits is provided by returning to the example of the auto producer. In their corporate planning, a scan of all countries creates a list ranked according to various criteria such as political risk or size of car market. If, as some companies still do, they had adopted a smug policy of international expansion via only majority or fully owned affiliates, a great many countries in the middle and lower rankings would have been ruled out altogether. Certainly, some of these can continue to be supplied by imports, but tariffs, transport costs, quotas, and locally based competition would rule out this option in many nations. As it is, selective licensing-cum-assembly agreements contribute significant additional income to the global total. By careful selection and monitoring, two important fears or drawbacks, moreover, are minimized. First, by refusing licensees the use of their brand name, the fear of an inferior product hurting their image is eliminated. (This is in interesting contrast to our electronics company which promotes trademark licensing for quite a different strategy purpose.) Second, by licensing only particular models to technologically or financially inferior companies, or only in small territories with higher costs, the fear of present or future licensee competition is minimal. In short, these countries begin to yield cash flows that could not have been obtained by across-the-board policies of direct-investment-based operations. This is one of the theses of this book—many U.S. firms are neglecting incremental profit opportunities from licensing. Even if licensing were never to supplant equity investment (and this book does not propose that it will in the aggregate for the U.S. economy), it can still play an important selective role from the simple fact that the financial or managerial resources of even the largest companies can be stretched only so far to cover direct investment opportunities. The administrative, technical, and financial commitment required for a licensing program is by contrast small. But it requires careful organization and a commitment from the highest levels to have a licensing group do more than earn its keep several times over, which is easy. This is to say that while it is rather easy to generate high ROIs from licensing, it takes considerable organizational effort to have the program generate net cash flows to rival those from direct investments abroad. Chapter 7 treats the organizational issues, describing alternative designs of licensing groups as a function of the company's structure, diversification, industry maturity, and so on.

The global business climate has become more stringent vis-à-vis equity investment. In a ranking of markets in terms of their attractiveness as foreign investment locations, going down the list we hypothesized that the corporate planner would begin to encounter nations where licensing was an equally attractive option for some of the firm's technologies.[20] Toward the bottom of the list of course, one would encounter COMECON (Council for Mutual Economic Assistance) or socialist countries where no majority equity investment is usually possible and where licensing is often the only market entry method possible. Moreover the global business environment for investment has grown more stringent in general, that is, in both the emerging developing countries as well as the traditional advanced markets of Western Europe or Canada. On balance, licensing opportunities will appear attractive somewhat more frequently than in the past and in more nations than in the past. This is hardly saying that U.S. foreign investment will decline or even stop growing. It will not. The hypothesis is simply that the time is approaching for licensing or non-equity modes to play more than the minor or incidental role they have assumed hitherto in international strategy. Chapter 5 examines some of these changes in the last decade in the regulatory and competitive areas.

LICENSING IN SMALLER COMPANIES

Licensing is a particularly attractive strategy for smaller companies. Its dangers are also greater for smaller firms. For companies with sales below $100 million, equity investment becomes difficult in the best of foreign environments. Two factors are involved: there is often a constraint on investment capital but, perhaps more importantly, on management expertise. The opportunity cost, and hence the value of key managers, is greater for a smaller company. And foreign investments require the best a company can offer. Second, to the small or medium-sized firm, an additional investment, especially overseas, is a greater risk simply because it represents a substantial percentage of total assets. Exporting where feasible does not put any foreign capital assets at stake although for a concerted long-range program it requires a large expenditure on promotion and market development. Particularly for companies under $25 million in sales, licensing often seems to be the only viable foreign option—a means of generating income overseas without too large an incremental expenditure. Chapter 6 describes the case of a small New Jersey company with about $25 to $30 million turnover, a third of it in foreign licensing income, and illustrates a highly successful program in a small firm.

Yet for every successful program in a small U.S. business, there seems to be another story of plans gone awry, of proprietors and shareholders regretting the licensing decision. (There is very little empirical work in international licensing to start with, and, apart from case studies, no comprehensive data on small company licensing exist at all except for the data analyzed later in this book). Without advance planning, the drawbacks of licensing for small businesses can be painful indeed. We have defined the two principal ones as inadequate compensation for value transferred and creating competition. There are many cases of U.S. firms signing straight royalty agreements, without other income-producing features, without adequate thought as to territorial coverage or duration, and without consideration of the licensee's capabilities. At the time of signing the agreement, even a modest royalty percentage appears adequate since the company has expended practically nothing incremental on the deal. Later it may be discovered that the licensee has generated handsome annual sales which, of course, generate royalties. But in retrospect the total of royalties appears very inadequate compensation for the abdication of the foreign market for the duration of the agreement. Worse yet, the technology transfer may have so strengthened the licensees that they can effectively shut out the licensor even after its expiry. Small and medium-sized firms are particularly susceptible to this threat and are less likely to devise an appropriate package to compensate them for such an eventuality or forestall it with strategies such as obtaining patent and trademark coverage abroad.

NOTES

1. Whichard, O., "U.S. Direct Investment Abroad in 1981," *Survey of Current Business*, August 1982, pp. 11–29. To the $5.9 billion in net receipts of fees and royalties from affiliates, about $1.3 billion from independent licensees is added, making a total of about $7.2 billion. The Commerce Department's definition of "affiliates" is, however, rather broad (10 percent or more equity share) so that some of the $5.9 billion is paid by joint ventures that are effectively arm's-length foreign licensees.

2. This estimate is based on extrapolations from the last Benchmark Survey: U.S. Department of Commerce, *U.S. Direct Investment Abroad, 1977* (Washington, D.C.: U.S. Government Printing Office, 1981).

3. See Sato, M., and Bird, R., "International Aspects of the Taxation of Corporations and Shareholders," IMF Staff Paper no. 22, July 1975.

4. Kopits, G., "Intra-firm Royalties Crossing Frontiers and Transfer-Pricing Behavior," *The Economic Journal*, December 1976, pp. 791–803.

5. An excellent review for the non-specialist executive may be found in Finnegan, M., and McCarthy, R., "U.S. Tax Considerations in International Technology Transfers," *Licensing Law and Business Report*, April 1979, pp. 101–112, and May 1979, pp. 113–119.

6. Some of the earlier studies of international licensing include Lovell, E., *Appraising Foreign Licensing Performance* (New York: Conference Board, 1969); and Lightman, J., "Compensation Patterns in U.S. Foreign Licensing," *IDEA*, Spring 1970, pp. 1–26.

7. See UNIDO, *National Approaches to the Acquisition of Technology* (New York: United Nations, 1977).

8. Contractor, F., *International Technology Licensing: Compensation, Costs and Negotiation* (Lexington, Mass.: D.C. Heath & Co., 1981).

9. This was specifically addressed in a survey of forty firms having 4,055 unaffiliated foreign licensees by Bleeke, J., and Rahl, J., "The Value of Territorial and Field-of-Use Restrictions in the International Licensing of Unpatented Knowhow: An Empirical Study," *Northwestern Journal of International Law and Business*, Fall 1979, pp. 450–483. Of thirty-five firms having 1,606 combination patent and know-how agreements, "only 9 firms with 297 (18%) of the total combination licenses indicated that more than half of the revenue . . . may be attributed to the patent component," p. 461.

10. Business International, *Doing Business with Eastern Europe* (Geneva: Business International Corp., 1972).

11. Contractor, F., "The Composition of Licensing Fees and Arrangements as a Function of Economic Development of Technology Recipient Nations," *Journal of International Business Studies*, Winter 1980, pp. 47–62.

12. Billerbeck, K., and Yasugi, Y., *Private Direct Foreign Investment in Developing Countries*, World Bank Staff Working Paper no. 348 (Washington, D.C.: World Bank, 1979).

13. These are net current dollar amounts. The Development Assistance Committee nations are the United States, United Kingdom, Canada, West Germany, France, Japan, Australia, Austria, Belgium, Denmark, Finland, Italy, Netherlands, New Zealand, Norway, Sweden, and Switzerland.

14. This is legal, even under the stricter interpretation of U.S. laws, as long as the territorial restraints do not have the effect of restraining an activity outside the scope of the patent. See U.S. Department of Justice, *Antitrust Guide for International Operations* (Washington, D.C.: U.S. Government Printing Office, 1977).

15. The situation is delicate for process patents which may not be used to prohibit the sale of unpatented products, after *United States* v. *Studiengesellschaft*, G.m.b.H., in 1978. See also Brunsvold, B., and Farabow, F., "The Impact of Antitrust Laws on International Licensing," *Licensing Law and Business Report*, October 1978, pp. 41–52.

16. An example is Mexico: "Law on the Control and Registration of Transfer of Technology and the Use and Exploitation of Patents and Trademarks of December 29th, 1981," *Diario Oficial*, January 11, 1982.

17. For instance, McNamee, B., "A Primer on Patent, Trademark and Knowhow Licensing," *MSU Business Topics*, Summer 1970, pp. 14–22.

18. In the author's earlier study, *International Technology Licensing*, in a 1978 sample of 102 international agreements representative of U.S. licensing in general, licensors' costs in negotiations and meeting their agreement obligations averaged some $200,000 over the agreement life. This is corroborated in Teece, D., *The Multinational Corporation and the Resource Cost of International Technology Transfer* (Cambridge, Mass.: Ballinger, 1977). In comparing licensing and investment as options for a particular technology-country combination, we may ignore the otherwise important question of amortizing R&D costs and other central overhead, treating either cash flow projection on an incremental revenue and incremental expense basis.

19. Whichard, "U.S. Direct Investment Abroad in 1981," pp. 17–19. Data on "non-affiliated" licensing fees and royalties were obtained directly by correspondence and added to the figure for affiliate fees and royalties.

20. There are a number of ranking or country-scanning models used by multinational banks and consultants such as Business International. See Business International, *Managing and Evaluating Country Risk* (New York: Business International Corp., 1981). Statistical analysis relating the business method to environmental or country variables is found in Goodnow, J., and Hansz, J., "Environmental Determinants of Overseas Market Entry Strategies," *Journal of International Business Studies*, Spring 1972, pp. 33–50. For the non-specialist reader a detailed analysis of overseas business options is Root, F., *Foreign Market Entry Strategies* (New York: AMACOM, 1982). A classic primer, as an introduction, is Stobaugh, R., "How to Analyze Foreign Investment Climates," *Harvard Business Review*, September-October 1969, pp. 100–108.

2

Licensing in the Theory of the International Firm

A specific treatment of licensing in theories of the international firm is a relatively recent phenomenon dating to the late 1970s. Most previous work treats the choice between exporting and direct foreign investment. In all cases, the objective is to deliver a product into the hands of a buyer in a foreign market. Producing in the foreign market under direct investment or licensing eliminates the transport and tariff costs associated with the export strategy. Instead, it creates an international technology transfer cost. (To this we must of course add the cost of production, marketing, and administration in that location.) So far, focusing only on costs, we have not treated two other crucial aspects—the ownership of the company in that nation and the revenues that can be earned on the product. As we shall see, even for the same product, revenues earned are a function of the ownership of the operation. In pure arm's-length licensing, the ownership of the physical plant and organization remain with the local licensee firm which in strict legality does not "own," but licenses, the technology. In a direct investment, the foreign firm owns both the company and the technology.

A FRAMEWORK FOR STRATEGY DECISIONS

A schematic representation of international technology transfer costs and compensation under either licensing or direct investment is shown in Figure 1. Conceptually, there are five distinct types of costs that the strategist should account for and two categories of return. The costs are neither incurred in the same location nor over the same periods of time. When referring to costs and returns, we should take that to mean their present values over their relevant time horizon as indicated in Figure 1. Moreover, the unit of measurement is not the product but the technology.

On a technology developed by the firm, it will seek to maximize the present

Figure 1
Schematic of International Technology Transfer Costs and
Compensation in Either Licensing or Direct Investment

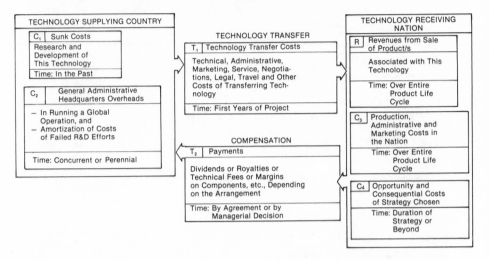

value of global profits. For simplicity let us initially assume that international markets or countries are segmented. If so, the strategic objective is to maximize profit in each country. But how to measure this profit properly from a long-term strategy point of view is the subject of the following discussion.

The sunk costs, C_1, are the past research and developmental expenditures on this technology. We may assume they were all incurred in the technology-supplying firm's home country; although increasingly the R&D function itself is being internationalized.[1] While these costs are sunk, i.e., they should not influence future negotiations with a prospective licensee or future strategy formulation, it is clear that, in general, a technology-creating firm would wish to recover these costs from global sales of the product (otherwise, it cannot long remain in business or generate further technologies).

Similarly, in the long if not the short run, and over all technologies and markets, the international firm must also sustain general headquarters overheads, C_2, which include the R&D costs of technologies that never came to commercial fruition. Where C_1 is the present value of research costs associated with the particular technology in question over a finite time interval, the general administrative and research overheads are perennial costs. Theoretically speaking, C_2 is the sum of their present values till infinity.

In classical economics, technology was viewed as readily digestible information, akin to a freely available public good, and its transfer was thought to be costless.[2] Of course this is not true in practice. D. Teece and F. Contractor measured significant costs merely to transfer technology between countries.[3] In our definition, transfer costs, T_1, are only those costs associated with transferring the technology to the foreign affiliate or licensee. They are specific to a technology, the nation, and the recipient firm. They comprise expenditures on technical matters such as engineering, blueprints, manuals, models, installation, plant erection for the licensee or affiliate, training of personnel, devising procedures and specifications, quality and prototype testing, etc.; on legal matters such as patent and trademark registration and enforcement in the nation, drawing up a technology agreement, etc.; on marketing and managerial assistance given to the other firm; on travel, negotiation, and management time specifically associated with the technology transfer; and last, on any other costs that the technology supplier bears to effectuate the transfer. T_1 is the present value of all such costs which are mostly incurred in the early years. Transfer costs may be incurred in either country. If our unit of measurement is a technology (assuming the firm has several), then C_1 is the cost of producing it, whereas T_1 is the cost of reproducing it in the foreign location—that is to say, its variable cost.

Once the technology is transferred, a product or products are sold and revenues, R, earned in the nation. (Alternatively, in the case of more efficient techniques or improvements on existing products, instead of new revenues, we consider the value of cost savings derived from the improvement.) C_3 represents the present value of the production, marketing, and administrative costs in the nation, specific to the products associated with this technology. Both R and C_3 have as their time horizon the product life cycle in the country and $(R - C_3)$ is the margin earned on the products.

C_4 is the opportunity and consequential costs of the ownership strategy chosen. The opportunity cost of a strategy is the profit on business that would have occurred were it not for implementing this strategy. For example, an exclusive license granted may eliminate existing exports to that nation and the profit that could have been earned on them for the duration of the license. If other investments exist in the nation, a licensing agreement may also detract from them. We can say in general that opportunity costs are more likely to exist with licensing or joint ventures than with fully owned subsidiaries which presumably would be instructed not to intrude upon other business opportunities. Moreover, these costs exist as long as the arrangement, and possibly beyond, if the licensee or joint-venture partner emerges as a formidable competitor even after expiration of the agreement. Exactly similar events may occur in other national markets if a license has the consequence of creating a multinational competitor in the licensee. The cost to the technology supplier is once again the lost profits on sales otherwise made. Some would prefer, however, to label these as consequential, and not opportunity costs, although the underlying concept is the same.

For the five types of costs borne by the technology supplying company, compensation T_2 is expected. This can be in the shape of royalties, lump-sum or per diem fees, etc., in the case of a licensing agreement over its specified life. Or compensation can be earned in the shape of the repatriated portion of earnings from an equity stake, which is naturally of indefinite duration. Additionally, there are other minor categories of compensation such as profit margins on components, products bought or sold to the company, tax savings at head-quarters, the shared fruits of foreign research, and so on.

The Basic Conditions for International Technology Transfer

Let us examine the basic conditions for technology transfer that flow from the above schema for either licensing or investment. Only later will we extend the argument to the act of choosing between them.

a. $R - C_3$ is the local margin obtained from the sale of the products in the nation. This margin is to be applied toward the remaining four costs, C_4, T_1, C_1 and C_2. Moreover, it is axiomatic that $T_2 \leq R - C_3$, i.e., the payment extracted from the nation cannot exceed $R - C_3$. (The only possible exception to this statement is when T_2 is defined to include markups earned by the technology-supplying firm outside the host nation, on materials or components bought or sold to the licensee or affiliate.)

b. $T_2 - T_1$ is the international or cross-border margin obtained from the technology as a whole, from the recipient nation. Ideally, the supplier company would like to see

$$T_2 \geq (T_1 + C_4) + \alpha_i C_1 + \alpha_{ij} C_2$$

where α_i is the share of this product's sales in nation i out of global sales of the product ($i = 1, 2 \ldots n$ nations the product is sold in) and where α_{ij} is the share of the product's sales in nation i out of global sales of all the firm's products ($j = 1, 2 \ldots p$ products). That is to say, they would like to have the compensation T_2 drawn from the nation cover the transfer costs T_1, the opportunity or consequential costs C_4, and furthermore also partially contribute toward costs C_1 and C_2. Here α_i and α_{ij} are some fractions (of costs C_1 and C_2, respectively). T_2 need only partially contribute toward C_1 and C_2 because, after all, the same technology will also have been transferred to and be earning a margin in other nations, i.e., cost C_1 for this technology is spread over several nations. Cost C_2, however, is not only spread over many nations, but also over all the company's technologies and markets. As opposed to this corporate desire, in some countries the margin actually available on a technology ($T_2 - T_1$) may not be very much greater than zero, i.e., $T_2 = T_1$.

c. $T_2 = T_1$ is the absolute minimum precondition for technology transfer, and an outcome desired by some governments in recipient nations, i.e., technology transferred at a compensation equal to only its transfer or variable cost. Some socialist and developing countries took this position in the recent United Nations debates. By imposing ceilings and controls on royalties, dividends, and other direct payments they are attempting to move toward this condition or at least lower the margin ($T_2 - T_1$).[4] In the Ricardian economics view, any excess of T_2 over T_1, or R over C_3 for that matter, is called a monopoly rent. In the Schumpeterian economics view, however, $T_2 - T_1$ is not rent but a necessary contribution toward C_1, C_2, and C_4—perhaps not necessary for any one particular deal but certainly necessary for the firm's survival in the long run.[5]

d. $(T_2 - T_1 - C_4)$, which we define as the "net technology margin," ought to be the focus of the strategy planner. A focus only on the net direct cash flow ($T_2 - T_1$) can lead to wrong decisions, particularly in companies with an international division or licensing department as a separate profit center to which ($T_2 - T_1$) accrues, while the opportunity costs C_4 are borne by the concerned product division. This organizational problem is treated in a later chapter. We may note in passing here that ($T_2 - T_1$) is directly measurable and the international group may be eager for it to accrue to them, whereas C_4 is more difficult to quantify and the product division may, in the extreme case, not even be aware of this cost until after the international group has already committed the company and it is too late.[6] Clearly, somewhere in the company the overall picture has to be obtained by estimating the net technology margin $(T_2 - T_1 - C_4)$. This is the focus of the next section where we ask, "Under what conditions will licensing produce a higher or equivalent margin compared to direct equity investment?"

WHAT THEORY SAYS ABOUT THE CHOICE BETWEEN LICENSING AND INVESTMENT

A priori, one may ask why the risk-adjusted net technology margin $(T_2 - T_1 - C_4)$ from a licensing agreement cannot be as high as or higher than the net margin from direct investment.[7] Indeed, in several instances, it must; otherwise, we would not have arm's-length licensing. Theory, however, suggests that it would be the preferred choice in only a minority of situations. Why? There are four related strands in the argument.

Transfer Costs T_1

The first strand of argument deals with the cost of transferring the technology. The transactions cost approach to the theory of the firm germinated by R. Coase, and recently elaborated by O. Williamson, has now been extended to the international company.[8] We can apply Coase's words equally well to international expansion via an extra subsidiary within the firm or via a technology "market" transaction with another firm as licensee:

A firm will tend to expand until the costs of organizing an extra transaction within the firm become equal to the costs of carrying out the same transaction by means of exchange on the open market or the costs of organizing in another firm.[9]

In most cases, M. Casson and others argue that transfer costs T_1 will be higher in licensing than in an internal transfer to an equity affiliate.[10] Technical information is akin to a public good only in the sense that its use in one location does not diminish its stock or availability in another. But its transfer is not costless because technology transfer is not the transfer of only codified information in patents, manuals, blueprints, and so on. Rather, it is the transfer of a production and distribution capability which may also require interpersonal contacts of a long duration. Technology may be embodied in documentation or in people, but it can also be embodied in organizations as a whole, their cultures, their established procedures, and their "ways of doing things." Thus, the very act of transferring this capability to another country can be expensive and perhaps even partially successful. Both Teece and Contractor have measured international transfer costs and found them far from small.[11] Moreover, they are likely to be higher in licensing because of the technological inferiority of the licensee and the latter's unfamiliarity with the technical or administrative standards and procedures.[12] (The fact that a license exists does not necessarily imply inferiority of the licensee in all instances. After all, two companies may be technically equal, but one cannot produce without a license because the other has an ironclad patent. But we saw in Chapter 1 that pure patent licenses are very infrequent and that most licenses involve know-how. This leads to the conclusion that most agreements are predicated on the licensee's need for assistance.)

An element of "transfer costs," T_1, not present when establishing a fully owned subsidiary but significant in licensing, is the cost of negotiating an agreement. This can be large because of "informational asymmetries."[13] The licensee as the less-informed party has to be educated as to the value of the technology without, paradoxically, revealing too much. This is usually a protracted and costly affair for the prospective licensor. Yet other elements of transfer cost that may not be present when dealing with an equity affiliate are the legal cost of the license agreement, patent filing, and enforcement, if any.

In brief, theory would say that transfer costs T_1 in licensing are likely to be higher; but they begin to approach the transfer costs of direct investment when the technology is standardized, codified, and easy to assimilate. Transfer costs are also lower if the recipient company is technologically on a par with the supplier firm, other things being equal.

The Product Revenues: R

The second strand of theory deals with the so-called monopoly power of the international firm in product markets overseas. The focus here is on the product revenues R. A venerable body of literature going back to R. Caves and S. Hymer has argued that, everything else being equal, the international firm is able to command higher prices compared to local competition (or in our argument, compared with a local licensee making an equivalent item).[14] A variety of reasons are enumerated, such as superior product quality, xenophilia on the part of consumers, superior organization, international brand recognition, and so on. These need not detain us here; but the point is, for the same production and distribution costs C_3, revenues R may well be higher in one's own subsidiary than those commanded by a licensee. (Incidentally, there is some evidence from my earlier study that licensees typically operate at smaller scale of production compared to the licensor's global average plant size.[15] This suggests that C_3 itself may well be higher for a licensee.) All in all $(R - C_3)$, the margin earned in the product market is likely to be higher in direct investment compared with the margin earned by a licensee—and after all, a licensee can pay the licensor only a share out of the product margin.

The Returns from a Country: T_2

The third strand of theory deals with the appropriability or extraction of returns from the foreign country. The focus here is on T_2, the cross-border compensation flow under licensing or direct investment. A licensor's problem is to try and restrict the licensee's share of local margin to a normal return on entrepreneurial investment, while appropriating the profit on the technology for themselves. Even in a fully owned subsidiary of course, the repatriated dividends are only a fraction of local profits, that is to say $T_2 \leq R - C_3$, but there is no problem of negotiating with an arm's-length party, which can be a vexing affair. A licensing agreement involves the negotiated apportionment of the margin $(R - C_3)$ between the two parties, in a relationship akin to a bilateral monopoly, with no theoretically prescribed equilibrium or determinate solution.[16] A prospective licensee usually places a higher uncertainty, and lower value, on the technology because of relative (or in some cases absolute) ignorance, so as to offer license fees below the repatriable profit that may be earned by an equity investment. Dividends, unlike licensing payments, are not constrained by an agreement formula nor are they of limited duration. Last, Casson suggests another constraint on licensing compensation, namely, the possibility that licensing the same technology in several countries puts pressure on the licensor to move to a uniform price for all licensees, which is sub-optimal compared to the discriminatory compensation possible in a global equity-investment strategy.[17]

Opportunity Costs: C_4

The percentage of international licensing agreements on an exclusive versus non-exclusive basis is unknown. By definition, an exclusive license is an abdication of the market in favor of the licensee. Nevertheless, all agreements have the consequence of creating, to a degree, some competition, which may in certain cases exist beyond agreement expiry. As we shall see later, in practice, licensors have a number of ways to curtail effectively this threat, but, in theory at least, opportunity costs are likely to be higher in licensing than in a controlled equity investment.

To summarize, the net technology margin extracted from a country $(T_2 - T_1 - C_4)$ is held by theory to be more often than not lower in licensing than from a company's own subsidiary because returns T_2 from licensing are likely to be lower, while transfer costs T_1 and opportunity costs C_4 are usually higher. In short, *a priori* reasoning would describe licensing as a strategy inferior to direct investment.

THEORY VERSUS PRACTICE: WHEN IS LICENSING FEASIBLE OR SUPERIOR TO EQUITY INVESTMENT?

In our theoretical reasoning we have used the words "usually" or "likely" to describe the corporate preference for direct investment and we conditioned the statements with the economist's favorite phrase "other things being equal." But of course when we consider the wide spectrum of industries, and the even wider variation among foreign markets, the "other things" do not remain the same, and licensing is often found attractive.

For instance, when a technology is easily assimilated by a licensee, which may occur because it is well defined, simple, mature, or standardized, transfer costs need not be appreciably greater in licensing. On the revenue side, in industries experiencing considerable price-based competition such as television receivers or steel, the appropriable product revenues R may have declined to an industry standard, making investment less attractive and the returns extracted from the market, T_2, more or less equal when licensing or investing. Take certain situations in the pharmaceutical industry: two firms may be technologically equally proficient but dominate different markets. One has a patent or proprietary formulation that can be very easily understood by the other, making licensing easy and transfer costs negligible. Licensing, with generous fees and royalties, may then be preferable to the large cost and risks of foreign investment in a market dominated by the other company.

Some of these considerations are illustrated in the case of ibuprofen, an antiarthritis drug sold in the United States by Upjohn Company under the brand name "Motrin." Ibuprofen was originally developed in Britain by an affiliate of Boots Company, which licensed it to Upjohn rather than invest in producing it in the United States. It was not simply a matter of production costs in the United States. More crucially, in prescription items it is the cost, time, and volume needed to build a reputation and presence with doctors who will recommend a particular company's brands. Boots, being a smaller foreign organization did not have these but Upjohn did.[18] Licensing to Upjohn would involve very little transfer cost and, in this situation, no opportunity costs to Boots. By contrast, to produce and establish a market presence *de novo* in the United States would be an expensive investment for one or a small range of products. To Upjohn it would only be one more item added on to an existing sales organization. In such a case, the technology owner must have found that the margin from a licensing strategy in the U.S. market can be superior to direct investment. Accordingly, Upjohn was signed on as licensee. (An interesting sequel to this case, illustrating other aspects of strategy, is described in an appendix to this chapter.)

We return to a theme of this book, that the choice between licensing and alternative strategies is a shifting and dynamic balance—it shifts from one industry to another, it shifts over a product's life cycle, and it shifts to favor licensing and contractual methods as the climate for investment gets more restrictive or competitive, not only in a cross-sectional sense (i.e., across countries) but also over time. The changing environment for international business, and how it affects the strategy choice, is discussed in Chapter 5.

APPENDIX

The Ibuprofen Case

In an interesting sequel to the case, in 1981 Boots won a court battle with Upjohn, allowing it to sell ibuprofen in the United States in competition with them, under the Boots brand name, "Rufen."[19] (Upjohn was their own original licensee.) So established, however, was Upjohn's marketing network that "Rufen" could gain only an 18 percent market share despite lower prices and rebate coupons. "We can tell doctors until we're blue in the face that they can save patients money by prescribing our product," said John Bryer, president of Boots, illustrating the lack of price-based competition in prescription items and a new entrant's difficulties in gaining market share. In a novel and controversial move, Boots now became established in Louisiana and initiated a TV campaign aimed directly at users who were expected to respond to a lower price signal and have the temerity to ask their doctor to prescribe "Rufen" instead of Upjohn's costlier "Motrin."

The case illustrates some points about licensing strategy. First, licensing can be used to "test" a foreign market for possible subsequent entry by the licensor, although there is no evidence that Boots so intended when it licensed Upjohn. Second, in the pharmaceutical industry, after signing the agreement, the degree of implicit control that can be wielded by one party over the other, or their mutual dependence, is lower compared to other manufacturing sectors where even after a patent right is passed to the licensee, a connection remains in the shape of continuing technical help, purchase of components, and so on. Thus, in pharmaceutical licensing a careful drafting of the agreement is even more important.

NOTES

1. See Lall, S., "The International Allocation of Research Activity by U.S. Multinationals," *Oxford Bulletin of Economics and Statistics*, November 1979, pp. 313–331; or Teece, D., and Romeo, A., "Overseas Research and Development by U.S.-Based Firms," *Economica*, May 1979, pp. 187–196; or Ronstadt, R., *Research and Development Abroad by U.S. Multinationals* (New York: Praeger, 1977).

2. Indeed, this results in the further assumption in classical economics that all producers somehow possess the same technology. The fact that they do not makes for one of the obvious explanations for international technology transfer. For the beginnings of the transition toward a more realistic theory see Arrow, K., "Economic Welfare and the Allocation of Resources for Invention," in National Bureau of Economic Research, *The Rate and Direction of Inventive Activity: Economic and Social Factors* (Princeton, N.J.: Princeton University Press, 1962), pp. 609–626.

3. Teece, D., *The Multinational Corporation and the Resource Cost of International Technology Transfer* (Cambridge, Mass.: Ballinger, 1977). Contractor, F., *International Technology Licensing: Compensation, Costs and Negotiation* (Lexington, Mass.: D.C. Heath & Co., 1981).

4. See Wallender, H., "Developing Country Orientations toward Foreign Technology in the Eighties: Implications for New Negotiation Approaches," *Columbia Journal of World Business*, Summer 1980, pp. 21–28.

5. Schumpeter, J., *Socialism, Capitalism and Democracy* (New York: Harper & Bros., 1942), Chapter 8.

6. There are several case examples and discussion of how companies have handled

this issue in Business International, *International Licensing: Opportunities and Challenges in World-Wide Technology Management* (New York: Business International Corp., 1977).

7. For simplicity let us assume that costs C_1 and C_2 are invariant to the strategy used, i.e., that the R&D costs as well as general administrative overheads at headquarters are assumed identical in either a direct investment or a licensing strategy. This is probably a fair assumption for a particular proposed entry into a country, but probably inaccurate for a fundamental global policy reorientation of the company.

8. Coase, R., "The Nature of the Firm," *Economica*, November 1937, pp. 386–405; Williamson, O., *Markets and Hierarchies: Analysis and Antitrust Implications* (New York: Free Press, 1975).

9. Coase, "The Nature of the Firm."

10. Casson, M., *Alternatives to the Multinational Enterprise* (New York: Holmes & Meier, 1979).

11. Teece, *The Multinational Corporation*; Contractor, *International Technology Licensing*.

12. This is empirically unverified and remains a hypothesis.

13. See Teece, D., "The Market for Knowhow and the Efficient International Transfer of Technology," *Annals of the Academy of American Political and Social Sciences*, November 1981, pp. 81–96.

14. Caves, R., "International Corporations: The Industrial Economics of Foreign Investment," *Economica*, February 1971, pp. 1–27; Hymer, S., "The International Operations of National Firms: A Study of Direct Investment," Ph.D. dissertation, Massachusetts Institute of Technology, 1960.

15. Contractor, *International Technology Licensing*.

16. For a bargaining model, again with no determinate solution but benchmarks and compensation ranges for licensor and licensee, refer to Root, F., and Contractor, F., "Negotiating Compensation in International Licensing Agreements," *Sloan Management Review*, Winter 1981, pp. 23–32.

17. Casson, M., "Introduction: The Conceptual Framework," in Casson, M. (ed.), *The Growth of International Business* (forthcoming), Chapter 1.

18. For a summary of recent developments in the case, see "TV Ads for Prescription Drugs to Start Today, Causing a Stir," *Wall Street Journal*, May 19, 1983, p. 37.

19. Ibid.

3

The Importance of Foreign Licensing Income to American Companies: An Analysis of Aggregate U.S. Data

This chapter focuses on aggregate data issued by the United States Department of Commerce on the foreign licensing of American firms. The data readily available are not subject to easy interpretation. The following discussion will serve as a map for the analyst and identify additional sources of data, while giving an overview of the importance of international licensing to the economy as a whole and a perspective on how important it is to companies relative to direct investment income. Wherever possible the statistics are accompanied by their interpretation and implications for corporate practice. For readers uninterested in the niceties of interpreting Commerce Department data, the ''Summary of Conclusions'' section at the end of this chapter, together with a review of the tables, will suffice.

An essay at the end of this chapter examines the arguments for and against the idea that the United States is giving away its technologies too cheaply.

INTERPRETING THE DATA

The objective of this section is to demonstrate that the contribution of licensing revenues to the balance of payments and to company income is considerably larger than commonly assumed, and that in these revenues the share of independent and less than fully controlled licensees is greater than immediately apparent. The last point stems from the Commerce Department's definition of direct investment as ownership by a single person, association of persons, corporation, or corporate group of at least 10 percent of a foreign business enterprise that is deemed an ''affiliate.'' A less than 10 percent interest is not considered direct investment and ''is not considered to have sufficient ownership to influence management.''[1] While the 10 percent cutoff is as good as any in that range it is clear that the definition of foreign affiliation is thus very broad and includes minority joint ventures where the U.S. firm has between 10 and 50 percent of equity. A great many joint ventures which may approximate an arms-length relationship are lumped into the "affiliate" category. There is only an approximate correlation between the percentage of shares held and the degree of control or influence wielded by a minority partner.

It would be fair to say that, to varying degrees, licensing agreements with foreign minority joint ventures tend toward, or even approximate, an arm's-length relationship between licensor and licensee over compensation and other agreement terms. The obvious fact is that while dividends are to be shared between the two equity partners, the licensor gets to keep all of the royalties and fees. A licensor will therefore negotiate for the maximum royalty, as with an arms-length party. On the other hand, in licensing agreements with U.S. companies' majority-controlled affiliates, there may well be a tax or strategy-induced bias in setting compensation terms, as G. Kopits has shown.[2] In short, the Commerce Department's classification of "affiliate licensing" and "non-affiliate licensing" tends to understate the importance of licensing as a primary international strategy and as an income generator or market-entry method (as opposed to its secondary role in controlled affiliates for tax and other strategy considerations detailed in Chapter 1).

This immediately raises the question of just what is the breakdown of majority versus minority affiliates, the extent of licensing in each category and the extent of licensing in the so-called unaffiliated category. The latest figures, released in 1981, come from the 1977 Benchmark Survey and are reinterpreted and summarized in Tables 2 through 10. Interpretation is slightly complicated by the fact that there are two statistical universes of U.S. licensors, one of unaffiliated licensing (with data gathered by the Balance of Payments Division on form BE-93) and the other of licensing with affiliates (with data gathered by the International Investment Division on form BE-577). The 1977 Benchmark Survey on U.S. direct investment involves an overlap, including in some tables the non-affiliate licensing of U.S. firms which also have other foreign affiliates.[3] This survey did not include the sub-set of U.S. licensors that have no affiliates abroad, and their number is unknown as shown in Table 2. One suspects that much of foreign non-affiliate licensing is done by firms that also have at least one other foreign affiliate. There is simply no information on this, however.

Table 2 shows some 3,500 non-bank U.S. companies with 23,641 non-bank affiliates. (In technology transfer or licensing terms the share of bank parents or bank affiliates is negligible). More than 1,000 U.S. companies had licensing agreements directly with unaffiliated foreigners. The total number is unknown. We do know that 905 of these U.S. firms (reported to the survey because they had another foreign affiliate) account for arm's-length agreements with at least 22,000 foreign companies. In addition there was an indirect transfer of U.S. technology to approximately 7,000 unaffiliated companies via agreements made by foreign affiliates with other foreign parties.

Table 2
U.S. Companies' Overseas Affiliates and Licensing, 1977

```
     Affiliated Relationship          Unaffiliated Relationship

                                      Well over one thousand
      3540 U.S. "Parents"                U.S. Licensorsb
  _____|_____             _____|_____
  ↓                    ↓           ↓                  ↓
  111               3429           905               Did
  Bank              Non-Bank       reported in       not
  Parents           U.S. Parents   the surveyc       report

  968     1,996     |2,705
  overseas with     |with          Agreements        Number
  affiliates majority|minority     with at           unknown
          affiliates|affiliates    least 22,000
          overseas  |overseas      foreignersd
  _____        _____        _____


      In all 23,641 affiliates
      overseas of both typesa
      _____
      1,701 of these affiliates
      licensed technology to --------->About 7,000
                                       unaffiliated
                                       foreignerse
```

Source: U.S. Department of Commerce, U.S. Direct
         Investment Abroad. 1977 (Washington, D.C., 1981),
         also called the Benchmark Survey.

Notes:

a. The actual figure is 23,698 affiliates, but 57 Bank
    affiliates were removed. From the survey it appears
    that no "Royalties and License Fees" are paid by bank
    affiliates at all. They did however pay $190 million
    in "Service Charges and Rentals," almost all of it to
    their bank parents. (See pages 20, 95 and 217 of the
    survey).

b. The Balance of Payments Division gets reports from
    only 650-700 reporters. There are reasons to fear
    significant under-reporting.

c. Of the universe of well over a thousand U.S.
    licensors having unaffiliated licensing agreements
    abroad, 905 reported under this survey to the
    International Investment Division because they had
    some affiliates overseas as well (see page 191 of
    the survey).

d. The estimate is derived thus: The survey indicates
    a count of 22,878 for the number of unaffiliated
    persons with whom there are patent and knowhow
    agreements; this should be a third higher if
    trademark agreements were included (see page 191
    of the survey). On the other hand we should account
    for the fact that page 191 figures are gross totals
    for technology transfers both to and from the U.S.
    company. (for this see page 190). Thus about 22,000
    is a reasonable estimate for the number of
    unaffiliated companies with which the U.S. firm is
    a licensor.

e. Please see the next table.

Table 3 examines licensing by U.S. parents to their foreign affiliates and the affiliates' licensing in turn to other foreigners. In Table 2 we saw that, already in 1977, the number of parents of minority affiliates exceeded the number of parents of majority affiliates. Counting the number of affiliates, there is an almost even fifty-fifty division of the total between 11,909 majority and 11,732 minority affiliates. We should quickly add, however, that this can be misleading. By assets, or number of employees, the share of minority affiliates was much smaller, as shown in Table 3. Of the 23,641 affiliates, 9,708 received technology or patent and trademark rights from parents. Affiliates numbering 1,701 licensed technology and rights to about 15,000 other foreigners. Of these, half were unaffiliated parties. Since licensees abroad are receiving technology directly from U.S. firms and indirectly from their foreign affiliates, this means that a small portion of the licensing income on U.S. technology is not reported as such. It accrues to the foreign affiliates, is merged with their profits, and may be then repatriated to the United States as affiliate dividends.

Next, let us examine the understatement that often arises because licensing dollar income figures are reported on a net basis; that is to say, gross receipts less payments by U.S. parents to their affiliates for other technology received. Before addressing this issue, one needs to understand the Commerce Department's terminology, which can be confusing. Total gross receipts are broken down into various categories in Table 4. "Fees and Royalties" is the term used to describe the grand total of all sums associated with technology transfer. This in turn is broken down into two broad divisions: "Royalties and License Fees" for intellectual property rights transferred to the licensee, such as patents, know-how, and trademarks, and "Service Charges and Rentals" for services to enable the technology transfer, such as technical, managerial, marketing, or research and developmental assistance. Thus, the principal conceptual distinction is between rights and services. This quite correctly recognizes that technology transfer is not merely an act of transferring proprietary information and rights to the other firm, but of the attendant services that have to be provided to facilitate and effectuate the transfer.[4] For historical reasons, there are two small payments extraneous to technology transfer thrown in to the pot, namely, "Rentals for Tangible Property" and "Film and TV Tape Rentals." These are, however, a tiny fraction of the total and ought to be subtracted.

Receipts of "Fees and Royalties" from unaffiliated licensees (which of course cannot be netted against affiliates) are reported on a gross basis.[5] These, added to "Fees and Royalties" from affiliates, gives the grand total of receipts of "Fees and Royalties" for technology directly licensed from the United States, amounting in 1977 to $5.848 million. To this, if one wishes, can be added the $295 million received by affiliates licensing technology to yet other unaffiliated foreigners, as shown in Table 8. By comparing Tables 6 and 7, for years 1972–1981, one gets an idea of the relationship between "Fees And Royalties" and "Royalties and License Fees."

Table 3
Licensing to Affiliates and Their Licensing to Others
(Non-Bank Affiliates of Non-Bank Parents, 1977)

	Total	Majority	Minority	Minority as % of Total
No. of Affiliates[a]	23,641	11,909	11,732	50%
Assets, $ Million[a]	490,178	352,357	137,821	28%
Employees[a]	7,196,691	5,368,826	1,827,865	25%

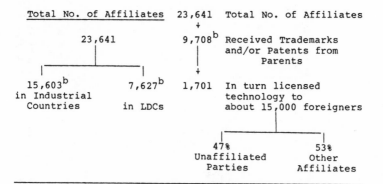

Source: U.S. Direct Investment Abroad, 1977

Notes

    a. Page 20 of the Survey

    b. Page 162 of the Survey

    c. 10,121 foreigners received patents and process technology in turn from the affiliates. Also we are told on page 166 and 167 of the survey that 9,526 foreigners received trademark rights from the affiliates. But since the two subsets overlap, i.e. have a partial union, the total number of foreigners is not the sum of the two, but less, perhaps 15,000 or so, at most.

Table 5 addresses the relationship between receipts gross, and netted against affiliates. The essential point is that netting deflated gross receipts by 20 percent in 1977.[6] Accordingly, the reported net figures in Table 7 for all the years 1972–1981 are inflated here by $\frac{1}{1-0.20} = 1.25$ to estimate gross receipts from affiliates in Table 8. This of course cannot produce a highly accurate estimate because

Table 4
Gross Receipts of All Fees and Royalties Directly by U.S. Licensors, 1977
($ Millions)

| | Breakdown of Affiliate Fees and Royalties | | | | | TOTAL AFFILIATE FEES AND ROYALTIES | TOTAL NON-AFFILIATE FEES AND ROYALTIES | GRAND TOTAL FEES AND ROYALTIES |
| | Royalties and License Fees | Service Charges & Rentals | | | Film & Tape Rental | | | |
		Services Rendered	R&D Assessment	Rentals for Tangible Property				
●All U.S. Parentsb	2,225	1,931	227	174	300	4,857	991a	5,848
●Non-Bank Parents/ Non-Bank Affiliatesc	2,225	<------------(2,143)-------------> Total			300	4,667	952	5,619
●Majority Non-Bank Parents/Non-Bank Affiliatesd	1,962e	<------------(1,935)-------------> Total			246	4,143	902	5,045

Source: U.S. Direct Investment Abroad, 1977

Notes
a. Extrapolated from the non-bank figure of 952 by multiplying by 4857/4667. This may still involve a slight underestimate because U.S. licensors with no foreign affiliates are not included in this statistical universe.

b. Pages 95 and 103 of the survey.
c. Page 217 of the survey. A breakdown of Service Charges and Rentals is unavailable in this category.
d. Page 426 of the survey. A breakdown of Service Charges and Rentals is unavailable in this category.
e. See also page 372 of the survey.

Table 5
Relationship Between Gross Receipts and Receipts Netted Against Affiliates, 1977
($ Millions)

	Gross Receipts	DIRECT INVESTMENT FEES AND ROYALTIES	
		Payments to Affiliates	Net Receipts From Affiliates
•All Parents[a]	4,857	974	3,883
•Non-Banks parents/ Non-Bank Affiliates	[b] 4,667	971	3,697
•Majority Non-Bank Parents/ Non-Bank Affiliates	[c] 4,143	863	3,280

Source: The Benchmark Survey, U.S. Direct Investment
         Abroad, 1977.

Notes:

a. p. 95 of the survey.

b. p. 217 of the survey.

c. p. 426 of the survey.

the ratio of gross to net, 1.2508 in the Benchmark Survey for 1977 which we have to use as the latest available information, must vary slightly for years after 1977. But the objective here is to give the reader an idea of the overall magnitude of licensing receipts, to compare these with equity-related receipts, and to show what portions of the total licensing receipts can be described as coming from independent or semi-independent foreign licensees.

The essential point in Table 8 is the little-realized fact that gross receipts from licensing are well over $8 billion in 1981. How does this compare with the returns that American firms are extracting by way of dividends on shares in foreign affiliates and by repatriated earnings of unincorporated affiliates? (Unincorporated companies need not declare dividends as such.) This is shown in Table 9. Here again, for want of data, the repatriated earnings of unincorporated affiliates are estimated by assuming that unincorporated affiliates will repatriate, each year, the same fraction of earnings that incorporated affiliates declared as dividends that year. This data collection problem is described by the Commerce Department as follows: "In practice, unincorporated affiliates . . . have difficulty separating the portion of their total earnings that is remitted from the portion

Table 6
Royalties and License Fees Netted against Affiliates, 1972–1981[a]

	1981	1980	1979	1978	1977	1976	1975	1974	1973	1972
Affiliated	3,650	3,693	3,002	2,697	2,173[c]	1,956	1,886	1,649	1,376	1,065
Unaffiliated	1,282[b]	1,170	1,068	1,055	923	844	757	751	712	655

Sources: 1. U.S. Direct Investment Abroad, 1977
2. Issues of Survey of Current Business
3. Unaffiliated data from Balance of Payment Division
4. Selected Data on U.S. Direct Investment Abroad, 1966–78 and its update

Notes: a. The netting of course does not apply to unaffiliated licensees
b. Provisional estimate
c. 1977 figures are from the Benchmark Survey

Table 7
Fees and Royalties Netted against Affiliates, 1972–1981[a]
($ Millions)

	1981	1980	1979	1978	1977	1976	1975	1974	1973	1972
Affiliated	5,867	5,780	4,980	4,705	3,863[d]	3,530	3,543	3,070	2,513	2,115
Unaffiliated[b]	1,369[c]	1,256	1,147	1,133	991	906	813	806	764	703

Sources:
1. Selected Data on U.S. Direct Investment Abroad, 1966–78 and updates
2. For 1977 the Benchmark Survey figures
3. Balance of Payments Division for unaffiliated figures
4. Issues of Survey of Current Business

Notes:
a. Netting is of course only against affiliates
b. Estimated by multiplying Royalty & License Fees figures by 991/923
c. Provisional Estimate
d. Page 95 of the Benchmark Survey

33

Table 8
Gross Receipts of Fees and Royalties, 1972–1981

	1981	1980	1979	1978	1977	1976	1975	1974	1973	1972
From Affiliates[a]	7,339	7,230	6,229	5,885	4,857[b]	4,415	4,432	3,840	3,143	2,646
Non-Affiliate[c]	1,369[d]	1,256	1,147	1,133	991	906	813	806	764	703
	8,708	8,486	7,376	7,018	5,848	5,321	5,245	4,646	3,907	3,349

Affiliates' Receipts from
unaffiliated Foreigners
295
6,143 (Grand Total, 1977)

Sources: 1. Various Issues of the Survey of Current Business
2. U.S. Direct Investment Abroad, 1977
3. Balance of Payments Division of the BEA

Notes: a. Estimated by multiplying netted receipts by 1.2508 = 3883 from
Benchmark Survey
b. Benchmark Survey, p. 95
c. Estimated by multiplying actual Royalties And Fees by 991/923
d. Provisional estimate

that is not." Just as dividends comprise only the repatriated fraction of foreign earnings of incorporated affiliates, all the earnings of unincorporated affiliates are not repatriated, regardless of their treatment in the data issued: "All earnings of unincorporated affiliates are treated as if they are remitted by U.S. parents even if in fact the earnings remain abroad . . . ."[7] At any rate, our rough estimate leads to the conclusion that gross Fees And Royalties are of the order of 50 to 60 percent of the total repatriation on foreign direct investment equity holdings, as shown by the ratio B/A in Table 9. (In 1981, the ratio is highest perhaps because the global recession depressed equity earnings, the denominator of the ratio.)

While this is true in a national balance-of-payments sense, we cannot leap from there to the conclusion that in corporate strategy licensing is 60 percent as important as equity investment. Hardly so. After all, most licensing income is derived from majority-controlled affiliates. But there are further practical and conceptual problems. For one thing, the effective multinational tax treatment on licensing income and dividend-type income is not identical as we saw in Chapter 1. Firms will often lower total tax liability if part of repatriated income is in the form of royalties and fees, as opposed to all being declared as dividends. Political and in some cases even exchange inconvertibility risk is lowered by having royalties and dividends as alternative channels. For these reasons we would suspect that there is a bias toward signing licensing agreements. On the other hand, from Table 3, we saw that a number of U.S. firms nevertheless simply do not bother to sign formal agreements with affiliates, remaining content to extract returns from only the one dividends-type channel (and of course from any eventual liquidation or sale value when the business is terminated).

In theory also it is difficult to disentangle the two types of returns. One can venture to say, with trepidation, that licensing income from an affiliate is a return on the firm's technical assets and past research, while dividends are a return on entrepreneurial capital. But this is an arbitrary distinction which may entertain tax lawyers; it does not yield much of prescriptive value to the corporate strategist. (One thing is certain though, licensing income is to be discounted to present value at a lower rate than dividend income.)

In the case of a minority joint venture, a consideration emerges that is irrelevant with majority affiliates. Quite apart from the tax and risk minimization motivations for signing licensing agreements, there is now the simple fact that while the U.S. firm will keep only a minority share of declared dividends, they will keep all of the negotiated licensing royalties and fees. The lower the percentage of equity held, the less control does the U.S. firm have of the timing and size of the dividends, besides of course having less say on revenues, costs, and operating strategy of the business in general. It is clear that in all joint venture situations, but particularly in minority joint ventures, there is every incentive to negotiate as large and lucrative a licensing payment as possible, as one would when negotiating with an independent licensee. This *a priori* reasoning leads to

Table 9

A Comparison between Licensing Returns to the United States and Repatriated Earnings on Equity in Direct Investment

	1981	1980	1979	1978	1977
·Gross Dividends[a]	10,541	11,783	10,042	8,762	8,217
·Estimated Repatriation of Earnings of Unincorporated Affiliates[b]	4,150	3,544	3,272	3,234	3,072
.Total Repatriation on Equity	14,691	15,327	13,314	11,996	11,289(A)
·Gross Receipts of Fees And Royalties	8,708[c]	8,486	7,376	7,018	5,848(B)
·Ratio of B/A	0.59	0.55	0.55	0.58	0.52

Sources: 1. Survey of Current Business, various years
August issues

2. Please see other Tables

Notes:

a. On common and preferred stock of incorporated affiliates before taxes.

b. This is a rough estimate derived for want of better data by multiplying each year's figure for the earnings of unincorporated affiliates by the ratio of gross dividends over earnings of incorporated affiliates for that year.

c. Provisional

the conclusion that licensing income ought to be relatively more important in minority than in majority affiliates. The data, however, show this is not so.

Table 10 shows the latest available information on the division of licensing income between majority and minority affiliates and unaffiliated licensees. The share contributed by minority affiliates is only 12 percent, or 15 percent of the affiliate total, whereas in Table 3 we saw that minority affiliates had a 28 percent share in assets and 25 percent in employment. There are two plausible explanatory hypotheses. Either U.S. firms are not attempting sufficiently to sign up minority affiliates, or their joint venture partners, aided in some countries by government policies, have sufficient negotiating strength to refuse licensing in addition to equity participation by the U.S. firm.[8]

The point nevertheless remains that 29 percent of total licensing income was derived, in 1977, from minority affiliates and unaffiliated parties. Assuming the same percentage has held constant since the last Benchmark Survey in 1977, that would amount to some $2.5 billion in licensing fees paid by such licensees in 1981, out of the gross total of $8.7 billion from all foreign licensees.

SUMMARY OF CONCLUSIONS

1. We estimated gross foreign licensing income earned by U.S. firms in 1981 to be $8.7 billion (Table 8).

2. This compared with a roughly estimated $14.6 billion as the actually re-

Table 10
Approximate Division of 1977 Gross Receipt of Fees and Royalties

			%
From Majority (Non-Bank) Affiliate		4,143[a]	71
From Minority Affiliates	714		12
From Unaffiliated Foreigners	991 / 1,705		17
Total		1,705 / 5,848	29 / 100
Add Affiliates' Receipts from Unaffiliated Foreigners 295[b]			

Sources: See above Tables

Notes: a. Page 426, U.S. Direct Investment Abroad, 1977
         b. Page 372, U.S. Direct Investment Abroad, 1977

patriated portion of equity earnings and dividends from direct investment (Table 9). In general, gross licensing fees and royalties amount to 50 to 60 percent of the repatriated return on equity investment, depending on the year. (In 1981, the percentage is highest perhaps because the global recession depressed equity earnings.)

3. The Commerce Department's figures appear to understate the significance of licensing to U.S. firms as a primary overseas strategy because

a. By its definition of unaffiliated licensees (who only contribute 17 percent of gross licensing fees and royalties), it excludes minority joint venture partners as licensees where the U.S. licensor has over 10, but under 50, percent in equity. (This latter group contributes an additional 12 percent of gross licensing fees and royalties). Thus independent and minority joint venture licensees together pay 29 percent of all licensing fees, amounting in 1981 to $2.5 billion (Table 10).

b. Unaffiliated licensing income is underreported.

c. The figures do not include the licensing of technology in turn by U.S. companies' foreign affiliates to other independent foreign firms.

d. Licensing income is often reported only as "Royalties and License Fees" which is a sub-set of "Fees and Royalties" (see Tables 4, 6, and 7).

4. Netting against foreign affiliates (for payments made by U.S. parents for technology received from their affiliates) may deflate the gross figure for U.S. licensing receipts by as much as 20 percent—and the Commerce Department usually reports the netted figures (Table 5). This tends to understate the volume of licensing from U.S firms to their affiliates.

5. Even by the Commerce Department's (stringent) definition of "unaffiliated" licensees abroad, and despite underreporting, in 1977 there were reported to be at least 22,000 of them (and 7,000 unaffiliated foreigners additionally licensed by the U.S. firms' foreign affiliates). By comparison, in 1977, majority affiliates of U.S. companies numbered only 11,909 and minority affiliates numbered 11,732—by number roughly equal, though by assets or employees, minority foreign affiliates comprise only a quarter of the total (Table 3).

6. While, *a priori*, there would appear every reason to sign up minority affiliates as licensees, 1977 data in fact show that licensing income is relatively less important in minority than in majority affiliates. Either U.S. firms are not trying hard enough to sign licensing agreements with their minority joint ventures, or host governments and local partners are resisting the idea of paying royalties and technical fees in addition to allowing the U.S. firm a share in dividends.

APPENDIX:

Is the United States Giving Away its Technologies Too Cheaply?

"Two and a half billion! Why, that's no more than the cost of two Trident subs!" cried a member of the audience at an academic conference after the author had finished presenting the figures for arm's-length licensing income accruing annually to U.S. licensors. The implication was clear, and serious, that American firms may be giving away their technical lead, in hundreds of new agreements each year with arm's-length foreign firms, all for a pittance in compensation compared with the total size of the U.S. economy.

The merits of this position are difficult to assess. Indeed, two-and-a-half billion dollars is a pittance compared to the U.S. GNP or even the profits of just the Fortune 500 companies. The erosion of the U.S. technological lead and the acquisition of U.S. expertise, especially by the Japanese and the Soviets, commands today not merely media space, but attention at the highest level of government. Scholars such as M. Boretsky or K. Calder have warned of the issue for years.[9] According to J. Abegglen:

Between 1950 and 1980, the Japanese essentially acquired all of the technology in the world that they considered worth having, for a small fraction of the current annual U.S. expenditure in research and development.[10]

Quoting Japanese sources, L. Lynn indicates that in this thirty-year period, the Japanese signed 36,000 agreements and paid out a cumulative total of only $11.6 billion, the overwhelming majority to U.S. licensors.[11] By comparison, the total R&D outlay in the United States in 1980 alone was $61.1 billion.[12] Implicit in such thinking is the idea that American managers are behaving irrationally, or at the least they are taking an extremely short-term profit maximization approach, to the eventual detriment of their company and nation. Indeed, F. Contractor's interviews and questionnaire on compensation design and negotiation in licensing agreements showed "satisficing" rather than optimizing behavior on the part of most of the American executives interviewed.[13] Moreover, the alleged short-term financial performance objective of U.S. managers has been unfavorably compared, in the popular press, with the allegedly wise, longer perspective of Japanese strategists. Last, the IRS has, for decades, espoused the concern that U.S. foreign subsidiaries are actually repatriating an insufficient return on U.S. R&D investment. (In the direct investment case, the "insufficient returns" argument would be even more acute since the sums involved are larger than in licensing. Certainly, with fully owned affiliates which comprise the typical investment (see Table 3) the U.S. multinational is said to retain control over its technology. But consider that almost all U.S. company foreign operations, whether fully or partially owned, are managed by local nationals. Ultimately then, there will be local diffusion of the technology.)

Let us now marshall the arguments on the opposite side. First, we should remember that the $2.5 billion in arm's-length fees and royalties may considerably understate the actual after-taxes cash value of the total technology transfer package including related sales to and from the licensee, etc. Second, arm's-length agreements are more likely to contain peripheral and maturing technologies compared with transfers of core technologies to controlled affiliates. Third, we may recall from Contractor's earlier study that transfer costs borne by the licensor in such agreements typically amount to less than 5 percent of the returns; i.e., over 95 percent of such licensing revenues are a direct contribution to cash profits.[14] Fourth, total U.S. R&D outlay in 1980 was $61.1 billion. However, R & D outlay by private industry in 1980 was only $19.4 billion, so that the $2.5 billion figure amounts to 9 percent of the private industry outlay. Fifth, if the U.S. economy's returns from foreign licensing appear small, so also are actually repatriated dividends of U.S. foreign affiliates which amounted in 1981 to "only" $10.5 billion, and these are returns not just on technology transfer but also on capital investment.[15]

All in all, barring specific situations involving military applications or cutting-edge technologies, the alarmists have not presented a strong case of the detriment to the economy from licensing. The erosion of the post-war American techno-logical lead in most industries need not be viewed as being caused by grand designs on the part of foreign governments, short-sightedness on the part of U.S. executives, or laxness and openness in laboratories and universities in the coun-try.[16] This may be true in some measure, but the primary causes lie elsewhere. The position of some protagonists in the public policy debate is strangely rem-iniscent of British government efforts to check the outflow of machinery and technicians in the years 1780 to 1843, described in a definitive history by D. Jeremy.[17] Despite great bureaucratic ingenuity, registration of skilled technicians, controls on machinery exports and emigration, and surveillance of foreign agents and recruiters, the British government effort was quickly perceived as futile and was eventually abandoned. As Jeremy puts it, "the central government seems to have been apprised of only a fraction of the leakage."[18] Even in pre-industrial times we find the same story: the diffusion of technology may not be instanta-neous, costless, or perfect, as in the economic theorist's world, but it is inex-orable. The second inexorable fact, if unpalatable to some, is that no country, not even the United States, can long remain pre-eminent in all fields. A quirk of history left the United States with nearly half of the world's productive capacity immediately after the second world war. This is now down to a fifth with the resurgence of Europe and Japan to their former relative positions. Moreover, the rapidly industrializing countries such as Korea or Taiwan are in hot pursuit of the "developed nation" status.

Ultimately, continued eminence can only come from the continued output of new products and technologies. In this light, foreign licensing revenues can make a significant increment to domestic corporate R&D efforts already contributing some 7 to 9 percent, as we saw. Of course, there is no guarantee that more spent on research and development will necessarily accelerate the rate of inven-tion or innovation, for much also depends on the social and economic context. But promotion of research is properly the centerpiece of any national policy. Viewed in a "technology cycle" perspective, corporations and nations may well, in many if not all products, try to maximize current returns from licensing, provided the money is put back into research so as to maintain the edge over competition.

NOTES

1. U.S. Department of Commerce, *U.S. Direct Investment Abroad, 1977* (Washington, D.C.: U.S. Government Printing Office, 1981), p. 3.

2. Kopits, G., "Intra-firm Royalties Crossing Frontiers and Transfer-Pricing Behavior," *The Economic Journal*, December 1976, pp. 791–803.

3. For example, on pages 190, 191, and 400. See *U.S. Direct Investment Abroad, 1977.*

4. For a further discussion of this conceptual separation and a cross-sectional statistical analysis based on this, see Contractor, F., "The Composition of Licensing Fees and Arrangements as a Function of Economic Development of Technology Recipient Nations," *Journal of International Business Studies*, Winter 1980.

5. In some publications they are occasionally netted against payments made by U.S. firms to some other unaffiliated foreign firms for technology licensed in.

6. The same is not true in Royalties and License Fees:

	Gross Receipts	Payment to Affiliates	Net Receipts
All parents	2,225	51	2,174
Non-bank	2,225	51	2,174
Minority non-bank	1,962	48	1,914

This means that the principal payments to affiliates are in the service charges category. We also see above by comparing the first and second rows that banks neither pay nor receive royalties and license fees, all their transactions being in the services category.

7. *U.S. Direct Investment Abroad, 1977*, pp. 16–17.

8. The share of LDCs in total Fees and Royalties, 1977, is 14.1 percent in minority affiliates and 15.8 percent in all affiliates, much lower percentages than their share in dividends. It is significant to note however that in 1981, the LDC share in (netted) Fees and Royalties was up to 21 percent. This would tend to support the former rather than the latter hypothesis, because no one will deny that the bargaining power of LDCs has increased in the last five years.

9. For instance, see Boretsky, M., "Trends in U.S. Technology: A Political Economist's View," in Kuehn, T., and Porter, A. (eds.), *Science, Technology and National Policy* (Ithaca, N.Y.: Cornell University Press, 1981), pp. 161–188; and Calder, K., "Technology Transfers, Promise or Peril?" in *U.S.-Japan Relations in the 1980's: Towards Burden Sharing*, 1981–82 Annual Report of the Program on U.S.-Japan Relations, Center for International Affairs, Harvard University, pp. 49–58.

10. Abegglen, J., "U.S.-Japanese Technological Exchange in Perspective, 1946–1981," in Uehara, C. (ed.), *Technological Exchange: The U.S.-Japanese Experience* (New York: University Press, 1982), pp. 1–18.

11. Lynn, L., "Technology Transfer to Japan: What We Know, What We Need to Know, and What We Know That May Not Be So," paper presented to the Social Science Research Council, Subcommittee on Science and Technology Indicators, New York, June 2–3, 1983.

12. National Science Board, *Science Indicators 1980* (Washington, D.C.: U.S. Government Printing Office, 1981), Appendix Table 2-4, p. 248.

13. Contractor, F., *International Technology Licensing: Compensation, Costs and Negotiation* (Lexington, Mass.: D. C. Heath & Co., 1981), Chapter 4.

14. Ibid., Chapter 5.

15. See Table 9. Of course, dividends are not directly comparable to royalties because to the dividend income stream one must add the present value of any future liquidation or sale. In practice, however, the latter is small.

16. See, for instance, Zinberg, D., "Training Foreign Nationals: An Examination of Science/Engineering Education as an Export Commodity," paper presented to the Social Science Research Council, Subcommittee on Science and Technology Indicators, New York, June 2–3, 1983.

17. Jeremy, D., "Damming the Flood: British Government Efforts to Check the Outflow of Technicians and Machinery, 1780–1843," *Business History Review*, Spring 1977, pp. 1–34.

18. Jeremy, D., *ibid.*, p. 13.

4

The Choice of Licensing versus Direct Foreign Investment: An Empirical Investigation

This chapter presents results of an empirical study that seeks to explain statistically the relative proportions of U.S. company licensing and foreign investment as a function of foreign country and industry-specific variables.

Its relevance lies in four areas: First, it tests theories of the international firm; in particular, the discussion of the concept of "internalization," which we treated in Chapter 2. This describes why a company is said to prefer, under a majority of circumstances, expanding overseas via internal transfer of technology and rights to controlled equity affiliates, rather than resorting to the market mechanism by selling the technology to independent foreign licensees. Second, this study follows on other empirical works, such as R. Baldwin, J. Dunning, or T. Pugel, which have attempted to model the determinants of foreign investment based on host country and home industry characteristics.[1] (None of these have, however, addressed the relative incidence of U.S. investment vis-à-vis licensing in foreign countries.) Third, this study relates to several public policy concerns of foreign governments, expressed in their growing preference for non-equity, contractual modes of acquiring technology, at least in some nations, and the debate over the international patent system. The data analyzed here include both industrial and developing countries, but a section of this chapter examines what differences exist between the two categories. Fourth, this study has significance for U.S. corporate strategy in its choice between licensing and equity investment.[2] Readers who are uninterested in the details of the statistical analysis may proceed directly to the section on conclusions and policy implications.

COUNTRY AND INDUSTRY VARIABLES INFLUENCING THE CHOICE

Practically speaking, the corporate choice amounts to this: a comparison of the risk-adjusted net present values of a technology transfer under direct investment versus licensing, keeping in mind that neither duration of the arrangement, costs of effecting the transfer, uncertainty associated with expected revenues, nor the opportunity costs of each method are identical. Under the theoretical framework developed in Chapter 2, Figure 1, this amounts to comparing $(T_2 - T_1 - C_4)$ under either option. Clearly, the relative attractions of the two methods are going to be influenced by both industry- or firm-specific factors, such as research intensity or patent incidence, and environment- or country-specific factors such as country risk, concessions, or inhibitions on foreign investment, the effective tax rate on affiliate income, the size of the country's market, and, finally, its indigenous technical capabilities. This is the empirical focus of this study.

Starting with a blank slate, we asked in Chapter 2 why risk-adjusted net margins earned on a licensing agreement cannot be as high as, or higher than, the income stream drawn from an equity investment in a country, even after accounting for the opportunity cost of licensing in vacating the market in favor of the licensee and the consequential costs of possible licensee competition in third countries. If licensing creates a bilateral monopoly from the act of sharing, via transfer, the technology with a licensee company, then the licensor's problem is to set fees and royalties high enough so as to restrict the licensee's share of local revenues to a normal return on capital investment of the licensee, while appropriating the incremental economic rent on the technology for themselves. Obviously, this is a problem not encountered with one's own controlled affiliate integrated within the boundaries of the international firm.

As K. MacMillan and D. Farmer or M. Casson develop the argument, not only are transactions or negotiations costs higher when dealing with an outside prospective licensee, the costs of effecting the technology transfer may be higher, particularly with complex technologies.[3] Moreover, on the returns side, extension of O. Williamson's market failure considerations suggest that a prospective licensee places a higher uncertainty and lower value on the technology, so as to offer license fees below the rent that may be earned by an equity affiliate in the country—unless, that is, the technology is well defined, mature, simple, or standardized.[4] In such cases, the balance may shift in favor of licensing. Moreover, while licensing carries the possibility of opportunity or consequential costs of the licensee competing in third markets with the licensor, F. Contractor asserts that in practice, this fear is often overblown and many licensees in fact do not have the export or sub-licensing capability.[5] Or, the rate of technical change may be rapid enough to retain the licensor's edge and obviate the fear of competition. In the next sections, we examine hypotheses to be tested.

Firm and Industry Factors Influencing the Choice

In any event, with patents, a licensee can, perfectly legally, be restricted to a particular territory. This would suggest that patented technologies are more amenable to licensing.[6] This is to be tested. We may be more bold in hypothesizing that, *ceteris paribus*, the more complex and proprietary the technology, the more the firm has to lose and to this extent will avoid licensing, as R. Wilson or W. Davidson and D. McFetridge indicate.[7]

Apart from a proprietary monopolistic advantage derived from the size of a company's R&D budget or its R&D intensity, important expertise may also be in adminstration and marketing. Pugel, Baldwin, and Dunning all find foreign direct investment positively correlated with measures such as the share of managers in total employment or the years of education of employees.[8] Since these studies did not, however, address their relationship with licensing, we have no *a priori* information on how such measures would correlate with the ratio of licensing over direct investment, the principal focus of this study. One could even argue, for instance, that the systematic organization of information in a company would favor its ability to license. Let us make no *a priori* judgment about the direction of the relationship between the ratio and the share of managers in total employment, except to propose a non-null hypothesis.

Finally, on the question of the relationship between firm size and the propensity to license versus invest, theoretical papers by R. Mirus, Casson, and P. Buckley and H. Davies all suggest that smaller firms, lacking the managerial and financial resources to make direct investments, would be more prone to favor licensing.[9] (Empirically, the variable has been used to try and explain the level of direct investment alone, as in C. Bergsten, T. Horst, and T. Moran, but disentangling absolute firm size from firm size relative to its industry remains a problem.)[10]

Country Factors Influencing the Choice

Country characteristics that would influence the choice of methods are the nation's level of development, investment environment and risk, indigenous technical capability, patent intensity, and, last, the incentives or concessions accorded to foreign investment in the country. (The operationalization and interpretation of these measures is subject to the usual data limitations and caveats that accompany a cross-sectional study, and this is discussed later.[11] Here we treat the rationale behind the use of the country variables.)

In nations where direct investment earnings attract a higher tax rate, or are eligible for fewer incentives, or where the investment climate is perceived to be risky, we can hypothesize licensing to increase relative to equity investment, *ceteris paribus*. In licensing, there are fewer or no assets at stake, and royalties being pegged to turnover, they are more stable than dividends, the latter being declared only out of profits, if any. Many agreements include minimum royalty clauses and front-end payments. Moreover, the planning horizon is shorter and net cash inflows begin sooner than in the case of equity investment. Last, in several countries, there are likely to be fewer restraints on the convertibility of contractual licensing fees than on dividends. The hypothesis to be tested is that as country risk increases, licensing would tend to be favored over investment, *ceteris paribus* in a cross-sectional sense.

As a country's indigenous technical capability increases, as measured by indicators such as local R&D expenditures or research personnel per capita, other things being equal, we hypothesize there would be a relatively greater use of licensing. Appropriable revenues available to the foreign investor would be lower as local companies and technologies compete more effectively and hold their own against foreign investment. By the same token, local companies as licensees would be in a better position to absorb the foreign technology with a lower cost to the licensor to transfer the technology, while at the same time be in a position to offer a higher compensation to the licensor. An opposite tendency, discouraging licensing, would arise, however, from the licensee's ability to compete in third countries as local technical capabilities are enhanced. However, studies show that, in practice, the cases where a licensee does actually export or produce in a third country in competition with the licensor are infrequent, and this consideration has only recently been given importance by U.S. licensor executives and that only in a few nations like Japan.[12]

How does the level of economic development, as measured by indicators such as per capita GDP, affect foreign investment and licensing? Several studies (e.g., W. Davidson, S. Kobrin, and R. Green and W. Cunningham) show a positive correlation between U.S. manufacturing direct foreign investment and per capita GDP.[13] (Licensing has not been analyzed.) But what does this measure? Considerable caution is required. To the extent that per capita GDP measures market potential or size for manufacturing technologies and products (this study's focus) we can connect with the analysis in Davies, Casson, and Buckley and Davies that licensing would tend to be favored over investment in less-developed markets and vice versa, other things being equal. It is argued that a less-developed market will provide a smaller appropriable rent on an equity investment, *ceteris paribus*. Moreover, the investment costs in financial and managerial terms may not be very much lower than in a large market because of minimum scale requirements or indivisibilities. A smaller market also represents a lower opportunity cost to the licensor (in abdicating the market to the licensee.) On the other hand, to the extent that per capita GDP measures through collinearity, other factors such as political risk or investment climate, we have, in that event, alternative underlying explanations (albeit with the same prediction as to the corporate choice of methods). For instance, *ceteris paribus*, licensing is said to be preferred over investment, the greater the perceived country risk. But if risk itself is negatively correlated to per capita GDP, then our hypothesis of increased propensity to use licensing in less-developed nations could be explained as much on the basis of risk and investment climate as on market potential.[14] Since the predicted direction of the statistical relationship is the same in either explanation, the alternative theoretical rationales are, at any rate, convergent; but there could be an operational difficulty with possible multicollinearity judging from the experience of other cross-sectional studies.[15]

Last, we will examine the relationship between patent intensity in a country and the corporate strategy choice. We argue here that the greater the patent intensity, the greater the relative propensity to use licensing because the very fact that a patent is filed indicates a degree of codification, as opposed to un-patented information or know-how that represents greater unknowns and uncer-tainty to a prospective purchaser. The mere act of patenting does not mean anything, of course, but it does lead to a higher price paid for patented tech-nologies, *ceteris paribus*, as confirmed in Contractor.[16] Last and perhaps most important, the patent system legally enables market segmentation, obviating the danger of licensee competition in third countries; at the same time, by conferring the monopoly on the licensee, a high rent is available to the licensee and some of it is, therefore, passed on to the licensor. As discussed above, the counter-hypothesis that patent intensity is symptomatic of relatively higher direct in-vestment would have to rest on the argument that the number of patents symbolize higher technology and, hence, the appropriability of rents via direct investment. But this is not verified. P. Stoneman's industry study, on the contrary, finds a negative relationship between the number of patents and the R&D cost per patent.[17] Filing fees for patents and their legal costs, in any event, remain modest in all nations and are no impediment to mere registration.

MODEL SPECIFICATIONS

Two basic models are tested, one using only country variables, the second with both U.S. industry and foreign country variables. The equations are shown below in their longest form; later, some of the independent variables are dropped because of statistical problems or lack of significance, and a shorter form of the model results.

Country variables: (for country i)

$$\sigma_i = f(\text{PERS}_i, \text{RANDEX}_i, \text{PERCAP}_i, \text{TYPE}_i, \text{RISK}_i, \text{CONC}_i, \\ \text{MANUF}_i, \text{PAT}_i) \qquad (1)$$
$$\text{UNRO}_i = f(\text{CONC}_i, \text{RANDEX}_i, \text{TYPE}_i, \text{PAT}_i, \text{DIP}_i) \qquad (2)$$

Table 11 defines each variable. Please refer to the appendix for data sources, constraints, caveats, and availability, which have dictated the number of usable variables and cases. For instance, on a U.S.-industry/country matrix, complete data are not available at that level of disaggregation because of the confidentiality and other criteria used by the Commerce Department. For countries alone, a complete data set can be assembled for thirty countries. With an industry clas-sification, however (food products, chemicals, metals, non-electrical machinery, electrical machinery, transport equipment, and petroleum), only three countries can be broken out (Canada, United Kingdom, and Japan); whereas complete data for the rest are available only as regions (EEC-6, Latin America, and Australia, New Zealand, and South Africa, as a group).

Industry/region variables: (industry j and region k)

Table 11
Variable Definitions

Dependent Variables

Symbol	Description
σ	Ratio of U.S. Receipts of Royalties and Licensing Fees from Unaffiliated Firms Over Various Measures of Direct Investment Activity, described below:

For Country i or For U.S. Industry j and World Region k

σ_i^1 or σ_{jk}^1	Ratio of U.S. Receipts of Unaffiliated Royalties and Licensing Fees Over U.S. "Direct Investment Position"
σ_i^2 or σ_{jk}^2	Ratio of U.S. Receipts of Unaffiliated Royalties and Licensing Fees Over U.S. Direct Investment "Income"
σ_i^3 or σ_{jk}^3	Ratio of U.S. Receipts of Unaffiliated Royalties and Licensee Fees Over the Sum of U.S. Direct Investment "Income" and Affiliate Licensing Income
$UNRO_i$ or $UNRO_{jk}$	U.S. Receipts of Unaffiliated Royalties and Licensing Fees ($\$$'000s)

Independent Variables

		Expected Sign
$PERS_i$	Research Personnel per 100,000 population in country i	+
$RANDEX_i$	Research and Development expenditures in Country i, $\$$	+
PERCAP	Per-Capita GDP in country i or region k, as indicated	-
$TYPE_i$	Dummy Variable Indicating Extent of country i government intervention or restriction on foreign investment (8 = Maximum and 1=Minimum) from Gottfried and Hoby;a.	+
$RISK_i$	Investment Environment Score (0 to 100 best) from Business International;b.	-
$CONC_i$ or $CONC_{jk}$	Fraction of U.S. Companies that have received specific Incentives on Investment, from 1977 Benchmark Survey	-

Table 11 *(continued)*

Independent Variables Symbol	Description	Expected Sign
$MANUF_i$	Percentage of Manufacturing in GDP (0 to 100)	−
PAT_i	Patents in force, thousands	+
DIP_i or DIP_{jk}	"Direct Investment Position", $ Billion	−
NET_{jk}	Ratio of Net Income to Sales in Direct Investment Affiliates	−
RAN_j	R&D Expenditures per Firm in industry j	−
MEM_j	Ratio of Managerial Workers in Total Employment in U.S. Industry j	non-zero
REM_j	R&D Scientists and Engineers per firm − average in U.S. for industry j	non-zero
$MEMP_j$	Number of Managerial Employees in U.S., thousands, industry j	non-zero
$REMP_j$	R&D Scientists and Engineers, thousands, industry j	non-zero
$ASSETS_j$	Assets per firm of Firms Investing Abroad, in Industry j, $ Billion	(Equation 3: −) (Equation 4: +)
$RAND_j$	R&D Expenditures by U.S. Parents of Equity Affiliates, industry j, $ Billion	−

Notes

    a. An eight-point scale constructed by Berweger, G., and J. Hoby, "Wirthschaftspolitik gegenuber Auslandscapital," Bulletin of the Sociological Institute of the University of Zurich, No. 35 (1978) with values for several countries calculated by them and presented in the above article.

    b. See Business International, Managing and Evaluating Country Risk, (New York: Business International Corporation, 1981).

    c. For data sources for the other independent variables please see the Appendix.

$$\sigma_{jk} = f(RAN_j \text{ or } REM_j, NET_{jk}, CONC_{jk}, MEM_j, PERCAP_k, ASSETS_j) \quad (3)$$

$$UNROjk = f(REMPj \text{ or } RANDj, MEMPj, CONCjk, ASSETSj, DIPjk) \quad (4)$$

In equations (1) and (3), the main focus of the analysis, the dependent variable is the *ratio* of income from unaffiliated licensees over three distinct measures of direct investment activity. These are: U.S. direct investment position as defined by the BEA;[18] U.S. direct investment "income";[19] and direct investment "income" plus royalties and fees paid by affiliates. Ideally, the dependent variable ought to be a ratio with an income measure both in the numerator and denominator, as will happen in the second and third measures above. However, being a stock measure, the direct investment position is a less volatile index over time, and is to be somewhat preferred for that reason to the "income" measures, which are subject to cyclical business conditions. For statistical purposes, such a ratio is acceptable. To check on the stability of the results over time, the analysis was repeated for the years 1977, 1978, and 1980, and, as it turns out, the statistics are not substantially different for the three years.

As an additional exercise, instead of the above ratios, the absolute value of dollar licensing fees and royalties from unaffiliated licensees was used as a dependent variable in equations (2) and (4) and regressed against certain absolute country and industry measures.

Using the country data, *a priori*, we propose that σ_i is positively associated with indigenous technological capabilities in foreign countries (expressed by the variables, PERS and RANDEX) and with the degree of government intervention or controls on investment which ought, therefore, to favor the licensing mode. (This is expressed by the variable TYPE). It is expected that σ_i will be negatively associated with the level of economic development and industrialization (expressed with caveats, discussed above, by PERCAP and MANUF) and negatively associated with the variable RISK (because of the way RISK is defined; refer to Table 11). Last, we expect σ_i will be negatively associated with degree of concessions given to foreign direct investment (measured by CONC), *ceteris peribus*, the more concessions that are given to investment in the denominator of the ratio, the ratio σ_i will be lowered.

The use of several of these variables together is subject to caution, not only for the mechanical problems of possible multicollinearity of per capita variables, but the complexity of interpretation of results. Other absolute variables such as R&D expenditure and the percentage of industrialization in GDP variable are included in the initial specification, at least, for this reason, and also since other studies indicate they may be more significant than their per capita counterparts.

In equation (2), we propose that the absolute value of unaffiliated licensing income, UNRO, is positively correlated, *ceteris paribus*, with absolute R&D expenditures, government intervention or restriction on foreign investment, and patent filings and then negatively related to the level of concessions to equity investment and to U.S. direct investment position in the country (DIP). This last relationship presumes that arm's-length licensing and direct investment behave as substitutes. If, on the other hand, we actually find a positive relationship, then unaffiliated licensing would have to be viewed as complementary to equity investment, perhaps from a foreign market "experience effect," proposed by Davidson.[20]

Theory does not tell us the functional form of the relationship between the dependent and independent variables. An "ordinary least squares" (OLS) form of regression is used, quite satisfactorily as it turns out. Later, a single and double logarithmic form was tried and some results shown in the appendix.[21]

In equation (3) we propose that σ_{jk} is negatively associated, *ceteris paribus*, with CONC and PERCAP, as above, and negatively associated with the profitability of direct investment in the region, as measured by the variable NET, once again presuming that independent licensing and direct investment behave as substitutes. For REM and MEM, as alternate indicators of internal firm advantages, let us posit simply a non-null relationship since the *a priori* theoretical arguments are weak on this score. A negative sign for ASSETS is proposed from the familiar hypothesis that larger international firms are better able to internalize technology transfers and are less likely to use licensing.

In equation (4), absolute unaffiliated licensing income is to be regressed against absolute industry and region measures. For the same reasons as in equation (2), the sign for DIP is hypothesized to be negative. The sign for ASSETS is expected to positive in equation (4), on the assumption that the absolute level of international licensing will be higher the larger the firm. (In equation (3) we expect a negative sign because the dependent variable is the ratio of licensing over investment.)

RESULTS

For cross-sectional data, the results in general are gratifying, in that the percent variation explained (R^2) is high in most equations, overall equation F-values are strong, the coefficients show stability over different years, and the signs of the coefficients in most cases are as hypothesized.

Results from equation (1) are shown in Table 12. At the outset, we should notice that the variable RISK turned out to be strongly collinear with PERCAP and had to be dropped.[22] Moreover, data from PAT were available for only nineteen of the thirty nations, reducing the degrees of the freedom.[23] In estimations 2, 4, 6, and 7, PAT is dropped in order to use all the data.[24]

The results confirm the hypothesis that the relative propensity to use licensing increases with the technology-receiving country's indigenous technical capabilities, as measured by research expenditures and research personnel normalized by population. Again, as hypothesized, the relative proportion of licensing decreases, and investment increases, with the level of economic development, measured by per capita GDP and with the level of industrialization measured by the percentage of manufacturing in GDP, although in the latter case, the statistics are weaker. For the variable PAT, the sign of the coefficient is consistently

Table 12
Regression Statistics: Equation (1) for σ_i
(For Years 1977 and 1980 Only)[a]

No.	Year	DEPENDENT VARIABLE	Const.	PERS	RANDEX	PERCAP	TYPE	CONC	MANUF	PAT;[b]	d.f.	F Value	R^2
1	1977	σ_i^1	0.40	0.85 (2.53)**	0.27 (1.70)+	-0.49 (2.15)*	0.58 (0.29)	-0.16 (0.71)	-0.85 (1.74)+	0.15 (0.54)	9,77	3.77*	0.75
2	1977	σ_i^1	0.32	0.54 (2.15)**	0.30 (2.79)**	-0.18 (1.36)+	0.10 (0.98)	0.57 (0.58)	-0.19 (0.68)		6,22	4.43**	0.55
3	1980	σ_i^1	0.50	0.77 (2.32)**	0.26 (1.66)+	-0.54 (2.42)**	-0.95 (0.48)	-0.26 (1.16)	-0.85 (1.79)+	0.10 (0.36)	7,9	3.75*	0.74
4	1977	σ_i^2	0.99	0.82 (1.70)*	0.66 (0.35)	-0.21 (0.89)	0.46 (0.26)	-0.11 (0.80)	-0.26 (0.54)		6,23	1.11	0.19
5	1980	σ_i^2	0.35	0.49 (1.83)*	0.24 (1.87)*	-0.34 (1.90)*	0.44 (0.28)	-0.15 (0.83)	-0.73 (1.89)*	0.37 (0.16)	7,9	3.01+	0.70
6	1980	σ_i^2	0.51	0.29 (1.49)+	0.22 (2.65)**	-0.13 (1.36)+	0.58 (0.84)	0.49 (0.55)	-0.17 (0.80)		6,22	3.95**	0.47
7	1977	σ_i^3	Overall equation not significant using all variables[c]										
8	1980	σ_i^3	0.25	0.32 (1.71)+	0.17 (1.94)*	0.24 (1.91)*	-0.19 (0.17)	-0.11 (0.79)	0.56 (2.07)*	0.11 (0.07)	7,9	3.06+	0.70

Notes: a. Results for 1978 are roughly similar
        b. Data for PAT available for only 19 of the countries.
            When PAT is not used, number of cases = 30
        c. However signs of coefficients congruent with hypotheses except for CONC.

Significance levels: **0.025
                       *0.05 } for one or two-tailed tests as specified. t-values in parentheses.
                       +0.10

positive, as predicted, indicating that patent filings are positively associated with relative use of licensing. The direction of causality in this instance, and what this finding means, remains an open question. For the variables CONC and TYPE, the signs of the coefficients are as predicted only in a majority of estimations, nor are the t-values significant. There is insufficient evidence to reject the null hypothesis for these two variables.

Regression results for the dependent variable UNRO shown in Table 13 are on the whole congruent with *a priori* hypotheses. The absolute level of U.S. licensing activity, as measured by unaffiliated licensing income UNRO, is confirmed to be positively associated with R&D expenditures in the nation at better than the 0.025 significance level, as is the case with patent filings. The negative sign of the coefficient for DIP would tend to confirm the idea that non-affiliate licensing, as a nationwide generalization for the United States, is a strategy substitute for, rather than a complement to, direct investment. A caveat that needs to be considered is that this variable was significant only in the sub-sample of nineteen cases, and we ought not to draw strong general conclusions.[25] The sign of the variable TYPE is positive, as expected, weakly supporting the idea that increased host government intervention and regulation of direct foreign investment tends to favor the alternative market entry strategy of licensing. The sign of CONC is consistently negative, supporting the idea that concessions given to equity investment lower licensing, as predicted. Overall F-values and R^2 of the equations are all high.

Turning now to the industry/region data, the equations have high F-values, and the overall picture confirms *a priori* hypotheses (with the exception of NET and ASSETS, whose signs are consistently contrary to expectation—we will discuss this in a moment). In estimating equation (3) in Table 14, we note at the outset that the variable RAN (R&D expenditures per firm) was dropped, being collinear with REM (R&D employees per firm). In any event, REM is not significant, so that we are unable to say that R&D intensity does or does not influence the corporate choice of strategies. The ratio of licensing over direct investment is shown to be positively associated, *ceteris paribus*, with the ratio of managerial employees in total employment MEM (at the 0.025 or 0.05 levels), and to be negatively associated with the incidence of concessions granted to direct equity investment (at the 0.025 level), as expected. The sign for PERCAP is consistently negative, as anticipated, but the coefficients are not significant.[26] The sign for ASSETS is opposite to the hypothesis that the relative use of licensing compared to investment increases in smaller firms, *ceteris paribus*. The variable was not significant, however, in any estimation.

The paradoxical result is for the variable NET. We hypothesized that, assuming direct investment and licensing behave as substitutes, *ceteris paribus*, we may reasonably expect that the ratio of net income to sales in direct investment affiliates, NET, will be negatively associated with our dependent variable; i.e., the more profitable equity investment, the lower we might expect the ratio of licensing over equity investment to be. The opposite was found, paradoxically.

Table 13

Regression Statistics: Equation (2) for $UNRO_i$

No.	Year	DEPENDENT VARIABLE	Const.	RANDEX	TYPE	CONC	DIP	PAT	d.f.	F Value	R^2
9	1977	$UNRO_i$	-10885.60	18.43 (4.59)**	2259.18 (0.63)	-4565.65 (0.11)	-2.35 (1.54)+	271.67 (2.09)**	5,13	14.04**	0.84
10	1977	$UNRO_i$	-8032.59	23.79 (8.78)**	2325.25 (1.03)	-4935.26 (0.19)	0.86 (0.10)		4,25	23.03**	0.79
11	1978	$UNRO_i$	-18760.21	24.37 (4.75)**	3524.46 (0.76)	-3722.77 (.07)	-2.49 (1.36)+	291.25 (1.76)*	5,13	12.62**	0.83
12	1978	$UNRO_i$	-8478.95	29.56 (8.66)**	2936.44 (1.04)	-10989.15 (0.35)	-0.14 (0.14)		4,25	22.66**	0.78
13	1980	$UNRO_i$	-22635.99	23.97 (4.06)**	4562.44 (0.87)	364.86 (0.00)	-2.16 (1.34)+	315.08 (1.67)*	5,12	9.83**	0.79
14	1980	$UNRO_i$	-10789.27	29.98 (7.79)**	3381.30 (1.06)	-7294.48 (0.20)	-0.17 (0.20)		4,25	17.94**	0.74

Notes: a. Data for PAT available for only 19 of the countries.
When PAT is not used, the number of cases is 30.

Significance levels: **0.025
*0.05 } for one or two-tailed tests as specified. t-values in parentheses.
+0.10

54

Table 14
Regression Statistics: Equation (3) for σ_{jk}

No.	Year	DEPENDENT VARIABLE	Const.	REM	NET	CONC	MEM	PERCAP	ASSETS	d.f.	F Value	R^2
15	1978	σ^1_{jk}	-0.42	-0.63 (0.08)	2.51 (6.86)**	-0.30 (2.32)**	4.39 (2.40)**	-0.16 (0.19)	0.78 (1.20)	6,35	13.63**	0.70
16	1978	σ^2_{jk}	-1.26	-0.16 (0.37)	7.63 (1.79)+	-0.16 (2.54)**	18.42 (2.02)*	-0.15 (0.37)	0.20 (0.61)	6,34	2.98*	0.34
17	1978	σ^3_{jk}	-1.01	-0.70 (0.15)	5.68 (1.76)+	-0.10 (2.24)**	13.51 (1.92)*	-0.27 (0.05)	0.85 (0.34)	6,28	2.75*	0.37
18	1979	σ^1_{jk}	-0.27	-0.70 (0.83)	0.41 (1.13)	-0.28 (2.16)**	4.10 (2.28)**	-0.37 (0.45)	0.48 (0.75)	6,35	2.43*	0.30
19	1979	σ^2_{jk}	-7.90	2.45 (1.62)	76.18 (12.60)**	-0.13 (0.64)	36.83 (1.24)	-0.82 (0.61)	1.64 (1.57)	6,34	42.25**	0.88
20	1979	σ^3_{jk}	-1.62	0.12 (0.31)	11.84 (7.54)**	-0.11 (2.06)**	16.71 (2.14)**	-0.14 (0.38)	0.22 (0.75)	6,29	15.97**	0.77

Significance levels: **0.025 *0.05 +0.10 } for one or two-tailed tests as specified. t-values in parentheses.

55

The relationship ought really to be examined in a time series. Perhaps we merely have anomalous data peculiar to the time of this cross-sectional study.

Table 15 shows the results of estimating equation (4) with the absolute value of non-affiliate licensing income as the dependent variable against absolute industry measures. At the outset, REMP, RAND, and MEMP were found to be collinear, and two of the variables dropped as a result. While the signs of the relationships are as expected, only CONC and REMP are significant (at the 0.025 level). We may notice that the negative sign of ASSETS suggests the idea that, *ceteris paribus*, as the absolute level of licensing decreases, the larger the total assets in the U.S. firm. Again, however, the variable was not significant, but the sign is contrary to *a priori* expectation.

FURTHER TESTS

In order to test the robustness of the model, the sample of thirty nations was partitioned and regressions run on each sub-sample. The partitioning was not random; rather, a group of sixteen countries normally regarded as advanced industrial countries were separated, leaving another group of fourteen nations conventionally regarded as LDCs. (Please see the appendix for details.) This was done specifically to see if the predicted relationships are in any way significantly different in the two categories for the overall sample.

In general, the direction of the relationships that we found in the full sample hold, but with weaker significance levels in the industrial national sub-sample, as shown in Table 16, and very little or no significance in the LDC sub-sample.[27]

The appendix also shows some results of logarithmic and double logarithmic form of the equations, using 1980 data. The overall results are congruent with the OLS form.

CONCLUSIONS AND POLICY IMPLICATIONS

The results lend credence to the idea that the strategy choice of arm's-length licensing versus direct investment made by U.S. multinational firms is influenced by both country factors as well as industry characteristics but in a complex way, since each significant finding is based on *ceteris paribus* assumptions. For instance, the ratio of U.S. licensing relative to U.S. investment (across countries in a cross-sectional sense) increases with indigenous technical capability in a country, a variable that can indeed be influenced in the long run by government policy, as in Japan. Licensing, however, decreases in relative importance with higher per capita GDP and industrialization, *ceteris paribus*. Similarly, we found weaker support for the idea that the proportion of licensing increases, *ceteris paribus*, with government scrutiny and regulation of direct investment and decreases, on the other hand, as more concessions and incentives are offered on direct investment.

This was exemplified by two countries that were sometimes outliers, Japan

Table 15
Regression Statistics: Equation (4) for UNRO$_{jk}$

No.	Year	DEPENDENT VARIABLE	Const.	REMP	CONC	ASSETS	DIP	d.f.	F Value	R^2
21	1978	UNRO$_{jk}$	53.77	0.40 (4.79)	-1.05 (2.99)	-15.14 (1.25)	-0.11 (0.52)	4,43	12.69	0.54
22	1979	UNRO$_{jk}$	52.76	0.40 (2.76)	-0.97 (4.26)	-19.10 (1.57)	-0.95 (0.44)	4,43	12.23	0.53

Significance levels: $\left.\begin{array}{l}**0.025 \\ *0.05 \\ +0.10\end{array}\right\}$ for one or two-tailed tests as specified. t-values in parentheses.

Table 16

Regression Statistics of Some Tests on a Sub-sample of Sixteen Industiral Nations

No.	Year	(DEPENDENT) Variable	Const.	PERS	RANDEX	PERCAP	TYPE	MANUF	d.f.	F Value	R^2
23	1977	σ_i^1	0.24	0.45 (1.38)+	0.37 (2.30)**	-0.29 (1.57)+	0.95 (0.73)	-0.68 (1.10)	5,10	3.68*	0.65
24	1980	σ_i^1	0.26	0.40 (1.33)	0.38 (2.53)**	-0.34 (1.66)+	0.83 (0.68)	-0.77 (1.33)	5,10	3.98*	0.67
25	1980	σ_i^2	0.22	0.22 (0.95)	0.30 (2.63)**	-0.19 (1.48)	0.45 (0.49)	-0.65 (1.48)+	5,10	3.40*	0.63

NOTE: The above three equations exemplify the similarity of results for the sub-sample with the overall sample. Results for 1978 and other versions of σ are also similar.

Significance levels: ** 0.025
                     * 0.05 } one or two tailed tests as specified.
                     + 0.10 } t-values are in parentheses.

and the United Kingdom. The ratio σ for Japan was well above its predicted value in many estimations, while that for Britain was under. U.S. international firms clearly favor the direct investment route in Britain, where, going back to the data, we find far more concessions and incentives and a less stringent regulatory climate for foreign investment than is found in Japan. On the other hand, on indicators of indigenous technical capability, Japan is significantly higher. Clearly, governmental policy influences the choice of business methods.

Licensing was shown to be positively associated with the number of patents filed in a country, but interpretation of this finding is difficult because the direction of causality, if any, is unknown. A plausible explanation may be that patents increase revenues extractable from licensing (as opposed to licensing of unpatented know-how), and that patents are effective means of segmenting the international product market so as to obviate an important drawback of licensing, being the fear of licensee competition in third countries. Or patents may increase global licensing revenues by effective market segmentation, with the international firm behaving as a discriminating monopolist. If we accept this hypothesis, then a weakening of the patent system sought by some LDCs would only diminish international licensing and drive firms to greater "internalization" of the technology in controlled equity affiliates. This may not be advantageous to technology-receiving countries because studies, as well as regulatory practices in Japan, Mexico, India, etc., which favor licensing over investment, suggest a belief that licensing may involve a lower long-run national cost of acquiring technologies, as compared to equity investment, at least for some nations.

Turning now to corporate policy, the absolute level of licensing in a country was shown to be generally negatively related to the level of direct investment, from which one may conclude that the two are strategy substitutes, rather than complements. The results are weak when analyzing data broken down by both region and industry, possibly because disaggregation beyond the two-digit level could not be obtained. Nevertheless, there are indications that the ratio of licensing to investment increases with the ratio of managerial employees in total employment but is inversely related to research intensity. Many of the predictions of theory are borne out. Firms may prefer direct investment under most conditions, but licensing, while remaining a subordinate strategy, may increase its role as the environment is more restrictive toward investment, as the technology is less research intensive, more codified, patented, and transferable and as the recipient country has greater indigenous technical capabilities.

APPENDIX:
Data Sources and Limitations

Data for the dependent variables were obtained from the Bureau of Economic Analysis, U.S. Department of Commerce, and from *U.S. Direct Investment Abroad, 1977* and *Selected Data on U.S. Direct Investment Abroad*, both publications of the BEA. Their definition of non-affiliated licensing is that ownership or control by the U.S. licensor not exceed 10 percent of the licensee enterprise's voting securities. This, incidentally, omits an important segment of licensing, where the U.S. firm has between 10 and 50 percent of equity on which data are not available. This and other factors, such as the figures not including auxiliary business that often surrounds the core agreement for royalties and fees, result in the BEA figures for non-affiliated licensing considerably understating its strategic importance to U.S. companies. Nevertheless, they are adequate for a statistical analysis.

The confidentiality criteria used by the Commerce Department in suppressing entries when very few firms are involved do not have the result of deleting too many numbers in the direct investment portion of the data (namely, direct investment position or direct investment "income") even when the data are disaggregated to the country level or the BEA equivalent of a three-digit SIC code. However, there is a problem disaggregating the unaffiliated royalties and licensing fees too far. In computing the ratio σ, complete matched data were therefore available only for a total of thirty nations (sixteen industrial advanced nations and fourteen LDCs)—Argentina, Australia, Belgium, Brazil, Canada, Chile, Colombia, Denmark, Egypt, France, West Germany, India, Indonesia, Ireland, Italy, Japan, Mexico, Netherlands, New Zealand, Nigeria, Norway, Panama, Peru, Philippines, South Africa, Spain, Sweden, Switzerland, United Kingdom, and Venezuela. Iran and Iraq, for which data were available, were not included because oil revenues considerably distort not only the U.S. direct investment figures, but also independent variables such as per capita GDP. Because suppression of data occurs most often in very small countries, with, for example, less than three U.S. companies reporting, it is reasonably accurate to say that the thirty nations above include most of the significant countries from which U.S. firms derive non-affiliated licensing income.

The problem of disaggregation was even more acute at the industry level, and breakdown on an industry-by-region matrix was available only by BEA "major industry group." (For details, see *U.S. Direct Investment Abroad, 1977* (Washington, D.C.: U.S. Government Printing Office, 1981), pp. 8–9 and 494–516.) There were seven groups under "manufacturing," namely, food and kindred products; chemicals and allied products; primary and fabricated metals; machinery, except electrical; electric and electronic equipment; transportation equipment; other manufacturing; plus one non-manufacturing category, petroleum. These eight groups cover the great bulk of investment and licensing activity. For instance, they comprise 87 percent of the total direct investment abroad in 1977 of U.S. industries other than banking, finance, and trade. On the industry/region matrix, confidentiality constraints on the licensing data again enable only a six-region disaggregation: Canada, United Kingdom, EEC (original six), Japan, Latin America and Australia, New Zealand and South Africa, as a group. Even so, there are some suppressed entries and, instead of forty-eight cases (eight industries times six regions), the usable number of cases is closer to forty.

Sources of data on the independent variables are as under:

Variable	Source
PERCAP, MANUF	Worldwide Economic Indicators Series, Business International Corporation, New York (1975 prices)
PERS, RANDEX	UNESCO Yearbook
TYPE	Berweger and Hoby (1978), see Table 11
RISK	Business International (1981), see Table 11
CONC	U.S. Direct Investment Abroad, 1977, Table II-K1, p. 168
PAT	World Intellectual Property Organization
REM, MEM, REMP	U.S. Direct Investment Abroad, 1977
MEMP, NET, DIP, ASSETS	(Group II data for non-bank affiliates of non-bank parents)

For REM, MEM, REMP, and MEMP, the data relate to U.S. investors abroad, rather than to U.S. industry in general. This presupposes that the universe of U.S. arm's-length licensors is roughly identical to the universe of U.S. companies investing abroad (rather than comprising distinct sub-sets of U.S. industry in general). There is no conclusive evidence that this assumption is accurate, and it remains to be demonstrated empiricially.

The eleven countries dropped when PAT is included are Chile, Indonesia, Nigeria, Panama, Peru, Venezuela and Australia, Italy, New Zealand, Spain, and Switzerland, a roughly equal number of LDCs and industrial countries.

Ordinary linear least squares models may be a problem if the dependent variable has both an upper and lower bound and if there is significant bunching of values. There is only a lower bound of zero in these equations and there is no bunching of values. In any event, when the dependent variable is log transformed, the signs of the coefficients conform with the OLS model, as seen in Table 17. Since theory does not specify the form of the function, if OLS is satisfactory, further computer trials to squeeze out an incremental R^2 gain may not be warranted. In any case, we are using the regressions not so much for an econometric predictive ability as to identify the subset of relevant independent variables that influence the corporate choice in the anticipated direction.

NOTES

1. Baldwin, R., "Determinants of Trade and Foreign Investment: Further Evidence," *Review of Economics and Statistics*, Vol. 61, 1979, pp. 40–48. Dunning, J., "Non-equity Forms of Foreign Economic Involvement and the Theory of International Production," Working Paper, University of Reading, 1982. Pugel, T., "The Determinants of Foreign Direct Investment: An Analysis of U.S. Manufacturing Industries," *Managerial and Decision Economics,* December 1981, pp. 220–228.

2. Licensing with one's own affiliates is done for various strategy and tax reasons, as detailed in Chapter 1. Here we are concerned with licensing to independent and less

Table 17
Alternative Specifications

Because the ratio σ has a theoretical lower bound of zero, it is useful to try out an alternative model with the dependent variable log transformed, in order to see if the signs of coefficients are in general conformity with the linear model. This was done on 1980 data as an exercise whose results are reproduced below. Natural logarithms were used. The results are in general conformity with the linear model, although the statistics are weaker.

DEPENDENT VARIABLE	Const.	PERS	RANDEX	PERCAP	TYPE	MANUF	d.f.	F Value	R^2
$\ln\sigma_i^1$	-2.41	0.17 (1.32)+	0.74 (1.38)+	-0.58 (0.93)	0.44 (0.96)	-0.12 (0.89)	5,24	1.79	0.27
$\ln\sigma_i^2$	-1.89	0.65 (0.44)	0.73 (1.16)	-0.34 (0.47)	0.45 (0.84)	-0.55 (0.34)	5,22	1.04	0.19

DEPENDENT VARIABLE	Const.	ln(PERS)	ln(RANDEX)	ln(PERCAP)	ln(TYPE)	ln(MANUF)	d.f.	F Value	R^2
$\ln\sigma_i^1$	-2.42	0.75 (0.39)	0.15 (1.10)	-0.01 (0.00)	0.51 (1.64)+	-0.53 (0.95)	5,24	1.22	0.17
$\ln\sigma_i^2$	-2.36	0.56 (0.17)	0.16 (0.10)	-0.88 (0.20)	0.47 (1.22)	-0.57 (0.58)	5,22	0.56	0.12

than fully controlled foreign companies, where the license is presumed to be a substitute for, and not a complement to, direct foreign investment. In the data, the Commerce Department's cutoff of less than 10 percent equity interest in the licensee is used. See the appendix on data sources and limitations for further details.

3. MacMillan, K., and Farmer, D., "Redefining the Boundaries of the Firm," *The Journal of Industrial Economics*, March 1979, pp. 277–285. Casson, M., *Alternatives to the Multinational Enterprise* (New York: Holmes & Meier, 1979).

4. Williamson, O., *Markets and Hierarchies: Analysis and Antitrust Implications* (New York: Free Press, 1975).

5. Contractor, F., *International Technology Licensing: Compensation, Costs and Negotiation* (Lexington, Mass.: D. C. Heath & Co., 1981).

6. The opposite argument that patenting activity is indicative of research intensity or "higher" technology that a firm would prefer to share only with controlled affiliates is a weaker one. Stoneman, in fact, found a negative regression of the number of patents on the R&D cost per patent. See Stoneman, P., "Patenting Activity: A Re-evaluation of the Influence of Demand Pressures," *The Journal of Industrial Economics,* June 1979, pp. 385–401.

7. Wilson, R., "The Effect of Technological Environment and Product Rivalry on R&D Effort and Licensing of Inventions," *Review of Economics and Statistics*, May 1977, pp. 171–178. Davidson, W., and McFetridge, D., "International Technology Transactions and the Theory of the Firm," *The Journal of Industrial Economics*, March 1984, pp. 253–264.

8. Pugel, "The Determinants of Foreign Direct Investment"; Baldwin, "Determinants of Trade and Foreign Investment"; and Dunning, J., "Towards an Eclectic Theory of International Production: Some Empirical Tests," *Journal of International Business Studies*, Spring 1980, pp. 9–31.

9. Mirus, R., "A Note on the Choice between Licensing and Direct Foreign Investment," *Journal of International Business Studies*, Spring 1980, pp. 86–91; Casson, *Alternatives to the Multinational Enterprise*; and Buckley, P., and Davies, H., "The Place of Licensing in the Theory and Practice of Foreign Operations," Discussion Paper no. 47, University of Reading, November 1979.

10. Bergsten, C.; Horst, T.; and Moran, T., *American Multinationals and American Interests* (Washington, D.C.: Brookings Institution, 1978).

11. The collinearity found in cross-sectional studies between per capita GDP and other per capita measures of market size, such as energy consumption, roads, advertising expenditures, etc., is by now a familiar story.

12. Contractor, *International Technology Licensing*.

13. Davidson, W., "Location of Foreign Direct Investment Activity: Country Characteristics and Experience Effects," *Journal of International Business Studies*, Fall 1980, pp. 9–22; Kobrin, S., "The Environmental Determinants of Foreign Direct Manufacturing Investment: An Ex-Post Empirical Analysis," *Journal of International Business Studies*, Fall 1976, pp. 29–42; and Green, R., and Cunningham, W., "The Determinants of U.S. Foreign Investment: An Empirical Examination," *Management International Review*, Vol. 15 (2–3), 1975, pp. 113–120.

14. The negative correlation between political risk and per capita GDP is only partially validated. For example, Root and Ahmed, in seeking a discriminant function to classify fifty-eight nations into categories of investment risk, used per capita GDP combined with other variables such as urbanization. Because of multicollinearity they could not assess

the relative importance of the factors nor the direction of causality. See Root, F., and Ahmed, A., "Empirical Determinants of Manufacturing Direct Foreign Investment in Developing Countries," *Economic Development and Cultural Change*, July 1979, pp. 751–767.

15. Besides Root and Ahmed, the reader is referred to Kobrin, "The Environmental Determinants of Foreign Direct Manufacturing Investment," and Green and Cunningham, "The Determinants of U.S. Foreign Investment."

16. Contractor, *International Technology Licensing*.

17. Stoneman, "Patenting Activity."

18. The reader is referred to any August issue of the *Survey of Current Business* for a detailed definition. In essence it is the book value of U.S. direct investors' equity in, and net outstanding loans to, foreign affiliates.

19. As defined by the Bureau of Economic Analysis (U.S. Department of Commerce), this is earnings of affiliates, plus interest, less foreign withholding tax on dividends.

20. Davidson, "The Location of Foreign Direct Investment Activity: Country Characteristics and Experience Effects," pp. 9–22.

21. Ordinary least squares linear models may be a problem if the dependent variable has both an upper and lower bound and if there is significant bunching of values. There is only a lower bound, of zero, in these equations and there is no bunching of values. In any event, in the appendix the dependent variable is log transformed and the signs of the variables conform with the OLS model. Also, since theory does not specify the form of the function, if OLS is satisfactory, often further computer trials merely to squeeze out an incremental R^2 gain may not be warranted.

22. RISK is a composite index, based on numerous underlying factors, that ranks countries in terms of their desirability as equity investment locations. See Business International's *Managing and Evaluating Country Risk* (New York: Business International Corp., 1981) for details on its construction. If, however, such measures turn out to be collinear with per capita GDP, then one cannot help wonder whether corporations that buy this data are spending their money well when all they need are per capita GDP figures. A too-hasty indictment must be tempered, however, with the observation that the collinearity was observed only in this sample and may not occur in general. This remains an open question.

23. The eleven countries dropped in the sub-sample are Chile, Indonesia, Nigeria, Panama, Peru, Venezuela, Australia, Italy, New Zealand, Spain, and Switzerland, a roughly equal number of LDCs and industrial nations. Superficially, there would appear to be no bias on that score.

24. Paradoxically, with the full number of cases, the R^2 values are lower. There is no discernible bias in the eleven countries eliminated. (See note 23.)

25. See note 23.

26. This is not surprising when we recall that, as compared with equations (1) or (2) with thirty nations, here we have only six regions.

27. In no case was a significant coefficient found whose sign contradicted that in the full sample—where an opposite sign was found, the t-value was generally extremely low.

5

Licensing in International Strategy: The Corporate Planning Perspective

Over the last thirty years, much of the focus of corporate strategy in international companies has been on expansion by establishing controlled overseas affiliates, so as to exploit certain advantages internally in the firm. These advantages may range from special technologies, patented or otherwise, to a well-recognized brand name to marketing and managerial skills. The internal transfer of technology and proprietary assets in a foreign direct investment was presumed to be a superior strategy to their external sale in a licensing arrangement in the comforting belief that the profits extracted from a foreign market are higher when a direct investment is made. Licensing as an overseas expansion option has been relatively neglected by scholars. Worse, some U.S. corporations, despite changing conditions in the international environment, continue internal policies that almost reflexively rule out licensing. Studies show that several, on the other hand, have upgraded licensing departments in the last few years.[1] In some firms, the number of global licensees already considerably exceeds the number of international equity affiliates. For the U.S. as a whole we saw in Chapter 3 that the number of arm's-length licensees is greater than the number of controlled equity affiliates.

This book does not take issue with the general contention of theory that the large multinational firm should, in the majority of cases, still prefer direct investment over licensing. But this generalization often breaks down, and this chapter's first objective will be to define the theoretical and practical conditions under which licensing may, in fact, be the preferred strategy. Even when internal expansion via majority affiliates is the preferred option, in the emerging regulatory and economic environment it may be difficult for certain firms to attain it. The second objective of this chapter is to review the worldwide changes in the economic environment that are forcing companies to take a fresh look at licensing and other contractual modes for generating foreign income. An ap-

pendix outlines how organization design and strategy change over the technology
or product life cycle.

OVERSEAS EXPANSION STRATEGIES: SEQUENTIAL OR SIMULTANEOUS?

Older theories of international expansion implied sequential progression from
exporting and/or licensing to eventual equity investment. As the firm evolved
overseas, it was said to improve its knowledge of foreign markets, become less
ethnocentric, and finally muster the financial and managerial expertise to take
the greater risks of direct investment.[2] Similarly, in some presentations of the
internalization concept, licensing is presented as a ''last'' stage in the technology
cycle, a strategy to be considered upon incipient standardization of the product
or process.[3] While these are useful taxonomies, empirical evidence on their
actual use by firms is lacking. Two empirical studies by P. Telesio and F.
Contractor (admittedly focused on U.S. licensor companies and possibly biased
toward larger multinationals) indicate evaluation of overseas strategy options to
be simultaneous rather than sequential.[4] Firms appear at all stages to at least
consider the licensing alternative.

BASIS FOR EVALUATING LICENSING AGAINST OTHER STRATEGIES

While several detailed descriptions of the overseas expansion decision process
exist (e.g., Y. Aharoni, P. Buckley and M. Casson, or F. Root), the guiding
principle of comparative assessment is to choose the strategic option that maximizes the risk-adjusted present value of the net income stream from the nation
in question.[5] As we saw in Chapter 2, this must take into consideration the
opportunity costs and externalities associated with each option, such as the effect
on other product lines or other territories the firm is in or hopes to be in. For
exporting, projections of incremental margins on the sales to be achieved are
computed. For licensing, from projected payments of royalties and fees over the
anticipated life of the arrangement are subtracted the incremental costs of transferring the technology to the licensor, as well as the costs of possible licensee
competition in third country markets. This involves cash flow projections no
more tenuous than in the case of a proposed direct investment and often less so.
At any rate, recent evidence shows licensing income obtained by several U.S.
firms to be very respectable, especially considering the much lower risk associated with licensing returns compared with direct investment.[6]

The figures in Table 18, while they are after subtracting the technology transfer
costs borne by the licensor firms, do not include the possible opportunity costs
of licensee competition in third country markets and/or in the licensee's own
market subsequent to agreement expiry. But Telesio's findings, summarized in
Table 19, show that executives (at least in U.S. firms that actively license

Table 18

**Averages of Present Values of Net Cash Flows over Agreement Life from a
Global Sample of 102 Manufacturing-Sector Agreements Made by U.S. Firms**

($Thousands)

Industrial Market Economies	East Europe	LDCs	
3720	1717	3004	(Undiscounted)
326	226	284	(Discounted at 15 percent)

Source: F. Contractor, International Technology Licensing, See Footnote 4 to this
         chapter.

Table 19

Questionnaire Responses by Managers concerning Costs of Licensing

Scale: 7 = very concerned; 1 = not very concerned

(Mean responses shown below for selected questions.)

Question	Companies that li- cense (for income) and not for recip- rocal technology	Companies that do license for reciprocal tech- nology	Number of Observations
Creation of potential competitor when pre- sent agreements and patents expire	4.0	3.2	41
Lack of control over the export activities of licensees	3.8	3.9	40
Little or no control over the licensees' markets and market development	3.7	2.6	39

Source: P. Telesio, Foreign Licensing Policy, See Footnote 4.

internationally) are not overly concerned with this question of eventual licensee competition.[7] This would belie the universal applicability of statements such as the "ever-present danger of the firm's information monopoly being compromised by the licensee."[8] Studies show technology hardly corresponds to freely available information or a public good (except in the sense that its use in one location does not diminish its stock in another). They show technology transfer between firms to be an arduous, costly, and often less than thorough process, involving far more than the transference of mere blueprints, patents, or specifications, since most technology transfers include an important component of unpatented (or even undocumented) knowledge in organizational skills, production management techniques, and, occasionally, marketing.[9] In the majority of cases then, the licensee remains, in a degree, technologically and organizationally inferior, and sometimes dependent on the licensor for materials or trademarks. In most cases the licensee is bound under the purview of the agreement to the assigned territory. Thus, Telesio's findings summarized in Table 19, and echoed by Contractor's study, do not betray an excessive concern with the issue of licensee competitiveness in third markets. (In specific industries, however, such as semi-conductors, bio-sciences, and some chemical processes, this consideration is so dominant as to preclude licensing to non-affiliated firms.) But, one may ask, what about recent prohibitions on the part of several governments on placing territorial limitations on the licensee, even during the life of an agreement? Here again, the licensee's relative technical inferiority, smaller scale of output, tariff and transport impediments, and dependencies are shown to make their export propensity low, even in the absence of specific restraints in the agreement. In comparing the export behavior of U.S. firms' licensees in developing versus industrial countries, LDC licensee propensity to export is 57 percent of the already modest propensity for industrial nation licensees.[10]

The objective of the foregoing discussion was to show that in the increasingly stringent environment for direct investment, firms can no longer afford a policy that automatically rules out licensing. That licensing in many selected situations is not only very profitable, but superior in a net risk-adjusted comparison with alternatives is an idea gaining ground. Licensing income from royalties related to licensee sales has helped in many multinationals to smooth out the downturn in foreign dividend income in the last recession, profits being by definition more variable than output volume. In the next section, the circumstances under which licensing becomes an attractive option are explored.

POLICY VARIABLES UNDER WHICH LICENSING CAN BE A SUPERIOR STRATEGY

The 1970s saw the beginning of a reversal in the favorable climate for equity investment and trade in the twenty-five years after the second world war. Increasing transport rates, more discriminating government rules for investment and income repatriation, erosion of commanding technical leads, the ability of local firms to make competitive products or at least reasonable facsimiles, market saturation in Western Europe, and emergence of European- and Japanese-based international competitors are factors forcing U.S. firms to take a more discriminating look at alternative methods of doing business. Few firms today have the kind of technological and market lead which enabled an IBM to have an across-the-board policy of internalization. Given the changing conditions, licensing often comes out to be a preferred option. It is certainly superior to doing no business in a country, as in East Europe, where licensing is most often the only possibility. With by-now sophisticated bureaucracies, literally scores of developing nations, as well as some OECD countries, passed legislation or rules in the 1970s broadly emulating the Japanese example, which until recently sought to inhibit equity investment and replace it where possible with contractual means for technology transfer.[11] As opposed to the relatively unconstrained climate of the 1950s and 1960s, in the last decade governmental discrimination as to the entry conditions for foreign business had to be matched by corporate discrimination as to entry methods. This is the attempt of the following discussion, summarized in Table 20.

Strategic factors that impinge on the decision and which form the basis for corporate policy discrimination are:

Product cycle standardization and maturity. The idea of an international product cycle is familiar, where more mature, standardized products facing increasing competition and declining margins are produced, in the extreme case, in the least-cost global locations. Several studies confirm that production in LDCs involves relatively older and more standardized technologies.[12] But the Telesio and Contractor studies based on executive responses showed explicitly that product-cycle maturity also affects the mode of overseas business, and that more mature products within the firm are singled out as being amenable for licensing. (This directly confirms the expectations of the theory that maturing products within a firm that no longer confer an internalized advantage be offered for licensing. Product maturity, however, is but one of at least a dozen strategy variables that impinge on decision-making.)

Some companies have formalized this in their planning procedures. A product list is drawn up and given to the licensing department with a mandate to go all out and maximize licensing receipts. For other products, central coordination is required to ensure that a proposed licensing agreement does not interfere with the product division's export or equity intentions in a particular nation.

Similarly, a firm that knows it is due for a model change or technology jump will find itself willing to license the older version, secure in the knowledge of a continuing technical gap between it and their licensees. Alternatively, for example, executives in a U.S. aerospace firm related circumstances in which they were faced with the inexorable erosion of their lead and emergence of European competition in the international technology market and they decided they may as well license and lock up some income before their competition did. (In this case, the military nature of the industry precludes foreign investment and inhibits trade.)

Constraints on direct investment and direct investment income. The prohibition of foreign investment in certain industrial sectors, local participation requirements, stronger local competition, "fade out" clauses, and restrictions on repatriation of dividends are the environmental constraints over and above normal entrepreneurial risk facing investments in both LDC and OECD nations in varying degrees.[13] By the 1970s, in several industries in Europe, market saturation and strong domestic firms were factors providing further disincentives. In regions

Table 20

Licensing as a Preferred Strategy under the Following Circumstances

Strategic Concept	Conditions	Empirical Support/Studies **
1. Product Cycle Standardization	-Obsolescing products considered for licensing -Imminent technology or model change -Increasing competition in product market	Stobaugh(1971),Telesio(1977) Contractor(1980)
2. Environmental Constraints on FDI or FDI income	-Government regulations restricting FDI to selected sectors only -High political risk in nation -Market uncertain or volatile, licensor lacking in requisite marketing abilities, or market too small for FDI.	UN(1978), Ozawa(1979), UN(1977), Hayden(1976), Sagasti(1979)
3. Constraints on imports into licensee nation	-A high ratio for transport cost to value for item -Tariff or non-tariff barriers	Dunning(1980), Contractor(1981)
4. Licensor firm size	-Licensor firm too small to have financial, managerial or marketing expertise for overseas investment -Licensor firm too big (see 12 below)	Telesio(1977)
5. Research intensity	-Licensor firm will remain technologically superior, so as to discount licensee competition in other markets	Hayden(1976), Telesio(1977), Baranson(1978)
6. High rate of technological turnover	-Change so rapid, and technologies so perishable (e.g., semi-conductors) that even with equally proficient licensees, a design or a patent may be transferred with little fear of significant competition.	Contractor(1981)
7. Perpetuation of licensee dependency	-Even without or beyond the licensing agreement, effective licensee dependency maintained by trademarks, required components, or licensee hunger for technical improvements.	Davies(1977), UN(1975), Lall(1976)
8. Product vs Process Technologies	-licensing opportunities in auxiliary processes (e.g., galvanizing in the steel industry, or anodizing aluminum) even if the basic product technologies not licensed.	Teece(1977), Contractor(1981)

Table 20 *(continued)*

	Strategic Concept	Conditions	Empirical Support/Studies
9.	Reciprocal exchanges of technology	-Licensing as a valuable tool for obtaining technology or market rights, in industries characterized by high R.& D and market development costs and product diversity (e.g., Pharmaceuticals, Electricals, Chemicals).	Telesio (1977)
10.	"Choosing" competition	-With a patent about to expire, licensing gives a head start to a licensee firm favored by present patent holder. (May be illegal in some countries.)	Contractor (1981)
11.	Creation of auxiliary bus .ness	-Even if direct royalty income is inadequate, margins on components to or from licensee can be handsome (in the extreme, e.g., licensing automobile assemblers, licensing is tantamount to disguised imports). Other auxiliary business can be turnkey plants, joint bidding with licensee, etc.	Hayden (1976), Baranson (1978) Contractor (1981)
12.	Diversification and product-line organization in licensor firm	-Especially in large diversified firms, with divisional attention focused on the "product imperative", a centralized examination of the product / country matrix reveals neglected market penetration possibilities via licensing, (especially where considerable diversification puts a constraint on the financial and managerial resources available for equity ventures overseas)	Contractor (1981), Telesio (1977)

.. Please refer to the Notes at the end of this Chapter for full citations.

71

such as the COMECON countries and Japan, foreign investment and trade for that matter are options inhibited by government policy or lack of foreign exchange. In several LDCs, high political risk tilts the entry decision away from volatile dividends to more stable and agreement-bound income sources, such as royalties or fixed fees. Certainly these could be smaller, although not necessarily so, as suggested by average licensing income figures shown in Table 18. All that is suggested here is that, with higher risks and growing constraints on investment income, the neglect of licensing options will fail to maximize global profits.

Constraints on imports into licensee nation. Just as governmental regulations or political risk may rule out the direct investment option, transport costs (if a critical fraction of value) and tariff or non-tariff barriers often preclude the exporting option also. Government policy has been explicit in Japan, Brazil, India, Mexico, and Argentina on favoring the licensing method for technology acquisition by closing off the import alternative to indigenous companies, in the belief that in a balance-of-payments and dependency sense this is cheaper for the nation. Studies based on aggregate data lend tentative support.[14]

Licensor firm size. That the propensity to use licensing in an industry is inversely related to licensor company size, all other things being equal, was a statistically significant relationship in the Telesio study, although it was not supported in the analysis of aggregate data in Chapter 4.[15] The most immediately plausible explanation would be that the relatively smaller firm has a lower financial, managerial, and foreign marketing capability. Indeed, Telesio also confirmed relatively higher licensing propensity in companies with less experience in foreign operations, as measured by the proportion of total sales manufactured abroad by controlled subsidiaries.[16] While experience and size are often, though not necessarily, related, the direction of casuality between these two variables remains unknown.

At the same time, one encounters very large firms that undertake considerable licensing; but this may not be related to size *per se* as to product diversification. In many conglomerates, given large capital requirements and the magnitude of their product and nation spread, there is simply no way to internalize all production. Thus, one hears of a GE with hundreds of global licensees or an RCA licensing (with a buy-back provision) large-screen television designs to Hitachi.[17]

Research intensity of licensor company. How does research intensity relate to the question of strategic choice? At the moment, evidence is equivocal. Companies that spend relatively more on R&D as a percentage of sales in an industry were reported in the Telesio study to have a higher propensity to use the licensing mode over direct investment. (The study did not report which products in the R&D-intensive companies were licensed nor the product breakdown of the R&D expenditures, so that we are unable to say that this finding conclusively refutes the idea of greater licensing only with more standardized products.)

The finding does disprove the general contention that high-technology or R&D-intensive firms will uniformly opt for greater internalization or keeping the technology "in-house." Other evidence that casts doubt on this generalization is from the Contractor study, where licensing receipts were shown to increase with greater R&D in licensor firms.[18] An often applicable explanation may be that a firm is so comfortable in its technology lead and consequently fearless of imminent or eventual licensee competition, that it agrees to license (at an adequately high price) in all areas where investment is difficult or risky. Good examples are the several heavy equipment and basic industry firms that have extremely lucrative licensing arrangements in Eastern Europe. Payment may well be received in kind, but the margin on the buy-back arrangement is usually an extra bonus.

Rate of technological turnover. The rate of technical change (as opposed to R&D intensity) is another variable that, *ceteris paribus*, will induce significant use of licensing. Good examples are in the electronics and computer industries. Hypothetically, a company like Motorola may well license a chip design to a Hitachi, despite the fear that the licensee is technologically equal and already constitutes an international threat. This is because the rate of change is so rapid, i.e., the design is so perishable, that some licensing income may as well be generated on this design. The licensee is already proficient, so that the mere transfer of the design will not in itself improve the recipient's competitiveness. In the extreme case, the prospective licensee already has the specifications from patent filings or from "reverse engineering" and merely awaits the conferral of the right to the licensor's patent. (It is worth noting in passing that it is only in such relatively rare cases that technology comes closest to being akin to a "public good," in classical economics, i.e., where its use by one party does not entail costs or diminished use to another and where the costs of technology transfer are negligible.)

Perpetuation of licensee dependency. The disadvantages of licensing arising from licensee independence are often removed if the licensee is kept dependent for trademarks, required components, foreign market access, technical improvements, etc. This would be true even where the licensee government prohibits such explicit restraints as tied inputs. This is because, particularly in more protected environments, licensees' interests are likely to be closer to the licensor's than to their own government. Trademarks are a case in point: several studies (e.g., H. Davies, S. Lall, United Nations) show that often the licensee views the permission to use the foreign trade name as critical to marketing success and profit and, accordingly, craves it, where to the government it involves a balance-of-payments drain with little direct economic benefit over a local brand name.[19] (Not surprisingly, many nations like Mexico have come down hard on the inclusion of trademarks in technology transfer agreements.) Be that as it may, the point here is that it is licensees themselves who often desire such dependencies. Most importantly, once introduced, they lock the market and the producer into them, thus reducing the latter's freedom of action and bargaining strength when the agreement comes up for renewal.[20]

Similar situations exist with components supplied to the licensee, who often does not have domestic alternatives; with the licensee's exports through the licensor's international market network; and with technical improvements. In short, the inclusion of these features in the licensing "package" can often tip the balance in favor of licensing versus other options because they tend to constrain licensee freedom to compete with the licensor, thus removing an often important drawback to this strategic option.

Product versus process technologies. Several companies have realized that, even if the complete product technology is to be "internalized," there can be substantial incremental income possibilities in licensing associated or peripheral processes. For example, for a giant Pennsylvania steel producer for whom exports or foreign investment are out of the question, the licensing of oven door designs or galvanizing methods, to name but two examples, to scores of licensees all over the world involves little incremental costs (once the engineering and R&D costs have been incurred for their own operations), compared with the royalties that in the aggregate are extremely handsome. There is little likelihood of foreign steel companies as technology recipients increasing their international competitiveness vis-à-vis the licensor solely from a license involving a minor process. This is even more true for a globally oligopolistic industry like aluminum. Thus, you have an American aluminum producer aggressively seeking out licensees for anodizing processes or pull-top can technology, where a proposal to license the entire smelting or refining technologies would certainly be analyzed with much greater circumspection as to the future international competitive posture of the prospective licensee.

Many large U.S. firms neglect such licensing opportunities. A Detroit executive estimated that if his company were to organize internally to "collect" all the peripheral process technologies spread throughout the company, perhaps millions in incremental licensing income could be generated, even after subtracting the extra costs of personnel to administer such a program. As it is, the company does license processes like thermo-adhesion of coatings and special paint formulae. But this is completely incidental to its main strategic focus on building cars, and many licensing opportunities are ignored.

Reciprocal exchanges of technology. Reciprocal licensing has an important long-term strategic role apart from generation of income. In the pharmaceutical industry, not even the giants can do research on all biological fronts, or hope to go through testing and certification in all countries. Thus, exchange of knowledge and territorial rights is important for fuller representation in both a product range as well as territorial coverage sense. Thus, licensing out is the means for obtaining technologies and patents in a reciprocal licensing deal. Income is hardly a forgotten issue. If the perceived values of the exchanges are unequal, a compensatory cash flow is devised; but income is not the dominant objective.

Besides pharmaceuticals, this is an important consideration in some segments of the electrical and chemical industries.

"Choosing" the competition. Licensing has its strategic uses when a patent is due to run out. While this may be illegal in several countries, licensing transfers

the patent to a local firm that is favored by the patent holder in order to give the former a head start over other local firms. Even after the patent agreement runs out, a separate agreement covering non-patented information and assistance (commonly called "know-how") can be maintained. There are many other reasons for favoring a particular firm; there may be some present or future equity stake, a materials supply arrangement that will last beyond the patent expiry, joint ventures with that firm in third nations, and so on. The basic tactic is clear; that is, to perpetuate or extend by proxy the benefits of a patent beyond its legal life by a licensing arrangement.

Creation of auxiliary business. Any auxiliary business derived by the licensor from an agreement, whether mandated in the agreement or not, comprises extra income which often tilts the entry method decision in favor of licensing or makes licensing worthwhile (especially where otherwise no business is done in that country if exports and investment are not possible). In the foregoing sections, examples of auxiliary business have been given. A list of the main categories is given below:

1. Materials and components sold to licensee
2. Products bought back from licensee
3. Fees for future technical improvements given
4. Joint bidding and construction with licensee
5. *Ad hoc* technical assistance provided
6. Quality control and testing for licensee
7. Training of personnel

In several cases, the auxiliary business is so predominant that the licensing agreement is tantamount to being a cover. A good example is the licensing of automobile assemblers, who, at least in early years prior to the development of local suppliers, will buy much of the value of the automobile in parts from the licensor. Needless to say, for the licensor, the margins on parts (especially if taken on a variable cost calculation) will in early years far outweigh the royalties formally stated in the agreement. This is a form of disguised imports, aided often by lower tariffs on components than finished products, when the government wants local assembly. But even otherwise, for instance, in many nations that levy high duties on the import of TV sets and the parts and wish to reserve the consumer electronics industry for local entrepreneurship, a U.S. television firm has used licensing as means (or cover if you will) for entry into sheltered markets. Since licensees are heavily dependent for components, crave the U.S. firm's new models and trademarks, and since that nation's consumers are thereby "locked in," there is every reason to believe that in the absence of governmental intervention, this is a lucrative relationship of indefinite duration. The licensee will seek renewal anyway and get it, unless the government injects greater competition by allowing imports or mandates a minimum local value-added, or, worst of all from the corporate viewpoint, intervenes in the agreement renewal by limiting payments on both royalties and components prices.

Diversification and product line organization in the licensor company. Telesio's finding that companies with higher than average diversification are likely to choose licensing is subject to varying interpretation as to causes. The findings support the hypothesis that the greater the diversification, the thinner financial and managerial resources are stretched, and the firm has greater need for external support from joint venture partners or licensees, as opposed to internalized expansion via fully owned subsidiaries.[21] Alternatively, we may say that diversified firms have stronger central departments. For larger companies organized along product lines, there is usually a headquarters licensing department and/or corporate-planning function, which essentially performs a systematic market scanning and market entry method analysis. In such a case, licensing is likely to be favored somewhat more often for two reasons: first, central departments in such firms are more likely to have more complete information about a country and entry method options than a product-oriented manager. Second, they lack the bias of product managers for internal expansion over contractual methods.

It should be by now clear that there are at least a dozen policy variables that introduce complexity into the entry mode decision, and that generalizations about corporate preference for equity investments as an overseas expansion strategy ought to have limited use as far as corporate planners are concerned. Admittedly, licensing is superior in only selected circumstances. That these circumstances occur with moderate frequency is clear not only from the foregoing discussion, but also from the nearly $3 billon direct-licensing income received by U.S. firms from arm's-length parties. The next section details the hypothesis that the circumstances favoring licensing are increasing in number, intensity, and geographical spread.

CHANGES IN THE INTERNATIONAL BUSINESS ENVIRONMENT

This section summarizes the significant changes initiated in the last decade that would support the thesis of a marginal shift toward licensing at the expense of internal expansion of the multinational firm. We may note at the outset that, despite increased interest in licensing and a small increase in the relative share of licensing income in total foreign earnings of U.S. firms in the last recession, in the aggregate data for the U.S. reported by the Commerce Department there is as yet no conclusive evidence of such a shift. But this may well be because of inadequacies in reporting and classification in Commerce Department data. For example, there is a significant to serious underreporting problem in unaffiliated licensing data. Second, any auxiliary business such as sale of components is likely to enter the merchandise accounts even though such business is directly the consequence of the licensing deals. According to C. Oman, many technology transfers are not reported as such, but comprise part of turnkey deals, of which there has been an explosive proliferation in the last decade.[22]

An Environment-Scanning Checklist

The following summary is more in the nature of a set of hypotheses or an environmental-scanning checklist for the corporate strategist.

Saturation of traditional overseas markets for U.S. firms and the emergence of effective competition. The commanding technological leads of U.S. firms in a broad spectrum of industries has now eroded to the point where top managements are actively searching, in some industries, for ways to obtain European or Japanese know-how via in-licensing or acquisitions.[23] Thus, the higher profitability of direct investment in an oligopolistic environment is no longer available to many U.S. companies in the way that was possible in the 1950s. At the same time, licensing yields a surer return and preempts competition to an extent.

Proliferation of alternative sources of technology globally. For technology-importing nations, the availability of several alternative suppliers of technology puts them in a better bargaining position, where, on the contrary, an IBM could usually demand and obtain equity investment. In mature or consumer products, the availability of acceptable substitutes from Western European, Japanese, and even LDC sources has diminished the leverage of American companies significantly in the last decade.

Increased governmental intervention. The proliferation of schooled government regulators and the promulgation of legislation to control technology importation is a phenomenon not confined merely to LDCs, but is manifest even in OECD nations that have begun to formulate science and technology policies. For at least two decades until the late 1970s, Japanese technology policy discouraged direct investment, which by definition includes complete and ongoing transfer of production and organizational skills to the subsidiary, and substituted this, wherever possible, with licensing as a means of obtaining technology.[24] For government policymakers, the foregoing caveat "wherever possible" is the nub of a dilemma; for while non-equity arrangements are cheaper for the nation in terms of foreign exchange outflows for imported technologies, the value of the transfer is also lower than in a close equity association. For unsophisticated licensees, pure licensing arrangements, even with technical assistance, may not work. V. Balasubramanyam, studying Indian policy, suggests that, for complex technologies, direct investments there may produce a higher net benefit for the nation compared with arm's-length licensing.[25] Empirical work on this critical policy issue of modal choice from both corporate and governmental perspectives is very scant, and research is needed. An Organization of American States (OAS) Science Policy Research Unit study on Latin America reported that the incidence of pure licensing and contractual forms was correlated with the maturity of the industry and inversely related to patent protection and size of the technology-supplying firm. L. Mytelka similarly showed direct investment to be more frequent in complex technologies.[26]

The proposal for "collective bargaining" by technology recipients. This is today more a proposal than a reality. But the first steps in this direction have already been taken in some countries: government data banks have been set up to prevent duplication of technology imports, regulations prohibit technology suppliers from imposing restraints on affiliates or licensees who wish to sub-license, and governments have begun to exchange information on technology prices and sources.[27] These tendencies do not unequivocally portend an increase in licensing by U.S. firms. It may, in some cases, produce an opposite effect with companies seeking greater patent protection and refusing to license at all in some regions for fear that their technology will be widely dispersed with little gain to them and, in the worst case, eventual competition in third countries. Yet one can equally plausibly construct an opposite scenario, that this trend will force firms to seek as many licensees as possible on the presumption that some income from many licensees is better than no income from a region written off. The impact of these developments on corporate behavior must remain an open policy issue for now.

Weakening of the international patent system. Some developing nations are beginning to entertain the idea that, in many industries, the international patent system is detrimental to their interests in terms of the high costs of technology imported and continued dependence, as Lall asserts.[28] Patents, as government-sanctioned monopolies, are seen by critics as creating inefficiencies in the global technology market. The merits of this assertion and the long-run consequences of weakening the international patent system are treated more fully in later chapters. But as in the foregoing point, some scholars such as Dunning suggest the possibility at least that any such movement toward a more "efficient" global market for technology may force firms to "dis-internalize" technology where hitherto they had been reserved for equity affiliates.[29]

Increasing protectionism and transport costs. Higher tariffs, more non-tariff barriers, and costlier fuel compared with the period before 1973 are beginning to dampen the growth of trade. At the margin, it will tilt market entry decisions toward manufacturing near markets via the licensing and foreign equity investment alternatives. Obviously, this would affect certain industries more than others.

Higher interest rates. Higher interest rates are now a global phenomenon and affect borrowing and internal corporate calculations in all currencies. When companies face the choice of capital investment overseas versus a relatively quicker, less risky return with a comparatively negligible outlay, the latter contractual option would be preferred more often than when interest rates were low. This simple relationship is illustrated by Figure 2. *II'* represents the usual curve for the net present value of a capital investment as a function of the discount rate. The greater the time gap between cash outlays and net cash returns, i.e., the longer term the project, the steeper will be the slope of *II'*. Because licensing returns are more immediate compared with transfer of technology costs borne by the supplier, the slope of the curve *LL'* for the licensing alternative is far less steep. (Moreover, in many agreements, 54 percent to be exact in my earlier study, there is an instantaneous return in the shape of lump-sum or front-end payments). The net present value from licensing is lower than from an investment, in the range *OA* for the discount rate. Licensing however may yield a higher

Figure 2
The Strategy Choice as a Function of the Cost of
Capital Facing the International Firm

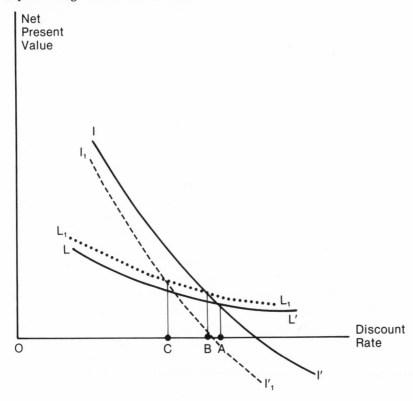

present value, for the same technology transfer, for any discount rate higher than A. The case in Chapter 8, appendix B, gives an example of this.

But this assumes that we are using the same company-wide discount rate for either strategy option, which is not correct. There are two factors to be taken into account: risk in licensing is lower because of the frequent linking of royalties to turnover, the fact that an agreement is a contractual commitment, and so on. Using a somewhat lower rate for licensing (lower than the standard rate for company-wide capital investments) yields the slightly displaced curve L_1L_1, and a break-even point B slightly lower than A. The differential effects of political risk are more pronounced. Since the effect of political risk on licensing is negligible, the curve LL' would hardly shift at all, but the curve II', using a higher discount rate for investment in a riskier country, does shift significantly to $I_1I'_1$, producing a new break-even point C. At all discount rates above C, licensing would be preferred. Thus in an era of higher corporate discount rates in general, the licensing alternative is preferred somewhat more often.

The dollar exchange rate. In the long run, under some certainty models, changes in the dollar exchange rate ought not to affect the capital investment decision.[30] (Practically speaking, however, the larger dollar outlays required to buy foreign assets when the dollar weakens against other currencies, as it did in the 1970s, may in some companies inhibit direct investment, making licensing at the margin a more attractive proposition and vice versa). However, a far more pervasive effect arises from the fact that exchange rates have floated since 1972. Under uncertainty about the exchange rate, not only is licensing less risky in the usual sense, but anticipated returns are much more immediate compared with the far longer planning horizons of a capital investment. This is particularly true when lump sum fees are paid at the inception of a licensing agreement.

CONCLUSIONS

The theoretical generalization that multinational firms will prefer "internalization" via direct investment over the sale of technology via licensing is a proposition that needs to be examined with greater circumspection in the emerging climate for international business. At least a dozen strategy variables or situations were presented where licensing could be a superior overseas market entry option. Recognizing that across-the-board policies can be sub-optimal, some companies are beginning to make entry strategy decisions on a case-by-case basis, formally including licensing as a possibility. In the extreme, a few firms periodically review the strategy decision for every combination on their product/country matrix. While aggregate figures for the U.S. do not yet show an unequivocal increase in the share of licensing in overseas income, the increased attention paid to this strategy option is manifested in the recent upgrading of licensing departments in international companies.

APPENDIX:

Technology and Organization Design: A Historical Parable

This appendix outlines how organizational structure and strategy change over the technology or product life cycle. Later we relate this to international licensing. The idea is to see how internal organization of the firm and its external expansion strategy are a function of the stage of evolution of the industry.

Technical change is at once the story of improved machinery or processes, as it is the story of organizational change. Let us take the hoary example of pin making. By the eighteenth century we find pin making had been transformed from an individual skilled worker operation to a sequential process, involving a division of labor. Let us examine this by a corporate allegory, the history of Q. Smith and Sons. Visiting their works in 1776, on the banks of the Coalbrooke river, one would have found each of the sons specializing in a different operation, one cutting the rods, another sharpening ends, another heat quenching the pins to make the metal harder, while the eldest was in charge of the most delicate operation of forging heads on each pin. The productivity gains of division of labor that the economist Adam Smith attributed to "facility" from task repetition, or what we today would call the individual worker learning curve, are also derived from the fact that each "assembly line" worker now does not waste time switching from task to task and materials are brought to him.[31] But such productivity gains are always partially offset by the costs of increased governance. The senior Quentin Smith, who previously had produced pins himself, now has his hands more than full with the task of buying the rods, scheduling the flow of semi-finished materials from one son to another, and marketing his now much larger output.

By 1825 the pin industry underwent another transformation in organization and scale as the result of engineering innovations—the use of precision metal-working equipment. Each rod or wire was now cut in a jig to an exact length, pin heads were now identically forged in a head-forming machine, and so on to produce standardized pins. The precision of the machines replaced the hand skill of the workers. What we see now is the birth of the modern organization characterized by the dual facets of hierarchy and departmentalization.[32] The locus of embodied skills has now apparently shifted from man to machine; but it has actually shifted from the worker to a caste of engineers, who design and tend the machines. Another caste of administrators would emerge above them to govern and control the increasingly complex flow of material and men, the wider distribution of the product, and the more stringent procurement and quality requirements that accompany the technical changes. Smith Ltd. is now also a large enough operation that wire cutting, head forming, heat treatment, etc., are now separate departments, each with its own "scientific manager."[33] Departmental specialization echoes, in larger scale, the individual worker specialization of fifty years ago. Once again, the greatly increased administrative or governance costs resulting from hierarchy and departmentalization are more than recompensed by the savings in production costs, as shown in Figure 3. (This process of increasing net returns to organizational scale would continue well into the twentieth century for most industries. But there are limits, as discovered by Ford Motor Co. who closed an automobile plant in 1979 because it was unmanageably big.)[34]

By the early decades of this century, Smith Ltd. was an even larger concern, not merely because demand for pins continued to grow as office paperwork, garment factories and other uses expanded. The company also "backward integrated" into wire-drawing factories to control their principal input. (In Williamsonian terms, this internalization or "vertical integration" substituted for a market transaction where wire used to be purchased from an arm's-length supplier.[35]) The company also expanded horizontally into related areas such as needles and sewing machines and into totally unrelated areas such as aircraft

Figure 3
Aspects of the Technology Cycle, 1776 to 1976

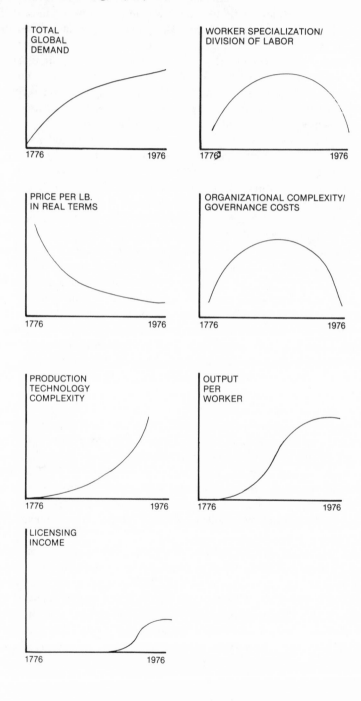

components. This evolution culminated in a multi-divisional, diversified firm called Smith Transglobal Inc., whose headquarters shifted in 1966 to the Netherland Antilles. Pin-making operations had in the meanwhile been established in the former British colonies such as Canada, India, Australia, and South Africa; but the pin division was treated as a sentimental relic, contributing less than a tenth of global turnover, though in 1966 it produced more pins than ever before in its history.

In production technology there had been another revolution. A single skilled operator, more an expert technician than a worker, now tended an automatic machine the size of a desk. What had been a five-department operation was performed in a single machine. Miles of wire drawn and wrapped to precise specification, onto standard spools, were loaded onto the machine, from which tons of pins were issued daily.

As a result of this technology, where one machine and worker does the entire job, organizational complexity and governance costs are once again down to levels comparable to the earliest years of the firm, thus tracing an inverted U-shaped curve over time. (See Figure 3). In the market, what had been a product for the rich in the founder's time, was now a commodity sold by the pound, with margins of the order of a penny or two. Worse yet, with the advent of alternative fasteners such as staples and tape, the market was distinctly "mature" or declining in industrial nations, redeemed only by continuing expansion of demand in Asia, Latin America, and Africa, whose increasing populations found the more "sophisticated" fasteners beyond their incomes.

In such a situation, what constitutes appropriate global strategy for the pin division? What is the role of licensing in international strategy? Clearly, direct investment in pin factories, if not impossible, would yield returns inferior to other products of the firm. Second, key managers and investable funds were occupied in larger, more lucrative ventures in other divisions of the diversified firm. Third, with declining unit margins in this fiercely competitive, standardized product, transportation costs were becoming important, so that pin factories tended, all over the world, to become smaller, geographically decentralized units, serving their immediate regions. But this was precisely what the Smith pin division could now exploit with the new technology; for if pins were thoroughly prosaic, standard items, their efficient production, on the other hand, was a relatively sophisticated, if small-scale operation whose technology could be licensed. Earning a few cents per pound of royalties is superior to earning the same few cents of repatriated earnings on capital investment. Even better, the pin division engineers and licensing executives, with few factories of their own to worry about, could set up licensee after licensee all over the world.

The years 1966 to 1976 were a surprise to higher management. The pin division, whose demise was anticipated by executives unmoved by history or sentiment, turned out instead to become one of the conglomerate's "cash cows," by signing up over ninety licensees worldwide. In-house turnover declined to less than 3 percent of the whole company's turnover, but in the recession years

1975 and 1976 the pin division contributed over 15 percent to company profits. What were the contents of these technology transfers? Agreements contained a variety of elements such as

For New Operations	*For Existing Operations*
Factory design and equipment layout	Improved heat-treatment methods to produce a superior quality pin
Organizational and marketing assistance	
Machine setup and technician training	Change of technology to use thinner gauge wire for significant cost savings
	Diversified uses such as small fasteners and nails for other industries (e.g., furniture)

A key to the success of the program was a small technology transfer team consisting of two licensee development executives who would seek, solicit, and negotiate with prospective licensees; an engineer and a business analyst to help licensees with technical and business development problems; and a buyer who supplied many licensees with the pin-making machines, precision-drawn wire, and related hardware. Needless to say, an important profit source was the margin earned on such equipment and accessories sold to licensees. In many nations in fact, other business opportunities were spotted with the help of the licensees, in the office equipment, textile, and related fields, information that was used to advantage by other Smith Transglobal divisions.

Over the ten-year life of the technology licensing program, $40 million had been earned in royalties and technical fees, after deducting for the team's salaries and expenses. Another $15 million or so was earned as margins on sales made to licensees, to make a total incremental cash flow contribution of $55 million. (The extra profits made by other divisions were not quantified.) But this could not continue indefinitely. There was approaching saturation even in some developing nations; several licensees did not renew the agreement since, after learning the technology and marketing, there was relatively little new expertise the licensor could supply; and 1975 was the first year the number of licensees did not grow beyond the peak of ninety-three worldwide. Wisely, the divisional vice president, with generous help from corporate planning at headquarters, had foreseen this day. The $55 million cash "throw off" had been used quietly to acquire a company that manufactured the leading pin-making machine, as well as other specialized fasteners. More money was put in to vitalize this unit's research and development activities since corporate planning believed the future lay in fasteners uniquely tailored to industrial applications. In 1977 the division was renamed the fastener division. Pin-producing units themselves were either sold off or abandoned, although some income still rolled in from existing licensing agreements. A posthumously commissioned bust of the founder holding a pin in his right hand continued to grace the entrance lobby as a reminder of the firm's origins.

NOTES

1. Telesio, P., *"Foreign Licensing Policy in Multinational Enterprises,"* DBA dissertation, Harvard University, 1977, describes practices in sixty-six U.S. and non-U.S. licensor companies. Also, see surveys in later chapters in this book.

2. For example, see Perlmutter, H., "The Tortuous Evolution of the Multinational Corporation," *Columbia Journal of World Business*, January 1969, pp. 9–18; or Johanson, T., and Vahlne, J., "The Internationalization Process of the Firm–A Model of Knowledge Development and Increasing Foreign Market Commitments," *Journal of International Business Studies*, Spring/Summer 1977, pp. 23–32.

3. Rugman, A., "A New Theory of the Multinational Enterprise: Internationalization versus Internalization," *Columbia Journal of World Business*, Spring 1980, pp. 23–29.

4. See Telesio, *Foreign Licensing Policy*, and Contractor, F., *International Technology Licensing: Compensation, Costs and Negotiation* (Lexington, Mass.: D. C. Health & Co., 1981).

5. Aharoni, Y., *The Foreign Investment Decision Process* (Boston: Harvard University Press, 1966). Buckley, P., and Casson, M., *The Future of the Multinational Enterprise* (New York: Holmes & Meier, 1976). Root, F., *Foreign Market Entry Strategies* (New York: AMACOM, 1982). A point to be noted is that, if under the country's tax rules, the treatment of income from export sales, licensing fees, and dividends is not identical, the calculations should be on an after-local-and-U.S. taxes basis.

6. The risk is lower, not just because the licensee bears the entrepreneurial risk, but because royalties (occuring in 80 percent of agreements) are keyed to output rather than paid out of profit. Moreover, 54 percent of agreements contain front-end or lump-sum fees payable regardless of licensee performance. (Data are from Contractor, *International Technology Licensing*, Chapter 5.)

7. Telesio. *Foreign Licensing Policy*, footnote 4, p. V-10.

8. Rugman, "A New Theory of the Multinational Enterprise," p. 27.

9. See Teece, D., *The Multinational Corporation and the Resource Cost of International Technology Transfer* (Cambridge, Mass.: Ballinger, 1977). Contractor, F., "The 'Profitability' of Technology Licensing by U.S. Multinationals: A Framework for Analysis and an Empirical Study," *Journal of International Business Studies*, Fall 1980, pp. 40–63. See also Killing, P., "Technology Acquisition: License Agreement or Joint Venture," *Columbia Journal of World Business*, Fall 1980, pp. 38–46, for a similar viewpoint from the technology recipient end.

10. Contractor, *International Technology Licensing*, pp. 116–121. The difference was significant at the 0.02 level.

11. For Eastern Europe, see Hayden, E., *Technology Transfer to East Europe: U.S. Corporate Experience* (New York: Praeger, 1976). For a summary of LDC rules and policies, see United Nations, *National Legislation and Regulations Relating to Transnational Corporations* (New York: United Nations, 1977). For a review of Japanese policy, see Ozawa, T., "Technology Transfer and Control Systems: The Japanese Ex-

perience," a paper delivered at the NSF Conference on Technology Transfer Control Systems in Seattle, April 1979.

12. There are several, ranging from Stobaugh, R., *The International Transfer of Technology in the Establishment of Petrochemical Industries in Developing Countries* (New York: United Nations, 1971), to Contractor, "The 'Profitability' of Technology Licensing."

13. See United Nations, *National Legislation and Regulations* and United Nations, *Transnational Corporations in World Development: A Re-examination* (New York: United Nations, 1978), for a general review. For Latin America, see Sagasti, F., *Technology, Planning and Self-reliant Development: A Latin American View* (New York: Praeger, 1979). For Japan, see Ozawa, "Technology Transfer and Control Systems." For Eastern Europe, see Hayden, *Technology Transfer to East Europe.*

14. Dunning, J., "Towards an Eclectic Theory of International Production: Some Empirical Tests," *Journal of International Business Studies*, Spring 1980, pp. 9–31. Also see Contractor, F., "The Composition of Licensing Fees and Arrangements as a Function of Economic Development of Technology Recipient Nations," *Journal of International Business Studies*, Winter 1980, pp. 47–62.

15. Telesio, *Foreign Licensing Policy*, pp. VI-9–VI-17.

16. Ibid., pp. VI-26–VI-30.

17. "Makers Bet Millions that Big TV Screens Will Be Next Rage In Home Entertainment," *Wall Street Journal*, March 9, 1981, p. 25.

18. Contractor, "The Profitability of Technology Licensing." Again, this does not necessarily prove licensing will gain in relative importance with respect to direct investment; only that licensing revenues are positively correlated with R&D intensity. However, it casts doubt on the generalization that high-technology firms will avoid licensing.

19. Davies, H., "Technology Transfer through Commercial Transactions," *Journal of Industrial Economics*, December 1977, pp. 161–191; Lall, S., "The Patent System and the Transfer of Technology to Less-Developed Countries," *Journal of World Trade Law*, January 1976, pp. 1–15; UNCTAD, *Major Issues Arising from the Transfer of Technology to Developing Countries: A Case Study of Chile* (New York: United Nations, 1975).

20. Lest this discussion sound too cynical, we need to remember that the inclusion of such features in a technology transfer agreement is a non-zero-sum game, as evidenced by the frequent licensee craving for such provisions. For instance, a 1972 study in Chile showed trademarks to be far and away the single most ubiquitous element in a sample of 399 agreements. See United Nations, *Major Issues.*

21. See Stopford, J., and Wells, L., *Managing the Multinational Enterprise* (New York: Basic Books, 1972).

22. Oman, C., "New Forms of International Investment," Working Paper, OECD Development Center, 1982. See Baranson, J., *Technology and the Multinationals* (Lexington, Mass.: Lexington Books, 1978).

23. Abegglen, J., "U.S.-Japanese Technology Exchange in Perspective, 1946–1981," in Uehara, C. (ed.), *Technology Exchange: The U.S.-Japanese Experience* (New York: University Press, 1982).

24. See Ozawa, "Technology Transfer and Control Systems." Only recently has this been relaxed and not for all industries.

25. Balasubramanyam, V., *International Transfer of Technology to India* (New York: Praeger, 1973).

26. Mytelka, L., "Licensing and Technology Dependence in the Andean Group," *World Development*, June 1978, pp. 447–459.

27. See Singh, R., "A View Favoring Collective Bargaining," paper presented at the UNIDO/LES Symposium on Licensing and the Proposed New International Economic Order, in New York, June 1976.

28. Lall, "The Patent System."

29. Dunning, J., "Alternative Channels and Modes of International Resource Transmission," a paper presented at the NSF Conference on Technology Transfer Control Systems, in Philadelphia, February 1979.

30. Assuming purchasing power parity and "international" Fisher effects, etc.

31. The pin-making example was first broached by the political economist Adam Smith, *An Inquiry into the Nature and Causes of the Wealth of Nations*, Cannan, E., (ed.) (Chicago: University of Chicago Press, 1976). Reprint of 1776 edition.

32. For a classic summary treatment see Chandler, A., "The United States: Seedbed of Managerial Capitalism," in Chandler, A., and Daems, H. (eds.), *Managerial Hierarchies* (Cambridge, Mass.: Harvard University Press, 1980), Chapter 1.

33. The term "scientific management" was coined by Frederick Taylor, the father of the discipline of industrial engineering. See, for instance, his 1911 work, *The Principles of Scientific Management* (New York: Norton & Co., 1967).

34. Of course, in the automobile and other industries we have the emergence of another factor that now enables the same productivity at considerably lower organizational scale: Computerization, or rather the implementation of management information systems, enables a descaling and decentralization of operations, while increasing organizational flexibility and response.

35. Williamson, O., *Markets and Hierarchies: Analysis and Antitrust Implications* (New York: Free Press, 1975).

6

Licensing Practice in U.S. Companies: Corporate and Public Policy Implications of Two Empirical Studies

This chapter discusses the findings of two studies of international licensing practice in U.S. firms. We have discussed the role of licensing so far in previous chapters in theoretical or normative terms or in terms of aggregate U.S. data. But what are companies actually doing? How are they responding to changes in the international business environment? What is the degree of their reliance on intellectual property laws protecting patents or trademarks? Which of the strategy variables discussed in Chapter 5 actually influence the level of licensing activity? The contents and industry distribution of technology agreements signed by U.S. companies also need to be analyzed since they have a bearing on these questions.

Corporate policy in U.S. firms is marking a retreat from an across-the-board insistence on majority or fully owned foreign affiliates. Already, in several of the largest companies the number of global licensees exceeds the number of foreign affiliates. Data from as far back as the 1977 Benchmark Survey of the Commerce Department (published in 1981) show 23,698 equity foreign affiliates of U.S. companies but licensing agreements with some 29,000 unaffiliated foreigners.[1] Of course, this is somewhat misleading since in the gross licensing income of $8.7 billion repatriated to U.S. companies in 1981, income from independent or minority joint venture licensees comprised only an estimated 28 to 30 percent, the rest coming from their own majority affiliates who are also licensees.[2] But the numbers are large enough in their own right (or when compared with foreign affiliate dividends, which were $10.5 billion in 1981) so that there is growing recognition of the need to formalize technology policy in companies, to inventory technical assets, and to consider explicitly alternative strategies to foreign direct investment so as to optimize global returns.[3] Of these, licensing is receiving increasing attention.[4] We need to ask, however, whether this is due to an awareness by executives of its role in strategy, or whether licensing now appears somewhat more attractive merely because the alternatives of exporting or foreign investment are nowadays more constrained. This question is also addressed in one of the studies.

Many nations in the 1970s began to limit the ability of foreign investors to form majority affiliates, allowing only minority equity or licensing agreements as the Japanese did earlier.[5] The policy objectives of several nations, on the other hand, particularly the less-developed countries, are not amenable to generalization because, while many have inhibited equity investment, some have also placed constraints on the terms of licensing agreements.[6] Developing nations also have been winning points at the World Intellectual Property Office (WIPO) talks to revise terms of the Paris Convention regarding patents and trademarks. Both developing and industrial countries are taking unilateral measures, such as the restrictions on foreign trademarks in Mexico or the Canadian proposal to forfeit foreign patents if they are not used within a certain time. In broader government policy terms, the international transfer of technology, patented or otherwise, is scrutinized as to its cost to the recipient country and its effects on the competitiveness of the recipient nation in international markets. The results discussed here will shed some light on corporate strategy responses to these environmental changes. A portion of the analysis also models statistically the level of a firm's licensing activity based on variables such as its size, internationalization, patent and trademark coverage, etc.

Another important objective is to draw out, wherever possible, implications for U.S. government policy on issues such as intellectual property protection and the role of medium and small firms, if any, in international technology transfers. The U.S. government interest in these developments springs from four interrelated considerations: (1) the effect of technology transfer overseas on the continued competitive posture of American industries in global markets; (2) the maintenance of patent protection in foreign nations in order to generate sufficient global revenues to enable U.S. companies to continue their investment in research and development; (3) encouragement of medium and small companies to utilize their technologies in overseas markets; and (4) balance-of-payments effects of technology transfer.[7]

Considering the significance of international licensing to these issues, surprisingly little empirical information is available in a comprehensive manner to aid U.S. or company policymakers. For instance, what is the relationship between company size and international licensing? Is it restricted to the larger firms? To what extent do patents, trademarks, or turnkey contracts figure in international agreements? Overall, if patents, for example, are not seen as critical by companies, then the almost isolated, hard-line U.S. position in the WIPO patent talks may not be warranted or necessary to protect U.S. technology.[8] On the other hand, if patent coverage is indispensable to a few industries, then perhaps the selective discriminatory powers proposed for the president under the revision of the Trade Act of 1974 (which specifically covers intellectual property) may be a more effective intervention for these industries. Under the proposed legislation, if there is "unjustifiable" denial of adequate protection in a foreign nation, such as unreasonable forced licensing or very short patent duration, practical inability to prosecute infringers, delays or only token fines inflicted on violators, impossible burden of proof placed on the patent holder, or too narrow an interpretation of the patent right (as determined by the U.S. trade representative), then the president is to be empowered to take actions that may include withholding of most-favored-nation treatment.[9] These issues are not the purview of this book, but the point here is that there have been almost no studies with a large, comprehensive sample size to answer basic empirical questions such as the content of technology agreements; their number and distribution by industry, region, and company size; the views of corporate executives as to the importance of patent and trademark protection in advanced industrial or less-developed countries; and the role of small and medium firms in technology licensing

The first sample, involving 241 companies, is based on the 1982 Technology Transfer Survey of the Licensing Executives Society, whose data I analyzed with permission after questionnaire responses were already received by the society. Apparently, in designing the questionnaire, complexity was sacrificed in favor of a comprehensive U.S.-wide, all-industry response from a very large, representative sample of firms. This approach was successful in that responses from as many as 300 firms were received, out of which I was able to cull 241 usable responses involving technology transferor companies (as opposed to law firms or consultants, unless the latter were filling out the questionnaire on behalf of a manufacturer firm client). The gratifyingly large response, which may involve as many as a quarter of all U.S. firms that license, was, however, at the expense of getting all the data in very simple categorical or interval measures or ratios. Statistical inferences can nevertheless be drawn and conclusions derived for policy formulation.

The second sample, involving forty-four companies' responses, provides greater detail and was initiated by me in 1982 to address specifically the corporate strategy issues raised in Chapter 5 and earlier in the book, to get actual measurements of licensing income, the ingredients of agreements, the degree of international competition in the technology, the organization of the licensing function, and so on—a level of detail that necessitated personal cultivation of these companies, some of whose policies are written up in cases at the end of this chapter. (see Appendix C.)

In this chapter we treat a few of the same hypotheses as in Chapter 4, but we use data from company samples instead of data for the United States as a whole. There is a minor degree of overlap between the two questionnaires and, where it does occur, a comparison of the two samples is of interest. Further details on each sample, its industry distribution, its representativeness versus aggregate U.S. data, etc., are presented later. Now we turn to a review of the theoretical background of some of the hypotheses tested in the data.

DISCUSSION OF EMPIRICAL ISSUES AND HYPOTHESES

The empirical issues investigated fall into four categories:

• *Characteristics of U.S. firms* that license technology overseas in terms of their size, industry, and products licensed.

• *Contents of technologies* and industrial property rights transferred. The perceived importance of intellectual property protection laws overseas.

• *Strategy role* of licensing and underlying reasons.

• *Modeling the incidence* of licensing in the firm as a function of industry and product variables.

Characteristics of U.S. Licensors

This is an area about which not much is known. A partially reliable idea of the industry distribution of U.S. licensors may be obtained from the Commerce Department, but only in broad categories equivalent to the three-digit SIC classification, the only information available is in the Benchmark Surveys, of which the most recently available has 1977 data.[10] For U.S. policy in international discussions over patent or trademark rights, the first question is just which U.S. industries engage in international licensing. In recent academic studies, such as R. Caves et al. or F. Contractor (see note 4), the sample size has either been small, as in the former case, or else the sample was designed to ape the Commerce Department distribution, as in the latter study.[11] It is only here that every member organization in the Licensing Executives Society was polled, and, apart from a possible non-response bias, this survey represents the only other credible industry breakdown of U.S. licensors. Further details are given later.

As far as the distribution of U.S. licensors by size is concerned, nothing so far is known. The issue of firm size is relevant because more attention has recently been paid in U.S. economic policy to the role of small and medium companies in job and technology growth. Empirically, their participation in overseas business or licensing in particular is not known with any degree of certainty. Theory itself can lead us to contrary conclusions about the use of licensing as a foreign expansion strategy as a function of firm size. On the one hand, since licensing does not involve a significant investment of capital or management time, licensing would be favored by smaller companies as a foreign market entry strategy.[12] On the other hand, if in fact most transferable technologies, patents, and valuable trademarks are possessed by large corporations, then they would be the ones to license. Indeed, the share of individuals and small businesses in patent registration is under 25 percent.[13] However, there is another consideration: while large corporations may be the possessors of most technologies, they are said to be reluctant to transfer these to any firms overseas other than their own controlled affiliates, in which case a licensing agreement, if one exists, is only an adjunct. In such large companies, arm's-length licensing may, on the other hand, be resorted to when a controlled equity investment is not contemplated, such as in politically risky environments or where controlled affiliates cannot be established or where tight patent registration in all major countries obviates fear of licensee competition or in mature or peripheral technologies. In short, the various *a priori* theoretical arguments are not congruent as to the relationship between firm size and the scope of licensing. There are so far no empirical data and the policymaker is even unaware whether small firms participate at all in international licensing.

As related questions (explored in more detail later) in developing nations where intellectual property protection laws are less effective, are smaller firms even less represented compared to their share in industrial country licensing? Do the smaller firms rely more on pure patent licensing as opposed to licensing of know-how, which requires more of a managerial or financial commitment by the licensor? This leads us to another fundamental issue, namely, to what extent are international transfers of technology predicated upon or dependent upon the transfer of patent rights and trademarks as part of the overall agreement? What is the incidence of patents and trademarks in international agreements in general?

Contents of Technology Transfer Agreements

We have seen that what is transferred to a licensee under agreement consists of a mix of

1. Intangible property rights such as
     • Patents
     • Trademarks
2. Services rendered such as   Occasionally this is included under
     • Technical assistance   the rubric of know-how
     • Managerial assistance
3. Information that is not patented but that can be vital to the competence of the licensee—this is labeled "know-how."
4. Tangible goods traded
     • Raw materials   Inputs to the licensee's
     • Components   production
     • Capital equipment
     • "Buy back" of
       licensee's output

Empirically speaking, the relative mix of the elements listed above continues to be of considerable relevance to corporations in their desire to maximize the overseas return on technologies, as well as to governments whose policies set the effective level of protection accorded to patents or trademarks registered by foreigners.

The frequency of patents in licensing. If technology were freely transferable information, akin to a public good in classical economics, then technology transfer of patented technology would involve no more than issuing permission to the licensee. Under this theory, since knowledge disseminates itself freely and without cost, a licensee already has the production and marketing capability and merely awaits the conferral of the patent or trademark to proceed.[14] How often is this true in practice? If this were true, then patent coverage would be absolutely critical to the patent holder, and the patent by itself would be a valuable, transferable asset. The literature tells of several instances, particularly in the chemical and pharmaceutical industries, of the prospective licensee being technologically capable and ready to proceed on their own with only a patent license. On the other hand, there are recorded instances of licensees failing to produce a viable product with a pure patent license and being forced to call on the licensors for further assistance in the shape of know-how or unpatented but proprietary information.[15] Many, if not most, international technology agreements are said to contain know-how in addition to the patent, which in many cases is not the important component of the "package." But there are no hard statistics so far.

For U.S. policy to protect American companies' interests, a hypothetical yet important question is this: What would be the effects of a serious erosion or absence of intellectual property protection laws in foreign countries? Would it retard licensing by increasing the fear of licensee competition, while reducing overseas income? Which industries would be affected? To what extent could foreign firms appropriate technology developed in the United States and operate on their own (and vice versa)?

Trademark incidence in licensing. On the utility of trademarks, there is a similar (inconclusive) theoretical debate between classical welfare economics theory, which considers trademarks a monopolistic advantage possessed by the firm, and marketing theory, which would contend that the benefits to consumers by way of quality assurance, standardization, and ongoing research outweigh the costs of trademarks to society. To the United States, the consequences of an erosion of trademark protection abroad may be somewhat less onerous than in the case of patents if trademarks do not figure as prominently in technology transfers or the erosion of foreign revenues from the inability to use international trademarks (or their debasement by imitators) will not lower the level of R&D or quality assurance programs in multinational firms.

Several developing countries that accept in principle the value of patents as an impetus to innovation and technology transfer consider that, for their countries at least, the costs of foreign trademarks outweigh the benefits to their populations. Moreover, they contend, the mere fact of the trademarks being foreign confers an advantage on the international firm in xenophilic societies and inhibits local competition. Also, licensee exports may be curtailed if they lack trademark rights outside their territory. In extreme cases, it is said that trademarks may become the dominant component in the agreements signed between the LDCs' licensees and foreign firms. For example, in Chile, a 1971 analysis of some 400 licensing agreements showed that trademark transfers were found in 78 percent of agreements, where by contrast transfer of rights to patented processes and inventions occured in 49 percent and 32 percent, respectively.[16] There are very few data to show whether this represents an extreme or typical example. (It is likely that the restrictions on foreign trademarks since the date of the above study have reduced their incidence in developing nations.). S. Patel reported that a quarter of the 4 million trademarks in force in 1974 were registered in LDCs and that of these half were foreign.[17] For our purposes, a relevant empirical question is whether trademarks are more or less represented in agreements in LDCs versus industrial nations, and what is their frequency of occurrence in general?

Auxiliary business accompanying the technology transfer. Our discussion in Chapter 5 suggested that the strategic importance of licensing to American firms would be considerably greater if the transfer of the basic technology, patents, trademarks, and know-how were used to create auxiliary business opportunities such as erection of manufacturing facilities and the sale of raw materials, intermediaries, and related products, whose profits conceivably could be much larger than nominal royalties. The reader will recall that theory describes royalties and other fees offered by a licensee in negotiations usually to be below the potential earnings derivable from an equity investment. But if the agreement could be sweetened from the technology seller's viewpoint by inclusion of other elements on which an auxiliary margin could be earned, that might tip the balance in favor of the licensing option. Empirically speaking, supply and counter-trade with Eastern European licensees is of course well known. But there is no overall picture for other nations.

The Strategy Role of Licensing

A firm that has expended funds to develop a technology will then seek to maximize global returns on it. This is done by considering, in each nation separately, the question of optimal entry strategy to the extent that the country comprises a segmented market.[18] From each nation the firm will seek to extract a "technology margin," defined as the present value of all receipts (from an affiliate or a licensee) such as dividends, royalties, or payments for materials, etc., less the technology transfer or any other costs borne by the international firm on behalf of its licensee or affiliate. We saw in Chapter 2 that the technology margin is usually not the same as the local earnings of a licensee or affiliate company since royalties or dividends are normally only a fraction of the local earnings.

How does an international firm choose, for a particular nation, equity ownership, licensing, or a combination of the two? In theory, there is no reason why a pure contractual licensing arrangement should not yield an equivalent or superior technology margin to that derived by a full equity position. But more often than not firms prefer investment over licensing. Why? There are three reasons, and all three ultimately devolve on fundamental questions of the nature of technology and the international legality of intangible property rights, a focus of the empirical analysis to follow.

Transferability and transfer cost. The first consideration is the transferability of the technology to an independent licensee and the cost to the licensor in so doing. If the technology is complex, uncodified in a patent, and the licensee firm unsophisticated, technology transfer costs would be much higher compared with a transfer to one's own affiliate. This makes the technology margin lower in licensing. Possible exceptions to this are when the product or process is older or standardized and when the firm is small and the cost of establishing overseas affiliates and creating technical capability there *de novo* is insuperably high.[19]

Low value offered by a licensee. The second consideration focuses on the value put on the technology by an independent licensee. Typically, because of ignorance or higher uncertainty or relative backwardness, an independent licensee or local joint venture partner in negotiations is likely to offer payment below the amount that a fully owned subsidiary can earn on that technology in that nation. That is to say that direct licensing income from royalties and fees may be seen by the technology-possessing company as too meager unless there is additionally indirect compensation such as reciprocally receiving technology from a licensee on signing an agreement or, later on, in the form of "grantbacks" and component supply or buy back or other profit-making avenues.

Opportunity costs of licensing. The third consideration has to do with the opportunity costs of a licensing strategy in the licensee nation or even in third countries. Since most agreements are on an exclusive basis, the licensor usually foregoes the opportunity of doing business in the nation such as exporting directly to it, for instance. However, these foregone opportunities may not be that valuable when

- The country's regulations or political risk inhibit forming majority-owned subsidiaries.
- Tariff barriers or transport costs preclude importing the product.
- With a patent expiring there may be competition, so if licensing is permissible at this stage, it can serve to co-opt some of the competition and generate income. By the same token, after patent expiry if the margins earned directly on the company's sales are going to drop, the "opportunity" costs of a licensing strategy will be lower.
- The firm has the opportunity in theory to invest in the nation but cannot do so because of internal management or financial constraints. This may happen when a firm is too small or, on the other hand, large but so diversified that strategic attention and resources are focused on other countries and products for direct investment purposes.

Furthermore, unless legally restricted to a territory by a trademark or patent coverage, a licensee may theoretically even compete with the technology seller in third countries. To summarize the strategic exceptions which minimize the fear of licensee competition:

- Divulging detail about a process (as opposed to the complete product) will not hurt the company's competitiveness. This is especially true for peripheral processes.

- The rate of technical change is so rapid that obsolescing technologies can be licensed without fear of licensees competing.
- The licensee's continued dependency is assured even after the agreement expires because of trademarks or the hope of receiving new models or because of their continuing need for components and materials from the licensor.

Thus the opportunity cost of possible licensee competition in third countries may be, and often is, negligible.

Modeling the Incidence of Licensing in the Firm

The objective of the regression analysis will be to model the level of licensing activity in U.S.-based firms as a function of size, internationalization, the incidence of patents or trademarks, the extent of international competition, and stage in the product cycle.

The two samples involving 241 and 44 companies, respectively, were independent efforts until I was asked to analyze the former. Hence, there is only a partial overlap in design and the kinds of data collected. Nevertheless, in Table 21 and hereafter the two are compared side by side to see in which instances conclusions support or contradict each other.

In the 241-company sample, most of the data are in categories. The "dependent" variable, that is, the variable whose magnitude we are trying to explain statistically, is either the number of agreements in various regions of the world

Table 21
Regression Models for the Incidence of Licensing

	241 Company Sample	44 Company Sample
DEPENDENT VARIABLES	TOTTS: Total no. of agreements (global) FORTTS: Total no. of agreements outside the U.S. DEVTTS: Number of agreements in developing nations INDTTS: Number of agreements in industrial nations P3:Ratio of agreements in industrial	INCOME: $ Licensing income in millions annually from independent licensees overseas LINC1: INCOME as defined above, divided by annual gross sales revenue of majority foreign affiliates LINC2: INCOME in $ Thousands, divided by annual sales

Table 21 *(continued)*

	countries over total P4:Ratio of agreements in developing countries over total	overseas by company directly and by its majority affiliates in millions
INDEPENDENT VARIABLE AND EXPECTED SIGN OF COEFFICIENT IN PARENTHESIS	SALES: Total Sales of Company[a] (+) MARKET: Degree of internationalization of company's market[b] (+) PATD: Dummy variable indicating inclusion of patent[c] (+) TRAD: Dummy variable indicating inclusion of trademark[c] (+) MAND: Dummy variable indicating inclusion of turnkey plant or equipment supply[c] (+) RAWD: Dummy variable indicating inclusion of raw material, components or product sale[c] (+) IMP: Degree of importance of industrial property laws for majority of companies' technologies[d] (?)	SALES: Total Sales of Company in \$ (+) SUPPLY: Number of international suppliers for the technology[e] (+) PATDUM: Dummy variable indicating inclusion of patent[f] (+) TRADUM: Dummy variable indicating inclusion of trademark[f] (+) RAWDUM: Dummy variable indicating inclusion of materials supply[f] (-) COMPETE: Likelihood of licensee competition[g] (+) PROCESS: Dummy variable for whether process is central or peripheral[h] (+) PRICE: Price of final product over its life cycle[i] (-)

Table 21 *(continued)*

Notes: a. Information was obtained only in categories, Under 100 Million (1); 100 Million to 1 Billion (2); Over 1 Billion (3).

b. Response on a three point scale for market purview, ranging from U.S./Canada only (1) to Global (3)

c. Values are (0): Not included; (1) Included. When the dependent variable is for a particular region, e.g., developing nations only, then the dummy variables will relate to that regional subsample. The suffix 1, e.g., PATD1 will refer to the LDC subsample. The suffix 2, e.g., PATD2 will refer to the industrial nation subsample only, and so on.

d. Perceived importance by the responding executive, (1) Not at all; (2) Somewhat; (3) Very important.

e. Unique technology supplier (5); Two to Five other global suppliers (4); Five to Ten (3); Ten to Twenty (2); Over twenty (1). Note that expected sign of coefficient is positive because of the way this variable is coded.

f. Not included (0); Included (1). Note that for RAWDUM the expected sign is negative only if we assume that supply of materials as part of an agreement lowers direct licensing income such as royalties, ceteris paribus.

g. Immediate competition from licensee (4); perhaps later (3); no likelihood of licensee competing outside their own country (2); licensee uncompetitive even in their own country (1).

h. Central (1); peripheral (2).

i. Dropped (1); same (2); risen (3)--in real terms after deducting for inflation.

or a ratio thereof. In the 44-company sample however, we are trying to statistically explain dollar foreign licensing income. This is the dependent variable
INCOME. On the other hand, one can argue that it is not so much the total
foreign licensing income of a firm that is of interest, so much as foreign licensing
income in relation to the income from other foreign strategies of the firm, such
as direct investment in majority affiliates or exporting, which comprise clear
strategic alternatives to licensing. Unfortunately, it is nearly impossible to obtain
profit margin estimates from companies on their exporting or their overseas
subsidiaries. (In some cases, this is on confidentiality grounds. In others, the
information exists but is widely scattered in the company. Licensing is by comparison a relatively more centralized activity at least in terms of a headquarters
accounting and monitoring of payments received from licensees.[20]) To get around
this difficulty one has to use substitutes or surrogates for exporting and foreign
affiliates profitability. In the denominator of the ratios LINC1 and LINC2 defined
in Table 20, foreign affiliate and export sales figures have been used.[21]

Each dependent variable shown in Table 21 is to be regressed against all
dependent variables. The parentheses show the expected sign of the relationship
of each with the dependent variable. We hypothesize a positive relationship with
all the variables in the 241-company sample except IMP; that is to say, the
number (or ratio) of technology agreements in each region is expected to be
larger, with larger sales, greater internationalization, and the inclusion of patents,
trademarks, plant erection, and material supply, the presence of which would
make technology transfer more likely by increasing total agreement revenues,
while at the same time increasing the level of control over the licensee.

In the forty-four-company sample we have some other variables such as SUP-
PLY, which measures the ubiquity or availability of the technology from alternative global sources. The fewer the alternative technology supplies the less the
competition among them and perhaps the more unique the technology and,
accordingly, the higher the compensation expected from licensing. (The expected
positive sign comes from the way the variable is defined. Please see note e in
Table 21.) The greater the likelihood and danger of licensee competition, the
higher the compensation should be if the technology is licensed.[22] This is represented in the variable COMPETE. Last, the variables PROCESS and PRICE
test the hypotheses that licensing increases with peripheral as opposed to central
technologies of the firm and increases, *ceteris paribus*, later in the product cycle.

The objective of the regression analysis is not econometric predictive ability.
Indeed, with much of the data available only in categories, it is not very mean-
ingful. We cannot place much reliance on such exercises as models that can
predict the level of licensing activity in firms. Rather, the objectives here are
more modest: (1) to identify a sub-set of independent variables that most pow-
erfully explains most of the variance (i.e., contribute to R^2)—that would indicate
that corporate practice is most influenced by these variables, and the rest are
unimportant; (2) by specifying a stepwise loading of independent variables,
starting with the most powerful, an indication of the relative importance of the

variables is obtained; and (3) to see if the direction or sign of the relationship between variables is as expected. For these relatively modest purposes, a regression analysis using these data is appropriate.

Before the regression results are discussed, however, we first look at the characteristics of the samples and discuss other general findings. The regression results may be found later in this chapter from Table 38 onward.

THE SAMPLES: CHARACTERISTICS OF LICENSORS AND PRODUCT TYPES

The 241-Company Sample

This sample consists of usable responses from 241 U.S. companies involving a total number of agreements probably well in excess of a thousand. Table 22 shows the industry and size distribution of the sample. The industry distribution is a reasonable approximation of the U.S. licensor industry distribution in aggregate Commerce Department statistics.[23] Nothing is known about the distribution of the universe of U.S. licensors, by size of firm. Table 22, therefore, contains entirely new information in this regard. The 241 sample companies include as much as 40 to 50 percent of the U.S. (and Canadian) companies represented in the Licensing Executives Society. The Society's research committee believes that most U.S. firms that license are represented in the Society. All of these received a questionnaire. Nevertheless, one must consider the normal caveats such as a non-response bias, particularly from smaller companies. There may be a slight bias in favor of firms significantly involved in licensing. But these are conjectural caveats.

As expected, a substantial fraction of firms are in the process industries, chemicals, petroleum, pharmaceuticals, and health care. By size, medium and small companies figure more prominently than expected, overall. (In the industry by size cross-classification they even dominate in the electrical, electronics, telecommunications, and data processing sectors of licensing.) Policy initiatives directed at them, therefore, would not appear to be wasted. Of the total sample size of 241 firms, less than half, or 111, have sales over $1 billion, as shown in Table 22. However, the large firms have a somewhat greater number of technology transfers, as statistically confirmed in the regression analysis later in this book.

The Forty-Four-Company Sample

In the forty-four-company sample, product classification was sought at the three-digit level, based on the company's principal technology in which most licensing was done. This is shown in Table 23. There is a wide range of product types, and there is a fair representation of the product distribution in the universe as estimated by the Commerce Department. A list of these companies is provided in Appendix A. Table 24 reclassifies the forty-four-company sample into the

Table 22
The Sample Distribution: Cross-classification of Firm Size vs.
Industry Type in 241 Firms

Number of Firms

-------$ Sales-------

INDUSTRY	UNDER 100 MILLION	100 MILLION TO 1 BILLION	OVER 1 BILLION	ROW TOTAL
-Electrical, Electronics, Telecommunications, etc., except as under.	6	7	9	22
-Computer, Data Processing and related equipment.	3	5	2	10
-Machinery, Motors, Autos and Structures.	3	11	14	28
-Chemical, Petroleum Photographics, Cosmetics, Health Care Products, Rubber, Glass, Pharmaceuticals, Paper and Foods.	22	35	63	120
-Other manufacturing including Optical, Textile, Fibers, Basic Metals and Aerospace.	13	13	19	45
-Non-manufacturing	8	4	4	16
	55	75	111	241

NOTE: The industry classification was devised by the Society before the author was involved with the survey.

Table 23
Product Types in Sample of 44 Companies

(When answering questions about one particular
technology on Page 2 of the questionnaire.[c])

BEA No. Classification[a]	Product[b]	No. of Companies
201	Meat products	1
204	Grain Mill Products	1
205	Bakery Products	1
230	Apparel and Similar	1
264	Converted Paper Products	1
281	Industrial chemicals, synthetics and plastics	3
283	Drugs	5
285	Paints and similar	2
289	Chemical products, n.e.c.	3
292	Petroleum refining	1
331	Primary metal products, ferrous	1
335	Primary metal products, non-ferrous	1
341	Metal cans and containers	1
345	Screw machine products like bolts, nuts, rivets, washers	2
346	Metal stamping and forgings	1
349	Fabricated metal products, n.e.c.	1
353	Construction, mining and material handling machinery	1

---

n.e.c. (not elsewhere classified)

103

Table 23 *(continued)*

355	Special industry machinery, n.e.c.	1
356	General industrial machinery	1
357	Office, computing and accounting machines	1
359	Machinery, except electrical	1
366	Radio, T.V. and communication items	1
367	Electronic components	2
369	Electrical machinery, n.e.c.	3
371	Motor vehicles and equipment	2
381	Scientific instruments	1
390	Miscellaneous manufactures, n.e.c.	2
891	Engineering and Architectural services	1
	No response	1
	Total	44

Notes: a. Adapted from SIC numbers by the Bureau of Economic Analysis (BEA) of the U.S. Department of Commerce

b. Product descriptions used by the BEA

c. While pages 1 and 3 were general questions relating to the company's international licensing program, on page 2 the questions were technology-specific. Respondents were asked to choose one "typical" technology licensed overseas.

n.e.c. (not elsewhere classified)

Table 24
Cross-Classification of Firm Size vs. Industry Type from
Smaller Sample of 44 Firms

	By number of Firms				
	------- $SALES ---------				
INDUSTRY	UNDER 100 MILL	100 MILL to 1 BILL	OVER 1 BILL	NOT MEASURED;a	ROW TOTAL
-Electrical, Electronics, Telecommunications, etc., except as under	1	0	3	0	4
-Computer, Data-processing and related equipment	0	1	2	0	3
-Machinery, Motors, Autos, and Structures	0	2	5	2	9
-Chemicals, Petroleum, Photographics, Cosmetics, Health Care Products, Rubber, Glass, Pharmaceuticals, Paper and Foods	1	2	14	0	17
-Other manufacturing, including Optical, Textile, Fibers, Basic Metals and Aerospace	1	5	3	1	10
-Non-Manuf.	1	0	0	0	1
	4	10	27	3	44

Note: a. When the company is very diversified and information on a particular division is not available.

categories used by the Licensing Executives Society so that we can compare it with the 241-company sample shown in Table 22. There is a parallel except in the chemicals, petroleum, photographics, etc., group. If this group is slightly overrepresented in the 241-firm sample, it is not in the forty-four-firm sample.

FINDINGS ON THE CONTENTS OF TECHNOLOGY-LICENSING AGREEMENTS

We now turn to the question of the content of technology transfers. In the forty-four-firm sample, respondents were asked to check items typically included in their company's foreign licensing and then score checked boxes on relative frequency of occurrence. Table 25 shows that know-how and technical assistance are components of virtually all companies' agreements, save one or two firms. Patent rights are transferred by thirty-five of forty-two responding companies. Other items such as trademarks, component supply, or managerial assistance occur in less than half the cases. This reinforces the idea that service rendered to a licensee and information that is not necessarily patented is of greater importance than the legal rights to patents or trademarks *per se*.

The larger sample gives us finer detail on this question and gives us cross-classification with respect to licensee country type. In Table 26 we probe further the issue of the extent of dependence of licensor firms on patents and trademarks. We find pure patent licensing in only about 5 percent of cases, this percentage being the same in all regions. (We see, however, that in terms of patent incidence with and without know-how, agreements in developing countries have a lower percentage of inclusion of patents.) Usually, patents are transferred with know-how, this being the most common combination, found in half the cases overall. If this suggests that licensees need technical assistance and know-how in addition to mere patent rights, then U.S. technology is not vitally threatened by the erosion of patent protection abroad. Table 27 gives a further breakdown of the top row of Table 26 to see if pure patent licensing is more common in some industries. As Table 27 shows, the chemical and pharmaceutical sectors would be most affected since pure patent licensing is concentrated in these industries. (While in the Society's survey these two industries are classified with others such as cosmetics, rubber, glass, etc., in fact, chemicals, petroleum, and pharmaceuticals dominate.)

Of course, the finding that most transfers of patent rights are accompanied by know-how does not mean that the loss of patent protection would be of no consequence. Other studies suggest that in the majority of instances, while the know-how is of greater value to the licensee, when patents do occur, they considerably augment the bargaining position and hence the compensation derived by licensors.[24]

On the question of the frequency with which trademarks occur, the two samples seem to differ. In the larger sample of 241 companies, trademarks (occurring mostly with know-how) are found in 13 to 20 percent of all cases overall,

Table 25
The Contents of Licensing Agreements From A Sample of 44 Companies[a]

Element	No. of Companies Which Checked Item[a]	Mean Score On Scale 0 - 8 Highest[b]	Ranking of Importance (1 = Most Important)
-Knowhow	41	7.26	1
-Technical Assistance	40	6.14	2
-Managerial Assistance	6	0.67	6
-Patent Rights	35	5.57	3
-Trademark Rights	20	2.67	4
-Component Supply	14	1.81	5
-Buyback of Licensee Product	3	0.26	8
-Other[c]	4	0.55	7

Notes   a. There were two missing responses, making the total companies for this question 42

b. After checking relevant boxes, responding executives were asked to score the checked boxes as 8 = most frequent, 7 = next most frequent and so on. Boxes not checked were scored zero. The mean scores include the zero values.

c. Under "Other", two respondents mentioned "marketing assistance" which could be lumped with managerial assistance, one mentioned "raw material supply" which could be classified with component supply, and one mentioned "grantbacks" which is an inappropriate comment because "grantbacks" are not a transfer of anything to the licensee. Rather they are requirements placed on the licensee to grant back to the licensor any technical improvements.

Table 26
Elements in a Majority of the Company's Technology Transfers

Involve: (241 Company Sample)

	FOR LICENSEES IN		
	U.S./ CANADA ONLY	DEVELOPING COUNTRIES	OTHER DEVELOPED COUNTRIES
	(By Number of Licensor Firms)		
-Patent license/ sale only	11	5	12
-Know-how license/ sale only	23	28	17
-Patent and know-how license/sale only	135	63	143
-Trademark and know-how license/ sale only	28	23	26
-Manufacturing facility only	3	2	1
-Manufacturing facility and know-how license/ sale only	12	14	15
-TOTAL OF ABOVE[a]	212	135	214

Note: a. Since some firms gave a response in more than one of the above categories the above totals exceed the number of firms having at least one technology transfer in the relevant region.

TOTAL OF ABOVE	212	135	214
-No. of firms having at least one technology transfer in area	170	118	207
-Therefore max. no. of firms making multiple responses above	42	17	7

Table 27
Incidence of Pure Patent Licensing by Industry Type

(In Sample of 241 Firms)

By Number of Firms Licensing In:

CATEGORY [a]	U.S./CANADA	DEVELOPING COUNTRIES	OTHER DEVELOPED COUNTRIES
-Electrical, etc.	2	0	1
-Computers, etc.	0	0	0
-Machinery, etc.	1	1	2
-Chemicals, Pharmaceuticals, etc.	5	4	7
-Other manufacturing	3	0	2
-Non-manufacturing	0	0	0
TOTALS [a]	11	5	12

Notes: a. For more complete descriptions please see Table 22.

depending on the region. (See Table 28.) There is indeed a significant difference between developing and industrial countries in this regard, with a considerably higher incidence, percentage wise, in LDCs. Yet even for LDCs as a group, the 20-percent incidence means only one out of five agreements have trademarks. This is modest and nowhere near the large figure for Chile, related above. That case study must therefore be an extreme example. As Table 28 shows, the transfer of trademarks is concentrated again in chemicals, pharmaceuticals, cosmetics, and foods. The smaller sample presents a different picture. Table 29 shows the results from the 44 companies, cast in the industry groupings used by the Licensing Executives Society sample in Table 28, for comparison. In the smaller sample a regional breakdown was not asked for. Rather, respondents were asked to check off elements included in a typical foreign licensing agreement. We see in Table 29 that as many as 20 out of 44 firms checked the box for trademarks as included, typically, a higher percentage than in the 241-company sample, although even here the single largest industry grouping is the chemicals, pharmaceuticals, and foods group. So, while the question of the overall incidence

Table 28
Incidence of Trademark Licensing by Industry Type in Sample of 241 Firms

		Number of Firms	
			OTHER
		DEVELOPING	DEVELOPED
INDUSTRY.[a]	U.S./CANADA	COUNTRIES	COUNTRIES
-Electrical, etc.	3	1	0
-Computers, etc.	1	1	2
-Machinery, etc.	3	2	2
-Chemical, Pharmaceuticals			
etc.	14	13	14
-Other manufacturing	5	4	6
-Non-manufacturing	2	2	2
TOTAL [b]	28	23	26
AS % OF REGIONAL			
TOTAL [b]	16.5%	19.5%	12.6%

Notes: a. For a more detailed industry description please
see Table 22.

  b. Regional totals are 170, 118, and 207,
respectively.

of trademarks remains open, we can as a general conclusion say that the threat of a weakening of the international patent and trademark system would appear to hang heaviest over these industry sectors (which, incidentally, contribute a little less than one-third of overseas licensing income derived by U.S. licensors).

Unsurprisingly, on the question in the 241-company sample, asking how the company perceived the importance of industrial and intellectual property protection laws, it was these same industries that expressed the greatest concern. An interesting empirical question is whether the degree of concern can be related to any other variable in the data set. Analyzing the responses in terms of foreign country type we find no difference between the developing and developed nations, so that the companies' concern is not focused particularly on LDCs. (If anything, the degree of concern is slightly less in LDCs, but the difference is not statistically

Table 29
Inclusion of Trademarks in Agreements by Industry Type
in Smaller Sample of 44 Firms

		Number of Firms	
			Missing
Industry [a]	No	Yes	Data
-Electrical, etc.	1	3	0
-Computers, etc.	2	1	0
-Machinery, etc.	2	7	0
-Chemicals, Pharmaceuticals,			
etc.	10	7	0
-Other manufacturing	6	2	2
-Non-manufacturing	1	0	0
	22 +	20 +	2 = 44
			Firms
			Total

Note: a. For a more detailed industry description
please see Table 22.

significant.) Again, analyzing the degree of concern against the firm sales variable shown in Table 30, there is no significant difference among various sizes of U.S. companies. The degree of concern is strongly related to the incidence of patents (and the slightly lower level of concern expressed vis-à-vis the LDC group is probably related to the lower inclusion of patents in LDC transfers, both in absolute and relative terms). The only other variable that seems to influence the degree of corporate concern is the number of agreements the firm has. (See Table 31.) The result would *prima facie* appear paradoxical, that the perceived importance of intellectual property laws is greater to companies with fewer agreements abroad. However, plausible explanatory hypotheses may be that the firms with fewer agreements express greater concern because (1) they have less international experience, (2) they are smaller and therefore presumably more dependent on foreign government enforcement, (3) they have a higher incidence of pure patent licensing which requires a stricter enforcement. What do the data say about these hypotheses? The data do not cover (1), they support (2) as shown later in the regression analysis, and they reject hypothesis (3).

Table 30
Cross-classification of Firm Size vs. Perceived Importance of Intellectual Property Protection Laws in Sample of 241 Companies

Perceived Importance In

SALES[b]	DEVELOPING COUNTRIES				DEVELOPED COUNTRIES[a]			
	NONE	SOMEWHAT	VERY	TOTAL	NONE	SOMEWHAT	VERY	TOTAL
-Under 100 Mill.	7	12	16	35	4	16	30	50
-100 Mill. to 1 Bill.	10	19	23	52	6	21	37	64
-Over 1 Bill.	14	28	44	86	8	36	62	106
	31	59	83	173	18	73	129	220

Notes: a. Other than U.S./Canada.

b. There appears to be a positive correlation with sales, but the X^2 is low and has no statistical significance.

Table 31
Perceived Importance of Intellectual Property Laws as a Function of Distribution of Agreements in 241 Company Sample

NUMBER OF AGREEMENTS	IN DEVELOPING COUNTRIES				IN DEVELOPED COUNTRIES[a]			
	NOT AT ALL	SOMEWHAT	VERY		NOT AT ALL	SOMEWHAT	VERY	TOTAL
1 - 5	6	36	37	79	9	41	64	114
More than 5	2	13	19	34	2	28	59	89
Totals	8	49	56	113	11	69	123	203

Note: a. Other than U.S./Canada.

FACTORS INFLUENCING THE ROLE OF LICENSING IN STRATEGY

The Forty-four-Company Sample

We have seen earlier in Chapters 2 and 5 how companies may choose between a direct investment and a contractual strategy in an overseas market. The theory of the international firm specifies certain conditions under which licensing may be preferred. Several of these were listed in Table 20. (The reader is also referred to the section titled "The Strategy Role of Licensing" earlier in this chapter for specific theoretical justification of each factor.) My purpose here is to measure the actual use of these factors in corporate strategy and to get some sense of their relative importance across a spectrum of industries.[25]

Fifteen factors in random order were supplied to executives in the forty-four sample firms. These are shown in Table 32. After checking factors used in formulating overseas strategy in their company, the respondents were asked to score the checked boxes in descending order of importance: fifteen = most important, fourteen = next in importance, and so on. Factors not checked were scored zero. This enables us to rank the strategic factors by two criteria: the number of times the item was checked and by mean score. Table 32 shows a high degree of correlation between the ranking obtained under the two criteria.

We notice immediately that no factor came close to being universally applicable: as many as thirteen of the fifteen factors were checked by half of the companies. In short, there is a wide range of strategic reasons for using licensing.

The salient factor promoting licensing is that the country's regulations or political risk inhibit forming majority-owned subsidiaries, followed in second rank by transport or tariff barriers making exports difficult. Environmental rather than internal factors have thus been cited as the salient considerations, a kind of backhanded endorsement for the licensing option to be resorted to when alternative strategies fail or to augment income extraction when forced to share equity with a joint venture partner. The question of barriers to trade was also separately addressed in the questionnaire. Table 33 shows that most respondents did not consider transport costs impeding direct exports an issue, whereas thirty-four of forty-four indicated that tariffs did constitute a barrier in some nations. Whether in a more restrictive and protectionist international business environment this augurs more licensing is not a conclusion one can jump to. It does show a recognition among corporate strategists of licensing as an option and perhaps a greater proclivity to use it, where in years past, a market that could not be accessed by the other strategies may have been written off.

The next-ranked factor, namely, licensing as a means of rapid entry into a market, could be interpreted as either an external, market-related consideration or a factor related to internal constraints. Conditions in the market, such as regulatory hurdles or entrenched competitors dominating distribution channels,

Table 32
Strategic Factors Influencing the Role of Licensing in 44 American Companies

Strategic Concept (from Table 20)	Licensing Can Be a Viable/preferable Option in Foreign Markets When:	Number of Companies that Checked Factor (Maximum of 44)	Mean Score on Scale 0 to 15 (Highest);[b]	Ranking of Overall Importance (1=Most Important)	
				by Companies;[c]	by Mean Score
Product-cycle standardization	(Computer Code) ROL1 Products/processes are older or standardized	17	4.70	5	6
Creation of Auxiliary Business	ROL2 When items other than paent or know-how are included in contract: Component supply; buy back; trademark; other	13	3.61	8	8
Environmental constraints on FDI or FDI income	ROL3 The country's regulations or political risk inhibit forming majority-owned subsidiaries	29	8.91	1	1
Licensee uncompetitiveness	ROL4 Divulging detail about a process (as opposed to the complete product) will not hurt company's competitiveness	20	5.73	3	4
Constraints on trade in product	ROL5 Tarriff barriers or transport costs preclude exporting product	23	7.11	2	2
Reciprocal exchanges of technology	ROL6 Reciprocally receiving technology from licensee is visualized on signing agreement from future grantbacks	17	4.71	5	5

Factor		Mean score		
"Choosing competition"	ROL7 Selecting a particular licensee gives him a head start over other local firms; for future licensee business	5	1.36	13	13
Speed of market entry	ROL8 Licensing is the fastest way to introduce product in market	20	5.96	3	3
Perpetuation of licensee dependency	ROL9 Licensee's continued dependency on us is assured even after agreement expiry because of trademark; new models; components; other	11	3.00	9	10
High rate of technical turnover	ROL10 Rate of technical change is so rapid that obsolescing technologies can be licensed without fear of licensee competing	11	3.18	9	9
Loss of patent coverage	ROL11 Our patent is about to expire in a country anyway	3	0.80	14	14
Tax reduction	ROL12 Tax considerations (specify)	2	0.46	15	15
Internal resources limitation	ROL13 Our firm is so large; diversified that there is no way we can generate financial; managerial resources for equity investment in all countries/ products; hence licensing	15	4.34	7	7
Small firm size	ROL14 Our firm is still small so that we cannot invest in our own subsidiaries in every country or product line	6	1.89	12	12
Other	ROL15 Other (specify)	7	2.02	11	11

Notes: a. All 44 companies responded to this question. There are no missing data.

b. After checking relevant boxes, the responding executive was asked to score the checked boxes, 15-highest, 14-next highest, etc. Boxes not checked were scored zero. The mean score includes zero values.

c. In case of a tie the subsequent rank is unfilled in order to make this rank ordering compatible with the ranking based on mean score.

Table 33
Transport and Tariff Impediments to International Trade in the Finished Product

(From Sample of 44 Companies)

Tariffs Hinder trade?	No. of Companies
- No	4
- In some nations	34
- In most nations	3
- No response	3
	44 TOTAL

Transport Cost Impediment?	No. of Companies
- Distance is no problem	24
- Only short distances	7
- No international trade	5
- No response	8
	44 TOTAL

may make licensing, to a company already selling similar products, a much quicker means of reaching customers. Alternatively, it could be internal constraints in the firm, such as delays in organizing and retooling for the particular needs for that market, that makes licensing a more rapid alternative.

We recall that an important concern when using the licensing option is the fear of the licensee turning into a competitor. The question in Table 34 indicates that when asked, responding executives expressed only a moderate degree of concern. Thirteen of the forty-four indicated their licensees could conceivably compete with them internationally on agreement expiry, while another thirteen believed there was no likelihood of licensees competing outside their own country. Another sixteen said licensees could perhaps be a competitive threat a few years later. All in all, these results do not indicate that this consideration is a grave impediment to the use of licensing.

Furthermore, there are ways of maintaining a competitive edge over a licensee. For instance, the strategic factor ranked next in importance is divulging detail about a process (as opposed to the complete product) will not hurt the company's competitiveness. In such a case the licensor reveals information about only one or a few steps in the manufacturing process. Even if the licensee's end-product is similar, by revealing only a portion of the complete technology, the licensor retains either a quality, performance characteristic, or cost-efficiency advantage over the licensee.

Table 34
Fear of Competition from Licensees

On expiry of the current agreement, could a licensee compete with your firm internationally?	No. of Companies
- Yes, immediately on expiry	13
- Perhaps a few years later	16
- No likelihood of licensee competing outside their own country	13
- No likelihood of licensee being competitive even in their own country	0
- No response	2
TOTAL	44

The factor ranked fifth in strategic importance is the expectation of receiving technology or improvements back from the licensee in addition to cash income. The reader will recall that because of custom and tradition, if not theory, royalty rates generally fall in the 2 to 8 percent range.[26] In many cases that level of direct cash return is seen by companies as inadequate compensation for parting with the technology. However, an earnings package of royalties plus the right to receive technology back from the licensee may be attractive. We need to probe further just what is expected back from licensees. Receiving know-how and rights from a licensee immediately on signing an agreement is called "reciprocal licensing" and is quite different from the future possibility that the licensee may build upon the technology received, develop something of interest to the licensor, and grant the rights back to them. The latter, called "grantback" provisions in agreements, is usually a very minor consideration since the chance that the licensee will generate improvements of significance to the licensor is generally small. By contrast, an agreement provision calling for a swap of technology or territorial rights at the start of the agreement means that each party has already carefully assessed the value of the technology held by the other. In some cases, for example, in the pharmaceuticals sector, with protracted testing and certification requirements, the main strategic purpose is cross-licensing of territorial rights—each firm may have tested and secured territorial rights in certain countries and now perhaps both wish to augment their product ranges. In such a case it is inappropriate to use the licensor/licensee labels. Both firms are licensors. Royalty payments then constitute compensatory cash flows for the perceived inequality in the value of the technologies traded. Table 35 shows in effect that thirteen of the forty-four respondents consider reciprocally receiving technology at the inception of agreements as a way of augmenting the value of compensation received. Grantbacks constituted only a small percentage.

Table 35
Receiving Technology from Licensees

Total Number of Firms	44
Number of Firms Which Checked This Strategic Factor:	17
- Receiving Technology on Signing Agreement	3
- Receiving Technology on Signing Agreement and Later on as "Grantbacks"	10
- "Grantbacks" only	3

The next criterion cited involves the product cycle, the idea that licensing would be a strategy favored more often when products or processes are older or standardized. This may be because income extractable under direct investment or exporting declines later in the cycle, to a level comparable to that derived from the 2 to 8 percent royalty range mentioned above. Alternatively, with standardization, the costs of transferring the technology to licensees may decline later in the cycle to levels comparably as low as transferring technology to one's overseas affiliate. Empirical measurement of the stage in the product cycle is difficult in a multi-industry survey such as this one. However, the inflation-adjusted price history of a product, the question addressed in Table 36, gives us a very crude idea of how many of the products in the sample may be advanced in their cycle. Obviously, we cannot draw any safe conclusion from Table 36, except perhaps to say that in only eleven of the forty-four cases is there the possibility (by no means assured) that internal company margins have declined, making licensing relatively speaking more attractive, at least in some overseas markets. This is reflected in the low ranking of this strategic factor overall. It belies the high importance given by some writers to the product-cycle idea as the principal theoretical explanation for the use of licensing as an alternative to equity investment.[27] There are at least six other factors shown in the study to be more important, in practice, to strategists.

The next factor deals with internal constraints in even the largest of multi-national companies, especially those which are diversified. With hundreds of products and processes having a potential market in well over a hundred nations, corporate planners in a company like General Electric have to contend with over

Table 36
Price Levels of Final Product over Life Cycle

```
After adjusting for inflation over its life cycle, the

product made from the technology has:
                                              No. of Companies
     - Dropped in price                              11

     - Same                                          14

     - Risen in price                                11

     - No response                                    8

                                                     44    TOTAL
```

10,000 potential product/market combinations. All of these cannot possibly be filled by local production or imports, nor would this be necessarily more profitable than licensing. For a GE, or an equivalent international firm, there are at least several hundred product/market combinations best filled by the licensing option. Income at GE from purely arm's-length global licensees alone is substantial, exceeding the annual gross profit of many medium-sized companies.[28] But this takes organization, a headquarters licensing group empowered to cut across product division lines, identify licensable technologies, and work with line executives whose normal instincts would prefer investment and production within their own divisional jurisdictions. GE is probably one of the best organized in this respect. At other firms, the internal-production-via-controlled-subsidiaries mandate is so strong that overseas licensing opportunities are neglected even when in the aggregate they could earn significant sums.

One of the recommendations of this book has been to use the transfer of technology as only the centerpiece of larger and more profitable arrangements involving other income-producing elements, such as the trading of materials and components between licensor and licensee, so as to make many deals, on balance, acceptably lucrative for the licensor, where otherwise a bare licensing proposal may not be attractive. In terms of corporate practice, Table 32 shows this factor was ranked only eighth overall and was checked by less than a third of companies. (The percentage is even lower in the 241-company sample. See Table 37.) Why are more firms not using licensing as a means for creating auxiliary business? Certainly there are some environmental constraints: foreign governments that pursue protectionist policies frown upon their licensees seeking to import too large a fraction of the value of their production, although they would probably encourage exports by the licensee. Moreover, there is always the fear that trading between licensor and licensee, or other agreement clauses auxiliary to the tech-

Table 37
Strategic Reasons for Technology Transfer Program

```
- Current Profit/Return                        36

- Royalties over period of time               119

- New market development                        68

- Sale of raw materials and intermediate
  or related products                          16

- Other                                         36

- Total of above                              275

- Total no. of respondents                    241

- Therefore maximum no. of respondents
  who could have made a multiple response      34
```

nology transfer core such as trademarks, may be construed as "restraints of trade" or "tie-in" arrangements. It is quite possible that the middle to low ranking given this strategic factor is partially due to the skittishness of responding executives schooled in U.S. antitrust laws.

Nevertheless, the fact remains that, in international business, the boundaries between the three strategic options of investment, trade, and contracted transfer of technology are beginning to break down in some industries. In electronics, in automobiles, and in other industries as well we are seeing the formation of "strategic partnerships" between firms of different nationalities, joint ventures involving a mix of equity ownership, trade and licensing, all in one package.[29] Chapter 8 develops this further.

The idea that licensing is more frequent in mature industries as opposed to high-technology sectors is partially contradicted in the next strategic factor. A high rate of technical change may in itself provide opportunities for licensing. (See the factor ranked ninth in Table 32.) The speed of change, for instance, in the electronics area, may make it difficult for firms to invest rapidly enough in many markets and technologies on their own. If a firm has a new or superior technology at an advanced stage of development, say an integrated circuit design that will be more powerful than the existing ones, then this design alone can confidently be licensed even to a competitor. By the time the licensee converts the design into actual production, the licensor hopes they will have further improved their own so as to remain one step ahead of the competition.

The strategic factor ranked tenth overall deals also with how to lower the danger of licensee competition by keeping licensees dependent. There is a delicate line between violating and not violating antitrust laws when licensees depend on licensors for components, access to foreign markets, renewal of trademark rights, and the hope of being given model improvements. Even under U.S. law, with one of the longest case histories, interpretation of when the line is crossed keeps lawyers busy; there is, moreover, considerable variation in the laws of other countries.[30] Nevertheless, one suspects that the cases where licensees actually welcome dependence on the licensor, or at least tolerate it, vastly exceed the few cases where the licensee is actually acquiescing to the situation under duress. This is because licensing is a positive-sum game where both parties gain. The arrangement is entered into voluntarily, and in many instances the licensees see such continuing benefit that they seek renewal of the agreement. The word "dependency" has its perjorative connotations; it can also have a healthy use in corporate strategy.

The remaining strategic factors in Table 32 were scored by relatively few firms. Under the "other" category, respondents were asked to write in their reasons. Two of the seven written responses in this category amounted, in different words, to the strategy considerations already discussed above. The other five were somewhat different:

- "To legitimize a pirate competitor by forcing him to be a licensee under threat of legal action"
- "Pollution control laws have driven production off-shore"
- "Foreign market too small for our own production; his cost lower than ours"
- "Technology no longer of interest to us but is to licensee for special reasons"
- "Product discontinued"

Six of the forty-four companies indicated in Table 32 that their small size was a factor inhibiting investment abroad. The constraint was managerial in more cases than financial. In Appendix C are case studies of licensing programs in both large and small firms. Many small firms, with U.S. sales under $50 million, have very successful overseas licensing records. For some, it is their principal foreign business method. The data show an immense growth potential for foreign licensing on the part of small American companies otherwise preoccupied with domestic market development. Once again, the larger constraint is executive time rather than capital in most cases. However, compared to exporting, or certainly investment, licensing is the least time consuming—although even in the simplest licensing agreement several hundred executive hours should be put in at the minimum.

Licensing a technology as a patent is about to expire and, more specifically, selecting a licensee at that stage to give him a head start over competition are again considerations that could be land mines under U.S. antitrust law if the express intent is to restrain competition even after patent expiry. (See factors ranked thirteenth and fourteenth in Table 32.) Other countries' interpretation and enforcement may be less rigid. Nevertheless, the fact remains that despite incipient expiration of the patent, a license agreement may still have an intrinsic justification. As we have seen earlier in the chapter, the unpatented information labelled "know-how" is generally speaking more valuable than the patent, *per se*. It may simply be that at this stage in the product cycle, margins have eroded or technology may have changed to the point where a firm now wishes to cease its own production in that market but may, however, wish to continue receiving some income from a license. Under law, the issue may come down to whether the intent of the license was to reduce competition even beyond patent expiry or whether licensing is simply an alternative strategy to switch to in the latter part of the product cycle.

The strategy factor ranked the very last, and checked by only two firms, was tax considerations. The two respondents cited the favorable capital gains tax treatment of licensing income as the reason.

The 241-Company Sample

In the Licensing Executives Society's survey, the strategy role of technology licensing was only incidentally probed in one brief question. Respondents were asked to check off possible strategy motivations, of which the four important ones are immediate return in the shape of front-end or lump-sum fees, royalties over time normally keyed to licensee output, new market entry and development without investment by the licensor, and auxiliary business accompanying the technology transfer such as supply or purchase of materials, intermediates, or related products. Respondents were given a chance to check off more than one category and write in alternative strategy reasons in the "other" category as well if necessary.

Table 37 suggests that the survey respondents were more interested in the income from licensing as opposed to using licensing as a market development device *per se*. Earlier, we had observed that licensing can be particularly effective if it is the catalyst for other related business that can be far more important than the technology transfer itself. However, Table 37 suggests that, so far at least, this has occurred in a very small percentage of cases, and the principal motivation for licensing overall continues to be direct income generated by direct fees and royalties. Similarly, the results here corroborate what we saw in Table 26, that the erection of manufacturing facilities or plant on a turnkey basis occurs overall in very few cases in the 241-company, all-industry sample. In general, companies still have a way to go before they fully exploit the strategic opportunities of licensing in international operations.

THE LEVEL OF TECHNOLOGY TRANSFER ACTIVITY ANALYZED IN REGRESSION EQUATIONS

The regression equations seek a statistically significant association between the number or level of technology agreements in various regions, as shown, and variables such as the firm's size, internationalization of the company's market, the inclusion of patents, trademarks, manufacturing plant, raw materials or components, the number of international suppliers, and so on. The hypotheses to be tested were summarized earlier in Table 21. The expected sign of each coefficient is also shown in Table 21 and the reasons discussed in that section of the chapter. We now check whether the directions (or signs) of the relationship between the "dependent" and "independent" variables are as expected, *a priori*. The second objective is to find out which of the independent variables are more critical than others. This is achieved by specifying "stepwise loading" of the independent variables, starting with the "most powerful" and discarding variables that do not meet a minimum significance criterion. (This was done using the NEW REGRESSION PROGRAM on SPSS.[31])

Regression Results from the 241-Company Sample

The results are shown in Table 38. Every one of the signs of coefficients are positive as hypothesized, and the overall *F*-values are strong, indicating significant equations for all countries and for the sub-samples also, comprising developing and developed nations. Overall, the size of the firm (indicated by the sales variable) is a salient explanatory factor for the number of agreements, with the market purview variable also having some importance (except in the ratios P3 and P4). This confirms the idea that the larger and more international companies do more licensing. The patent, trademark, manufacturing plant, and raw material dummies are also significant. Two comments are in order here: first, the fact that the supply of raw materials or intermediates and manufacturing plant have a low frequency of occurrence overall in the sample is not inconsistent with the significance of these dummy variables in the regression analysis. The regression equation merely indicates that these are significant (to promote licensing agreements) when they occur. Second, the fact that the first three dummy variables are significant in the developing and developed country sub-samples, but not in the all-nation or all-foreign-country groups is an artifact of the way the questionnaire was designed and does not imply a paradox in the analysis. (The question of the inclusion of patents, trademarks, and manufacturing plant was treated separately for developing and developed country groups. By contrast, the question for the raw material dummy was asked only overall and not separately by region, so that its lack of significance in the sub-samples comes as no surprise.) We can conclude that all four dummies are significant. Last, we see that the variable describing the importance of intellectual property laws is significant for developed but not for developing nations. This confirms our earlier suspicion that the degree of concern is lower in LDCs. In this and other cases we hardly need remind ourselves that statistical significance does not necessarily imply a cause-and-effect relationship. Here, all we can say is that the level of licensing activity is positively associated with the independent variables, and that, of these, the size of the company and patent incidence are two factors likely to be more important than the rest judging by the average order of inclusion in stepwise loading.

Table 38
Level of Technology Transfer Activity in Large Sample as Explained by
Characteristics of the Company and Technology
(Please Refer to Table 21 for Variable Definitions)

DEPENDENT VARIABLE	CONST	SALES	MARKET	PATD	TRAD	MAND	RAWD	IMP	d.f.	F Value	R^2	
TOTTS	1.49	0.22 (5.41)** [1]	0.20 (3.19)** [2]	φ	φ	φ	0.33 (2.62)** [3]	0.08 (1.43)+ [4]	(4,215)	14.79**	0.17	All Countries
FORTTS	0.98	0.48 (5.56)** [1]	0.39 (2.88)** [3]	φ	φ	1.07 (1.46)+ [5]	0.55 (1.99)* [4]	0.36 (3.32)** [2]	(5,211)	11.12**	0.21	Foreign Countries
DEVTTS	0.43	0.24 (3.99)** [2]	0.19 (2.03)* [5]	PATD1 0.62 (5.83)** [1]	TRAD1 0.45 (3.08)** [4]	MAND1 0.50 (2.86)** [3]		φ	(5,165)	14.48**	0.31	Developing Countries
P4	0.53	0.04 (1.69)* [4]	φ	0.16 (4.25)** [1]	0.15 (2.80)** [2]	0.15 (2.28)** [3]	φ	φ	(4,166)	7.02**	0.15	- do -
INDTTS	0.69	0.20 (4.26)** [2]	0.13 (1.86)* [5]	PATD2 0.47 (4.65)** [1]	TRAD2 0.24 (1.86)* [6]	MAND2 0.45 (2.79)** [2]	φ	0.17 (2.85)** [3]	(6,213)	11.22**	0.24	Developed Countries
P3	0.69	φ	φ	0.12 (4.00)** [2]	0.12 (3.12)** [3]	0.08 (1.67)* [4]	φ	0.05 (2.80)** [1]	(4,215)	9.13**	0.15	- do -

Notes:
** Significance level better than 2.5 percent
* Significance level better than 5 percent
+ Significance level better than 7.5 percent
φ Variable not included in equation because of very low significance
[ ] Order of inclusion in stepwise regression
( ) t-value

Regression Results from the Forty-four-Firm Sample

In the smaller sample, the dependent variable is either licensing income or, alternatively, a ratio of foreign licensing income over foreign sales, as defined in Table 21 (which also specifies the independent variables, some of which are similar to those in the regression on 241-company data).

Unfortunately, in the smaller sample, the extent of missing data, while not severe, is widespread enough among the eight independent variables so that the degrees of freedom are substantially reduced to the point where, even though statistically strong results were obtained, there is reason to worry about the representativeness of the small number of cases actually used in the analysis.[32] Of course, this also has the effect of making several of the independent variables non-significant, where otherwise they might have been.

Nevertheless, the results are worth looking at because, with one exception, they corroborate the results obtained in the large sample and confirm *a priori* expectations about the signs of some of the coefficients. (See Table 39.) In two of the three equations we find once again that the single most powerful independent variable is the sales of the company. Licensing income both on an absolute and relative basis correlates positively with the size of the company. Absolute licensing income also correlates positively with the SUPPLY variable (see Table 40), which measures the "fewness" of the international suppliers of the company's technologies, and with COMPETE, which gauges the likelihood of licensee competition. A larger licensing income should naturally be extracted, the more likely and more immediate the threat of competition from the licensee. The positive sign for the variable PROCESS supports the idea that more arm's-length licensing is done in peripheral rather than in "core" or central technologies. Last, the sign for the variable PRICE did turn out negative as hypothesized. With caveats discussed earlier in the chapter, we can say that this weakly supports the idea of lower licensing revenues, *ceteris paribus*, later in the product cycle. (At the least, if the sign were positive, contrary to expectations, there would then have been cause for some concern.) The positive sign for RAWDUM is contrary to expectation. We will have to drop our earlier hypothesis that the supply of materials as part of the package lowers direct licensing income such as royalties, *ceteris paribus*. Apparently, having a materials supply agreement with the licensee does not influence the direct compensation level in licensing.

SUMMARY OF RESULTS

The threat of a weakening of the international patent and trademark system appears to hang heaviest over the chemicals, pharmaceutical, petroleum, and food-processing sectors, which exhibit the highest incidence of patents and trademarks. Apart from these industries, however, while the bargaining position of technology licensors would be eroded, there is in general no vital threat in terms of the loss of important technologies since pure patent licensing, an indicator of a technology-receiving company's ability to "go it alone," occurs very infre-

Table 39
Licensing Income as a Function of Firm and Industry Variables in Smaller Sample

(Please refer to Table 21 for variable definitions)

DEPENDENT VARIABLE	CONST.	SALES	SUPPLY	PATDUM	TRADUM	RAWDUM	COMPETE	PROCESS	PRICE	d.f.	F Value	R^2
INCOME	-40.43	0.96 (9.12)** [1]	5.34 (5.46)** [2]	θ	θ	θ	3.93 (3.63)** [3]	5.75 (3.22)** [4]	θ	4,14	22.89**	0.87
LINC1	-0.05	θ	θ	θ	θ	0.03 (2.52)* [2]	θ	0.05 (4.67)** [1]	θ	2,7	11.76**	0.88
LINC2	5782.29	0.38 (4.22)** [1]	θ	θ	θ	θ	θ	θ	-3059.40 (-2.62)* [2]	2,5	10.96**	0.81

Notes: ** Significance level better than 2.5 percent

* Significance level better than 5 percent

() t-values

[] Order of inclusion in stepwise regression

θ Variable not included in equation because of very low significance

Table 40
Alternative International Sources for Technology from a Sample of 44 Companies

To a well-informed prospective licensee seeking your technology:

CODE	NO. OF COMPANIES
5. You are the unique technology supplier	12
4. Two to five other global suppliers	20
3. Five to ten other global suppliers	4
2. Ten to twenty other global suppliers	3
1. Over twenty other global suppliers	2
9. No response to this question. Missing value.	3
TOTAL	44

quently. Trademarks occur overall in only one out of seven technology transfers. Though higher in developing countries—one out of five—their incidence is much lower than the concern expressed by LDC spokesmen would have us believe. Although licensing activity is positively related to company sales as demonstrated in the regression analyses, medium and small companies in the United States comprise a larger fraction of international technology transfers than expected.

Strategic factors motivating the use of licensing in international strategy are many. Top ranked were constraints on direct investment and trade, indicating an awareness that licensing could be a viable alternate foreign market entry option in restrictive foreign environments. Other important factors were the use of licensing as a quick market entry method, as a means of generating additional income by licensing only selected portions of a process (which would not hurt the firm's overall competitiveness), as a means of reciprocally receiving technology from the licensee, as a strategy to be used late in the product cycle, and as a selective strategy for some country/product combinations that are attractive but cannot be covered by the firm itself because of internal personnel and financial constraints. In general, the main motivation of licensing remains short- to medium-term income generation as opposed to longer-term objectives such as market development. Auxiliary business accompanying the technology transfer, such as supply or purchase of raw materials, related products, equipment, or plant, occurs infrequently in the samples. However, when such auxiliary business does occur, it augments income, thus reinforcing the idea that more firms ought to use technology licensing, not as an end in itself to generate extra income under selected conditions, but rather as the centerpiece of larger and more profitable arrangements.

APPENDIX A:

List of Companies in Smaller Sample

Below is an alphabetical list of companies in the forty-four-firm sample. Note that in a few cases it was only a division of a company that was represented: Alcoa, American Can, American Cyanamid, Beckman Instruments, Beloit, Bendix, Bethlehem Steel, Boeing, Bristol-Myers, Budd, Celanese, Chevron, Eaton, Foster-Wheeler, General Electric, General Motors, General Signal, Goodyear, Hart Schaffner & Marx, Hormel, Ingersoll-Rand, Kaman Sciences, Marion Laboratories, McGraw Edison, Microdot, Monsanto, Pillsbury, Pritchard, Rexnord, Robertshaw, SCM, SPS, A. E. Staley, and Stromberg-Carlson.

Also included but not identified are:

- A mechanical engineering and construction company, principally in industry codes 356 and 359
- An East coast chemicals and pharmaceutical firm; codes 281, 287, 262, 270, 283, 284, 285, 289, 307, 310, and 291
- Chemicals division of a major oil company; code 289
- A New York–based conglomerate
- A paper products company; code 264
- An East-coast electronics firm; code 367
- One of the larger pharmaceuticals companies in the United States.
- Two medium-sized pharmaceuticals companies
- A consumer products and pharmaceuticals company

For product coding, see Table 23.

APPENDIX B:

The Questionnaire

Responding Firm's Name:
(Optional, but please see guidelines)

☐ Check box only if you are so diversified or
decentralized that there is no headquarters
policy at all and this page is filled in by a
product division. If so SIC code _____
(for product type from guidelines.)

PART 1: GENERAL CORPORATE STRATEGY

1. A buyer in a foreign market can, in theory, obtain your company's product in three ways: Sales by your own subsidiary or equity affiliate,
sales made by an independent licensee of yours, or by exports from the U.S. or a third country. Has your firm formulated a policy which enables
a choice to be made between the three options?

FOR EACH BELOW, PLEASE WRITE TWO SALIENT CRITERIA

Rank (check one or more)
- ___ ☐ By country or region (e.g. licensing acceptable
  only in politically risky nations)
- ___ ☐ By product type (e.g. prefer to export light
  weight products from U.S.)
- ___ ☐ No generalizations: We analyze each case (a product in a country) separately.

  ☐ Done as necessary
  ☐ Done routinely as planning exercise
  ☐ Risk-adjusted "Present value is calcu-
  lated for all three strategic options,
  then choice made.
  ☐ Other (Please write in)

(Lastly, rank the criteria in order of importance,1 is highest.)

2. Role of licensing (to independent firms) and contractual methods in international strategy.

a. Licensing can be a viable/preferable option in foreign markets when

Rank (Check appropriate boxes)
- ___ ☐ Products/processes are ☐ Older ☐ Standardized
- ___ ☐ When other items besides patent or knowhow are
  included in contract ☐ Component supply ☐ Buy back
  ☐ Trademark ____ Other
- ___ ☐ The country's regulations or political risk inhibit
  forming majority-owned subsidiaries.
- ___ ☐ Divulging detail about a process (as opposed to the
  complete product) will not hurt company's competitiveness.

b. Annual licensing income from independent foreign
licensees (include licensees where you have less
than a 50% equity stake) _____ $Thousands approx.

c. By what % would your R & D expenditures decline if
such return from foreign licensing was precluded? _____ %

d. Examples of discount rates used in present value
calculations for prospective business in countries

	With High Risk	With Low Risk
· Licensing	___	___
· Equity Investment	___	___
(or give minimum internal rates of return)		

Appendix B *(continued)*

e. Annual Gross Sales Revenue of majority-owned subsidiaries abroad _____ $millions approx.

A rough distribution of above by per cent in each region

Canada _____ %		Latin America _____ %
W. Europe _____ %		E. Europe _____ %
Asia _____ %		Africa _____ %
Australia/New Z. _____ %		Other _____ %

f. As a very rough estimate (indicative of your policy intentions), for all projects under current research and development, what percentage of future revenues or returns do you expect to come from licensing to arms-length parties or to minority joint-ventures (as a percentage of total foreign profit or net income) _____ %

g. Under the broad definition of "independent" licensees as including minority joint ventures, please give a percentage breakdown:

   No. of completely arms-length licensees _____
   (where you have no equity interest)

   No. of licensees where you have a less than _____
   50% equity stake

☐ Tariff barriers or transport costs preclude exporting product.

☐ Reciprocally receiving technology from licensee is visualized ☐ on signing agreement ☐ from future grantbacks.

☐ Selecting a particular licensee gives him a headstart over other local firms; for future licensee business

☐ Licensing is the fastest way to introduce product in market.

☐ Licensee's continued dependency on us is assured even after agreement expiry because of ☐ Trademark ☐ New models ☐ Components ☐ Other _____

☐ Rate of technical change is so rapid that obsolescing technologies can be licensed without fear of licensee competing
☐ Our patent is about to expire in a country anyway.

☐ Tax considerations. Please specify:
☐ Our firm is so ☐ large, ☐ diversified that there is no way we can generate ☐ financial ☐ managerial resources for equity investment in all countries/products. Hence licensing.

☐ Our firm is still small so that we cannot invest in our own subsidiaries in every country or product line.
☐ Other (Please specify)

PLEASE NOW RANK ALL CHECKED BOXES: 1 IS HIGHEST. This is very important for the research

3. BLANK SPACE FOR ADDITIONAL COMMENTS

130

PART II: FOCUS ON A PARTICULAR PRODUCT TYPE OR PROCESS

In order to reduce generalizations, questions on this page relate to one process or product type of your choice where you have independent licensees abroad. Please fill in product SIC code [ ] (from guidelines)

1. A typical "licensing" agreement will include (CHECK APPROPRIATE BOXES AND RANK)
   - [ ] Know-how, [ ] Technical Assistance, [ ] Managerial Assistance, [ ] Patent rights, [ ] Trademark rights,
   - [ ] Component supply, [ ] Buyback of licensee production, [ ] Other ____ Please rank by degree of importance of value in the total package (1 is highest, etc.)

2. The technology involves : [ ] A Product   [ ] A Process
   (Please check boxes)
   - [ ] Finished   [ ] As a cost-saving or efficiency improvement
   - [ ] Intermediate   [ ] As part of new product introduction

3. If a process, is it
   - [ ] Central (e.g. smelting of copper to a copper producer)
   - [ ] Peripheral (e.g. Special paint coating to a car maker)
   - [ ] Other

4. Uniqueness: Is a well-informed prospective international licensee seeking your technology
   - [ ] You are the unique technology supplier [ ] Two to five other global suppliers
   - [ ] Five to ten [ ] Ten to Twenty [ ] Over twenty

5. Age of the technology (in general) ____ Years
   (Your process or model ____ Year)

6. Would you describe your technology as [ ] A radical departure [ ] Incremental advance over older mthods?

7. As an approximation, how many years will elapse before this technology is obsolete? ____ years.
   If there is a patent, how many years until expiry? ____ years

8. If this is a product, is there international trade in the item?
   [ ] NO [ ] Only short distances [ ] Yes, distance is no problem

9. Do tariffs or other restrictions hinder trade? [ ] No [ ] In some nations [ ] In most nations

10. In a typical agreement with an independent licensee:
    What is the duration of an agreement? ____ Years
    Practically speaking, will it be renewed anyway? [ ] Yes [ ] No [ ] Maybe

    When estimating future royalties and fees in order to compute a present value, what discount rate is used? ____ % [ ] Not computed

    At the end of the agreement could a licensee compete with your firm?
    - [ ] No likelihood of licensee competing outside their country because: [ ] Yes immediately [ ] Perhaps later
      - [ ] They will be technologically inferior [ ] Transport costs
      - [ ] We will hold trademark anyway [ ] Other
      - [ ] In licensee's country [ ] In international markets
      - [ ] No likelihood of licensees competing even in their own markets. Why? ____

    Besides quality and advertising restrictions, what other legally permissible restrictions are written
    [ ] On Production [ ] On Sales territory [ ] Please specify ____

131

Appendix B *(continued)*

11. As a general policy, your strongest reservations about licensing this technology stem from: (Please check and rank appropriate boxes. 1 is strongest)

☐ Licensee competition: ☐ Inadequate ☐ Leakage of technical ☐ Other _____
Compensation   Secrets

{ ☐ Now ☐ Later
  ☐ Licensees Country ☐ Internationally }

12. If this is a product,would you say that over the years, adjusting for inflation, the price has ☐ Dropped ☐ Risen ☐ Same

13.
a. Could you please estimate as a % or ratio, $ Revenues from all "Independent" foreign licensees OVER GROSS Revenues of all majority-owned equity affiliates abroad using this technology _____
   (Please see notes below for definitions of categories)

	Canada	Lat. Amer.	W. Europe	E. Europe	Asia	Africa	Aust./N.Z.	Other	Now please circle those regions where the first market entry was by licensing rather than investment.
# of "independent" licensees	____	____	____	____	____	____	____	____	}
# of majority equity affiliates	____	____	____	____	____	____	____	____	}

b.

c. % Sales from exports: For U.S. plants _____ %, For overseas plants _____ %

d. · Annual Global Sales of this product division   Annual ☐ 1980 ☐ 1981 ($thousands)

   · Sales made abroad either by you or by majority equity affiliates

   · Revenues from agreements with "independent" foreign licensees (☐ counting ☐ Not counting, components)

NOTES

· "Licensing" is used in its broadest sense as including several elements of a contractual package (See Question 1 above).

· "Independent licensee" should include foreign affiliates (joint ventures) where you have less than 50% equity share.

· Majority-owned equity affiliate: Where your firm has more than a 50% equity share.

BLANK SPACE FOR ADDITIONAL COMMENTS

APPENDIX C:

Descriptions of Licensing Practices in Some Companies

There is a considerable variation in licensing practice among companies. The descriptions in this appendix will serve to illustrate the differences. Included are firms whose primary international strategy is licensing, as well as companies where licensing is incidental. In these case histories we are almost as interested in circumstances that lead executives to shun licensing as an international strategy, as we are in exploring reasons for its importance to others.

The firms interviewed range in size from under $10 million in sales up to some of the largest corporations in the world. There is a similarly wide product coverage. The idea is to give readers a flavor of how international licensing is viewed by executives in several corporations. These cases do not comprise a statistically valid sample.

Interviews followed a more or less standard outline presented below. The executives interviewed were in most cases either the chief executive (in small companies) or a vice president associated with international operations (in larger corporations) or a full-time licensing executive or corporate planner (in the largest firms).

A general outline of topics covered follows:

- Strategy role of licensing and contractual forms of overseas business
- The decision process whereby some products or technologies are reserved only for majority foreign affiliates, whereas others may be licensed to any parties for income
- How country variables (e.g., regulations constraining equity investment or political risk) and other environmental factors affect the choice of methods for doing business in a country
- How product or industry variables influence the choice
- In organization or personnel terms, who in the company makes these decisions and how these are integrated into longer-term corporate planning and R&D
- The organization of the licensing function and differences between licensing to affiliates and non-affiliates

CASE A: PRECISION FEEDER INCORPORATED*

Precision Feeder Inc. is a small, family-held manufacturer of very commonplace, even mundane, industrial equipment, with no unique technology, no crucial patents currently, and nothing that would overtly suggest a highly suc-

*Names and unessential facts have been altered to preserve confidentiality.

cessful foreign licensing program. The company makes hoppers, bins, and screw and belt feeders for dry bulk material handling.

Dry granules and powders are of course stored, moved, and processed in an enormous diversity of industries such as food packaging, mining, chemicals, lumbering, and agriculture. The technical ability to handle various materials provides a first clue to the company's success as licensors. An innovation for which the founder was originally issued patents was to add pulsating motors, which prevent clogging, material compression, and undesirable segregation by particle size. An uninterrupted, smooth, metered flow of uniform material are all indispensable requirements in any modern process industry with high productivity. By contrast, for instance, in a developing nation, if a hopper or bin clogs up, a well-aimed sledge hammer blow is adequate to restore movement for a while. Needless to say, neither high productivity nor precisely metered mixing or processing are attainable in such circumstances. This is detrimental to product quality and total output, to say nothing about labor costs.

Even so, the idea of mechanically pulsating a feeder or a hopper is, in principle at least, hardly a revolutionary one; nor is it unique to this firm. In engineering terms, it would appear to be simple to hook up a motor-driven gyrator to pulse a hopper or a feed tube—until you try it, that is. In practice it is complex. Not only does a firm's engineering experience have to span many industries, but even within an industry there are large variations in scale, hundreds of materials, and a wide range of particle sizes, to say nothing of their shapes, viscosities, moisture content, and so on. It is this design know-how in the company that is the crucial service to the equipment buyer (and therefore to licensees who custom make equipment), more than the quality with which the equipment is built or their possession of some patents.

In a nutshell, the company's strength lies in its files going back a quarter century, which contain specifications of 75,000 jobs spanning 5,000 materials. When a new job is undertaken, going back to this data base instead of designing a materials-handling system from scratch not only saves engineering time and cost but greatly increases the probability of design success on the first try. This is a key service that licensees value.

The profitability of the licensing operation in this small ($15 million U.S.-based sales) company is in part due to the fact that they have no incremental fixed cost beyond one full-time international executive. On this small financial commitment, the company has built up over the past decade a foreign licensee turnover of nearly $9 million, on which generously high royalty rates are earned, well above industry averages. Total licensee turnover approaches two-thirds of U.S.-based sales—and this from a mere eight foreign licensees. There yet remain several other nations that could successfully sustain a licensee; however, the task of identifying a prospective licensee and developing a proper arrangement is time consuming. The single full-time international executive has a considerable portion of his time devoted to the close marketing and technical liaison with existing licensees. As we saw above, licensees remain partially dependent on the company for technical design support and for sales to third countries. Licensees are wont to refer to them for technical advice on one out of every two of their sales on the average. It is not surprising then, that several licensees have signed up for a second term (of ten years, usually), despite there being nothing the least bit technically complex embodied in much of the equipment.

The predominant use of licensing in overseas business is dictated by a mix of factors. Equity investment proposals, if not dismissed out of hand, are viewed cautiously because of the obvious managerial and financial constraints of this small company. Exports of hoppers, screws, bins, and belts do occur from the United States and from licensees to other third countries that are covered by manufacturers' representatives. But this is not always feasible. Transport costs vary from 15 to 25 percent on FOB, and tariffs can be high, especially in developing countries. Finally, technical needs of the end users often require a local manufacturing presence. Several European markets are served by a Scandinavian licensee; Japan by a Japanese licensee; and Latin America by local licensees as well as U.S.-based production. U.S.-based exports, when they occur, are often to developing nations, where the lack of significant competition enables a price high enough to cover the extra transport and tariff costs. Many of these sales are initiated not by the ultimate user but by a U.S. or European engineering firm erecting a factory and original equipment on a turnkey basis for local client.

Three additional points need to be made about their licensing strength. First, even though the existing patents held by the firm are not crucial to the entire technology package (and can be worked around or are unenforceable—as in the United States, where courts overturned a patent), they comprise a negotiating chip with prospective foreign licensees and are an outward symbol of technical capabilities. Second, licensees may renew agreements because they value continuing technical help. But in several cases they also renew to preempt possible competition from other licensees or the licensors themselves. Last, licensees value and use the company's brand name, supported by a worldwide advertising program costing up to 3 percent of global turnover. This expenditure is thrice the industry norm, but it maintains the company's claim to having the best technology in the minds of industrial equipment buyers and engineers overseas. This may be insurance against a licensee's wish not to renew an expiring agreement, although none have expressed such a wish in any event because the more significant result of the advertising is to increase sales, thus illustrating and reinforcing the idea of successful licensing as a positive-sum game for both parties.

CASE B: MACOMBER PRODUCTS, INC.*

Nervously crossing and uncrossing his legs, Bill Macomber sat in the Small Business Development Center office. His $4 million business was at an important

*Names and unessential facts have been altered to preserve confidentiality.

crossroads in its growth. Within a few months, he would have to decide on whether to go ahead with licensing or joint venture arrangements with partners in three states and some foreign countries. The business had grown to its present size from internal resources, and customers everywhere were being served from two small East Coast plants.

As suppliers of specialty chemicals to the textile-finishing industry, the success of Macomber Products depended significantly on Bill Macomber's technical skills as a chemical analyst, aided by "a half million dollars' worth" of equipment, such as spectrophotometers and radioscopes, with which his staff would concoct customized formulae for individual buyer requirements. By contrast, his giant competitors were content to supply standard formulations in bulk. Macomber Products were known in the U.S. and, to some extent, abroad as a technically innovative firm willing to take on small tailor-made batches.

"Well, what exactly would you offer a licensee or a partner?" asked the consultant, mystified after learning that the company had no patents, written processes, nor any capital to contribute. "You don't patent in this business without giving the 'secret' formulae away," said Bill, "and there are so many end applications, you can only put the manufacturing processes on paper in the most general terms.

"Let's take it from the beginning," continued Bill, outlining how his company had grown rapidly in the 1970s and orders even came to him from Britain, Japan, and South Africa. But recently, the strength of the dollar had priced his chemicals out of foreign markets, and a double blow was struck by inexorably rising transport costs over the years. Margins were being squeezed and it had gotten so bad that, in some competitive product areas, he could not effectively supply customers too far away from the company's Northeastern U.S. base. His existing arrangements with distributors in Los Angeles, Chicago, and Atlanta, to say nothing about importers in Tokyo, London, and other foreign locations, were strained from static or declining business. Worse, some of his agents, themselves educated in chemistry, and having learned of the specialized niches in their markets, might strike out on their own. "We can't expand into these territories ourselves," he continued, indicating lack of capital and "people I can trust." From these events Bill Macomber had concluded that some "franchising type" arrangements with distributors were now needed, and he had come to the Small Business Development Center for help in defining strategy.

"First, we must define what licensees or franchisees would get that they don't already have. Next, we should define the types of arrangements that protect your long-term interests and keep your licensees on a tight leash. Last, we should examine different compensation arrangements," the consultant said, outlining the morning's discussion, summarized below:

1. What licensees or partners would get is the use of the Macomber name, which enjoyed a reputation, set up assistance, and centralized chemical analysis from the expensive

equipment and analytical expertise already in place at Macomber Products. (The value of the company's name was unpleasantly brought to Bill Macomber's attention when he found one day a letter from a former Canadian agent, who had registered the Macomber name in Canada and was now offering to sell it back to him for a healthy consideration. Similarly, in South Africa, even as he had made tentative overtures to the distributor to discuss a possible licensing arrangement, the distributor had rushed to register the name in that nation. [In this case, the relationship was still on a very friendly basis—yet it put Bill Macomber at a slight disadvantage in any forthcoming negotiation, with one less bargaining chip.])

2. The consultant returned to the question of how licensees could be kept on a leash. The issue was important because there was nothing intrinsically unique or indispensable about what Macomber Products was offering. Once licensees obtained the analytical equipment, expertise, and market knowledge Macomber had, they could go their own way eventually, and there was no point creating competition. After some discussion, a consensus emerged on how to retain licensees "in the family" over the long term:
   a. A uniform international name and image;
   b. Licensees encouraged to use Macomber Products' central analytical and research facilities, which would be cheaper for licensees compared to each of them buying their own equipment;
   c. A similar, if not identical, package of services offered by each licensee so as to create a worldwide network. This would better serve national and multinational clients and would cut delivery time and transport cost.

3. As to compensation design, royalties alone would be inadequate. An equity stake in the licensee would be desirable. But would potential partners agree? How would Macomber Products contribute to equity, and, especially in distant locations, how could management performance and profitability of the venture be monitored? In an ideal, but not necessarily attainable scenario, Macomber said he would like to be 51 percent shareholder with no cash but with only intangible assets and know-how as contribution, while the 49 percent partner contributed the capital in that location. This was an idea quickly discounted. The consultant also reminded Bill Macomber to give careful thought to the question of whether an agreement with a partner should include "all and future products" or whether future technical developments should be separately negotiated and licensed for separate compensation. These issues could not be resolved in one meeting. The consultant suggested, as a final thought, that Bill Macomber should forget about using "franchising" as an expression because often that meant uniform terms to franchisees. There appeared to be substantial variance in the technical and marketing capabilities of potential partners and the size of each territory, and that implied a separate package and separate compensation design for each to maximize global licensing revenues. Otherwise, Macomber's "global profits" would be "sub-optimal." The only problem would be to keep individual licensees or partners away from each other and ignorant of the terms the other got.

Bill Macomber left the meeting looking somewhat more perplexed than when he came in. There were now several more variables that had been presented to him; but, at any rate, he was satisfied that most of the crucial strategy issues had now been uncovered and identified, as a first step toward their resolution.

CASE C: LICENSING IN AN APPAREL COMPANY*

America may have lost much of its apparel industry, but its labels still carry their mystique and prestige. Textile production may be a mature industry now, but quality and productivity improvements continue to be made and valued in the context of strong global competition. On these statements rests the international licensing program of company C, a $1 billion sales, apparel and accessories firm.

Started in the last decade of the nineteenth century as a corset and attachable collar manufacturer, the company has never had an extensive overseas presence in terms of its own investment. However, especially since the end of the second world war, the company's brand name in apparel and its proprietary process in textile manufacturing have become instantly recognizable symbols of quality everywhere.

Corporate headquarters in Atlanta guides a collection of apparel (inner wear such as shirts or blouses), clothing (outerwear such as suits and jackets), and retailing companies, including overseas plants in Canada and three Latin American countries. For the rest of the world, products are exported where feasible, or, failing that, the company is represented by licensees in each nation. Exports have dried up with increased protectionism since World War II, and many former distributors have now become licensees. Thus, most of the company's customers outside of North America are buying licensees' production, with the company's brand name on it. Licensing has come to be not only the company's principal overseas strategy but has contributed up to one-third of the firm's entire profits in recent years.

The principal asset being licensed on the apparel side is the firm's brand name, although the interviewed executives were loath to put it that way. In their view, a licensee also got garment designs, fabric analysis, quality control assistance, and the ability to purchase fabric and accessories such as buttons and darts. But while most licensees were eager to renew agreements at the end of a typical ten-year term, at that time licensees usually wanted only the brand name, having learned the "technical" aspects already. However, since most licensees serve their own presumably profitable sheltered markets (excepting their Japanese and other Far Eastern licensees) and since the difference in the royalties for the entire package and for the brand alone is not significant, many licensees sign on for the whole package anyway.

On the textile-manufacturing side, although the company itself is not in textiles it has a patented and trademarked process to eliminate creasing and shrinkage in natural fibers like cotton. This process is licensed to textile mills all over the world. There is a significant R&D and technical content to this, and a team of engineers is dispatched to licensees for setting up the operation and for trouble

*Names, the company's products, and other facts have been changed to preserve confidentiality. This does not alter the essential strategic considerations involved.

shooting. Processes of this kind, making natural fibers crease and shrink resistant have contributed to the renewed acceptance of cotton and wool fabrics among customers used to the "easy care" aspects of polyester materials. This has been especially welcome to countries like the People's Republic of China, whose mills were geared to cotton, or nations that find that importing petroleum feedstocks for synthetic fiber production is expensive, uses too much scarce foreign exchange, or does not use local natural fibers in which the country has a comparative advantage.

But even in the licensing of this process, while the principal emphasis is technical, their globally recognized brand name for the process has been carefully built up over the years, unobtrusively but persistently. Confidentiality precludes mentioning the brand, but a good comparison is the "Woolwork" label, recognized by consumers and fabric buyers worldwide as signifying a certain quality standard in wool fabrics. In the same way, textile manufacturers gain an advantage not only by using the process and making their natural fabrics crease resistant, but also by proclaiming on the fabric or in their advertising that treatment was done under license from the company. This is a particularly relevant consideration when fabrics or apparel made from these fabrics are exported to quality conscious North America and Europe.

All in all, licensing is perceived by management as highly profitable in a short-run sense, but as a strategy they wish they did not have to follow. (See note below). Even in an industry as mature as textiles, executives still remember and yearn for a more active international role in terms of a direct sale of products from their own factories, an era that is now passing. With a billion dollars in overall sales nevertheless, the company is large enough to invest some funds in what they term "blue sky" research such as non-woven fabrics, elasticized paper, and disposable garments. While these developments may have specific applications in packaging or in service establishments such as hospitals, there is no prospect of a major breakthrough. It is not going to stem the inexorable tide of migration of the industry away from North America and Europe.

A Note on the Profitability of Licensing

The profitability of licensing depends on accounting procedures used. At one extreme, almost all licensing revenue can be considered pure profit, especially from agreements that do not require the licensor to perform any ongoing services and incur costs specifically for the licensee. Toward the other extreme, one finds the view that many licensor company costs, even if not specifically linked to the licensee, may be partially charged against revenues derived from licenses. For instance, a company that undertakes "corporate image" advertising to promote its brands in general may try to prorate some of these costs over licensing operations in foreign countries, even if the advertising was done mainly in the licensor's home country, on the grounds that there will be an international "spillover" benefit from the advertising that will eventually rebound to the benefit of the licensee who uses the company's brand names. Inputing a profitability level for licensing is made even more difficult when royalties are collected by a headquarters licensing department, but the costs of executing the agreements are borne by the operating divisions. Suffice it to say that licensing contributes handsomely to cash flows (in a short-term sense) and that, even in companies that charge all possible costs against licensing revenues, the overwhelming majority of the licensing income is usually still "pure" profit.

CASE D: AVERSION TO LICENSING IN AN ELECTRICAL PRODUCTS COMPANY

With 35 percent of its roughly $270 million sales total outside the United States, this company is a multinational firm in every sense of the term. There are major plants in Canada, England, and Japan, and important sales and warehousing operations in France, Germany, Italy, Australia, and Sweden, additionally.

Why income from unaffiliated licensees is under 2 percent of profits before taxes is explored below. As their vice president for corporate development put it, managerial time is engaged in more profitable pursuits than licensing. In this respect the company typifies firms averse to or unable to use licensing as an effective strategy. The company makes hundreds of products used in electric and electronic equipment and installations, varying from flat cables and connectors to insulators, conduits, and terminals used in commercial and factory construction, electrical equipment, computer hardware, and communications. A key factor is that, barring few exceptions, the company's products are (1) specialized for specifications peculiar to industrial applications in each industry, as opposed to being "commodity" items such as ordinary cable; (2) innovative, in that they represent engineering or productivity gains for users; and (3) manufactured to the strongest quality and wear specifications needed by the high-technology industries these products go into such as computers or aircraft. In short, their customers are in large part high-technology, growth industries in advanced countries.

The low use of licensing as a strategy is attributable to the following factors: *Lack of significant markets in middle- and low-income countries.* A good example is their very flat "undercarpet" cable and connections for office installation. In a high labor cost context with frequent office layout changes even after original installation, the system provides speed, flexibility, and durability. The considerably higher per foot costs and connector costs are justified by lower labor time in installation and ease of later modification. In lower-income nations, much cheaper cable, permanently wired through conduits is acceptable because the higher installation or rewiring time is more than offset by low hourly wages and the low opportunity cost associated with disruption of commercial space while the job is being done. The same logic also applies to quality, since a poorer quality cable at much lower price may be quite acceptable in an economic environment that does not place a high cost on power outages resulting from cable failure.

No unique technology or high-technology salable proprietary information. In most cases, while the company does make innovative products to the specifications of user industries, there is very little technically sophisticated about them. Much of the company's R&D budget (at 5 percent of sales, high for their industry) is spent on developing applications in their large number of distinct industrial markets. Research is marketing oriented rather then devoted to radically new ideas. In short, a key element of licensing is missing, the ability to transfer an identifiable advantage to the licensee, either in a specific process technology or a patent or even in specific market knowledge.

Inability to codify the company's marketing expertise. Here we arrive at a cornerstone of the company's strength—their knowledge of the requirements of the many industries they serve, from aircraft to computers to office construction, and their design of specific electrical products for them. But even for one or a few product lines, marketing expertise is difficult to codify for transfer and sale to another firm. Not only are there hundreds of applications, but specifications can vary across countries. Licensing a particular design, say a connector, is feasible, but a licensee in one nation is unlikely to offer any significant compensation for it alone. By contrast, expanding overseas through the company's own subsidiaries enables the extension of the firm's administrative, marketing, and technical abilities over their entire product range. Together, these provide a justification for a direct foreign investment. Other advantages of direct investment accrue from rationalizing production in different countries and sales made to foreign affiliates of their U.S. customers—to the extent that technical standards are uniform or similar, as in the electronics sector, economies of scale are achieved by combining national markets.

Thus, the strategic strengths of the firm, which lie in a mix of production and marketing efficiencies, are exploitable only through controlled foreign affiliates and by selling to nations where exports are feasible with a sufficient margin of profit. Licensing may possibly be used in specific circumstances such as:

1. The investment climate is undesirable because of rampant inflation or other factors, and tariffs are high.

2. Local market specifications are so peculiar that local expertise is needed. In some cases setting up a licensee already in complementary lines in a small market may be better than bothering to learn the business there themselves.

3. Their product is so standardized as to become a "commodity" (e.g., certain cables) on which return on foreign investment is now unattractive due to lower prices and competitive pressure. By comparison, most of their products are not only specialized but are not treated as a bulk purchase, so that they are relatively price inelastic.

4. A licensee is also a supplier: markups on resale, of greater importance than royalties, may make the arrangement as a whole worthwhile.

5. Licensing to establish a market presence and learn about conditions there was done in the company's early international expansion. Originally a licensee, a British firm became a joint venture partner and was later bought out altogether.

The company has, as a result, only four independent overseas licensees, and there is no effort to seek out more. The conventional royalties in their industry (which do not exceed 5 percent) are not sufficient compensation for abdication of a market to a licensee, although in their case there is no fear of licensee competition in third countries.

CASE E: A LARGE PHARMACEUTICALS AND CONSUMER PRODUCTS FIRM

The basic strategy for international business in this $2 billion sales company is to establish fully owned subsidiaries wherever possible. In this attitude, their vice president in charge of planning reflected a fairly prevalent view among the larger pharmaceutical firms, whose overriding mission is to get a "return on research and development" with the least hinderance from joint venture partners and licensees. Fully owned subsidiaries provide the best vehicle for extracting the "large enough" margins from foreign territories that need to be repatriated to headquarters and put back into R&D. By comparison, royalties alone would be an inadequate return for any drug or product, even moderately successful.

Licensing is done, but as an exception. The company has approximately thirty arm's-length licensees worldwide, some in restrictionist nations like India or Japan (where licensing appears a viable option, given the difficulties in entering those markets by direct investment); they also have some licensees in Western Europe. The EEC is, however, beginning to insist that a firm be allowed to sell anywhere, so that their licensees now have to have a Europe-wide marketing territory. This makes licensing in Western Europe even more difficult or, rather, less profitable as compared to having one licensee in each EEC country. Nevertheless, for many drugs, Europe is still *de facto* segmented into one territory per country because European nations still have their own health and certification requirements.

One constant in their licensing is that the agreement includes purchase of an active ingredient by the licensee. In the past, royalties by themselves may have been "large enough," but today, ceilings on royalty rates in some nations and the general reluctance of licensees to agree to too high a royalty rate make the supply of ingredients a necessary element of the deal, on which additional profits are earned. There are some other reasons:

1. There are significant economies of scale in the production of active ingredients from a few centers such as Puerto Rico and Ireland from which all affiliates and licensees can be served.
2. Generous tax benefits in these locations also make them attractive centers to pool global earnings.
3. In several (though not all) cases, the production method of the ingredient is a company secret or involves sophisticated technology, such as recombinant DNA, so that high

margins of profit can be earned and the licensee remains dependent on the firm. (As we have seen, this does not necessarily imply something sinister or predatory or imply a power tussle between licensor and licensee as antagonists. Quite the contrary. In almost all instances it is a mutually beneficial and mutually profitable relationship. Both parties know and are glad that profits are made by the other.)

Licensees are required to make identical claims for the company's drug all over the world. An agreement usually includes the patent right, technical assistance, trademark, and supply of ingredients. Of growing importance to licensees of late is the testing and certification that the company may already have done with the Food and Drug Administration (FDA) or other countries' agencies. A slightly increased willingness on the part of governments to accept testing done in other countries helps speed the licensee's certification.

Some of their agreements are based on reciprocal licensing whereby the company may license its drug in Europe, for example, so as to receive the rights to market a European company's product in the United States.

If we were to consider European countries separately, then Japan would be this company's second largest single market after the United States. With 115 million relatively affluent consumers and a developing health care system, this is only natural. Historically, Japan has been dominated by indigenous drug companies that were inward looking and content with their own market behind protectionist barriers. Even today, out of their top twenty pharmaceutical firms, only one can be properly described as an international company. So until five or ten years ago, licensing was the best method for accessing that market. Now barriers to investment are being lowered; but to be successful, one still has to understand governmental and market distribution practices in Japan that may appear arcane to an outsider.

The typical duration of a license is ten to twelve years or equal to the remaining patent life, since the agreement cannot exceed that limit legally in many nations. A long duration in excess of a decade, if possible, is deemed necessary to obtain an adequate recovery of some contribution margin toward R&D. In practice, licensees tend to sign up again for new products or even for the same product, e.g., for unpatented "over the counter" body-care items or, in the case of drugs, when the active ingredient is still best purchased from the company. Even when the patent for the formula runs out and can be used by any other firm, it may still make economic sense to purchase an ingredient from the original licensor because the production method may be secret or efficient (i.e., low cost compared to a single licensee's own attempts at manufacturing the ingredient themselves).

Despite a formal planning department and structure, the company, in keeping with its policy, does not screen countries of the world for possible licensing opportunities. Since the pharmaceuticals division is organized along country or regional lines, licensing proposals do come up from the country level for approval or rejection and are treated as exceptions to the norm of foreign direct investment as the preferred strategy.

CASE F: A LARGE CHEMICALS COMPANY

A large ($4 billion sales) chemicals producer, the company manufactures in three broad product areas: (1) bulk chemicals (e.g., methanol) and specialty chemicals (paints, glues, coatings), (2) fibers (polyester, cellulosic yarn, cigarette filter acetate), and (3) specialty plastics (structural aircraft parts, engineering parts, resins).

Exports from U.S. operations alone comprise 15–18 percent of global sales, and sales by affiliates overseas comprise 21 percent of total sales, giving a roughly 40 percent share to "overseas business" in the company. Equity affiliates exist in fifteen countries besides the United States. Of these, subsidiaries of major note exist in England, Canada, Mexico, Belgium, and Brazil. The majority are joint ventures-cum-licensees. The company has followed a policy, since the 1940s, of encouraging local equity participation in order to understand the local market better and to improve government relations and access to locally procured raw materials. Moreover, particularly in developing countries, the greater number are minority joint ventures with technology agreements. In several such cases it is difficult to say whether it is the equity or contractual relationship that predominates.

International operations are organized under a separate international company from the product groups. The licensing department at headquarters liaises with both. The product groups "own" the technologies, while the international division is responsible for overseas markets and equity affiliates and licensees there. Technology is transferred internally, in a manner of speaking, from the product to the international division's overseas subsidiary. The returns or profit from the overseas operation are then shared between the international and product division. This is, however, only an internal accounting matter (as distinct from formal accounting for tax and reporting purposes). As a working formula, dividends of overseas affiliates accrue to the international company while royalties and technical payments are credited to the product company. Thus, licensing and technology agreements here perform an internal accounting and control purpose besides their normal function external to the company, namely, to report for tax purposes separate returns on past R&D investment and returns on simple capital investment and entrepreneurial risk.

The headquarters licensing department, consisting of four attorneys with technical degrees, acts as a service center whose costs are absorbed into general overhead rather than charged to a specific division or agreement. As elaborated below, since there is no strategy mandate to license any of the company's technologies, agreements are seldom initiated by the licensing department, nor does it always participate in any initial investigation of the prospective licensee or the market. The primary responsibility for that rests with the international division, which will, however, often consult with them on tax and legal issues when deciding upon licensing vis-à-vis equity investment. During any actual negotiating, the licensing department staff are always involved and participate in not merely tax or legal aspects, but in questions of compensation, technology, and quality control as well. The licensing department supervises the signing and registration of contracts and the licensee's compliance and progress up until the first payment is received. Then responsibility for monitoring and technical service is handed over to the international division.

The company spent $100 million in 1981 on R&D, which is not a remarkably high percentage of sales. This is reflected in several reciprocal technology and licensing-in agreements which have greater priority in long-term strategy terms over transferring technology out internationally.

In a ranking of strategic choices, exports, preferably from existing U.S. plants, rank first because of the usual considerations of capacity utilization, marginal costing, and U.S. employment. But practically, this is not often possible, particularly in standardized bulk chemicals, because of competition and transport and tariff costs. Predictably, the best overseas customers are the company's own equity affiliates. Even this is true mainly when economies of scale derived from a few very large plants make vertical integration desirable. For example, one large cellulose acetate flake plant serves affiliates in many countries.

The second strategic choice is to have some ownership in a foreign plant to serve that nation's market. As we saw, the company is very receptive to the idea of local participation, even accepting a minority equity position. These joint ventures are also licensees and quite often trading partners as well. There have been years when the royalties and technical fees have exceeded dividends received on shares held so that it is difficult to say whether in fact the contractual or ownership relationship predominates. In any event, actual control or influence over the affiliate is another matter again, being determined by a mix of factors such as the expectation of future technologies from the "parent" company, access to global markets through it, composition of the management, and so on.

While there are a "few score" licensing arrangements worldwide, four or five of the largest "are *far* more significant in terms of international strategy and royalty income" (emphasis by the interviewed executive).

In short, the many completely independent licensees contribute in total only a few million dollars of annual licensing income. Pure licensing, without some equity participation, is the last strategic choice. "There just isn't enough money in it." No effort is made to initiate such arrangements, but approaches from prospective licensees are not turned away and entered into if feasible without the licensee constituting international competition for the company. Such arm's-length relationships, without the restraint of equity partnership, are indeed a worry because, while the company owns many patents, in no case are the patents so crucial or strong enough to be able to constrain the licensee only to his territory.

Another strategic motivation for licensing overseas is the desire by important U.S. customers that the same products and technical services they buy in the U.S. be provided at all their facilities abroad. Thus, the needs of Ford auto plants abroad led to the creation of overseas licensees for special paints and coatings; the need of a shipping fleet for certain chemicals at overseas ports of call was similarly met by setting up licensees in each nation. These examples illustrate a case where equity investment would be infeasible or uninteresting because of the many locations where the product was desired and the peripheral or small-scale nature of the technology.

For the future, the company sees no important rethinking of strategic priorities that would increase the role of licensing. Indeed, with the recent creation of a separate international division and the present arrangement whereby royalties and licensing fees are credited internally to the product division (whereas dividends from foreign affiliates are credited to the international division), there is likely to be an even greater emphasis on exhausting the possibilities of equity participation in foreign ventures before licensing is contemplated.

CASE G: LICENSING IN ONE OF THE WORLD'S LARGEST CORPORATIONS

More than twenty executives in a central licensing department oversee a portfolio of over 400 agreements in some forty nations. Royalty and licensing income of about $60 million makes but a small increment to net profit of this giant corporation, although an equivalent or possibly much larger profit is made elsewhere in the company on other business created because of the agreements. For some product divisions, licensing is very important and has comprised almost all the profit in some years. For most divisions, however, licensing is minor.

Technology transfer from the company has three channels: pure patent licensing to U.S. licensees is handled by divisional patent attorneys. Some spin-off technologies that the company is not interested in are licensed away from the corporate R&D center. However, the principal vehicle is the international licensing group, which functions as a service center at headquarters. Licensing professionals there serve to identify opportunities, help find suitable licensees or joint venture partners, negotiate the agreements, and often arrange financing if needed. Royalty and other income accrues directly to the technology-holding division, but the licensing department ''charges'' it (in an internal accounting sense) a fixed fraction thereof as a fee for its services. When the department's licensing executives travel to negotiate an agreement for instance, the division is charged a *per diem* fee and out-of-pocket expenses in addition. It has been estimated that for the company as a whole, the costs of executing and maintaining the licensing program are well below 20 percent of direct agreement income. That is not counting the additional margins of profit earned from doing other business with licensees, or technology or information received from them, the value of which has not been quantified and cannot even be guessed at.

For this enormous, diversified company it is difficult to make generalizations about international strategy. Export from existing plants is naturally preferred where possible, followed by controlled affiliates as a next option. (Incidentally, affiliates are also licensees, almost always, for familiar reasons—to create another income stream less volatile than dividends, to lower foreign taxes, to fulfill IRS requirements, and so on.) Contractual arrangements with a technology transfer component are the third strategy choice. These include pure arm's-length licensing and hybrids of contract production, minority joint ventures, and licensing. For example, some licensees are formally called "manufacturing associates" where most of the profit is from the sale of components rather than from royalties.

As far as international licensing strategy is concerned, here again it is difficult to make across-the-board generalizations. One thing can be said, and was stressed—that licensing is optimized in the company, rather than maximized. An all-out attempt to license technologies could produce thousands of global agreements. But this would be sub-optimal since many overseas product/market combinations can be more profitably filled by other strategies.

As an example of an across-the-board rule: synthetic diamond technology may not be licensed anywhere. The company has good, defensible patents, a technically unequalled process that is capital intensive but has low variable cost, trade is possible, and transport costs are negligible. There is, therefore, nothing to gain and much to lose by licensing.

For other products, market entry methods are a country-by-country decision. In Eastern Europe, China, and Japan (until recently) licensing was often the only practical choice. For example, a large sale of turbines and generators, in which the company is a world leader and the Japanese still lag, was made to a Japanese utility. Their Ministry of International Trade and Industry (MITI) insisted that the sale be accompanied by a compulsory license and transfer of technology to a large Japanese group which is often a direct international competitor. This was agreed to reluctantly after considerable debate because

- The order was large and profitable.
- Licensing terms were attractive (the Japanese are said to be always generous and prompt in paying for imported technology).
- Other competition like Brown Boveri or Siemens were willing to license the Japanese anyway.
- The company has patent protection in third countries.
- The agreement consequently explicitly forbids the licensee from transferring the technology outside Japan for five years after expiry.

Specifically, the company has its eye on large, undeveloped markets like Brazil and China where there is perennial need for adding power generation capacity. The Japanese would be a threat in those nations particularly.

Another contrasting case was discussed, where the company will freely license anybody, anywhere in the world. Wire and cable and copper rod production are not sophisticated, though there are proprietary formulae for insulation and proprietary tricks of the trade and efficiencies that can be shared with another firm. International trade is small in such items because of transport and tariff barriers and because the product value is sensitive to the price of copper, that being the principal input. This case illustrates how, as a company policy, it is easier to license an intermediate product or process technology or an older "generic" technology, as opposed to an end-product, particularly if it is new in its product cycle.

Simplicity of the design of the product may make a technology licensable. For an example, take an item in the company's consumer products division: a significant innovation is their new light-weight iron for household use, made with many plastic parts. There is no "high" technology, just an elegant design, low manufacturing cost, and a light weight for the user. Eminently licensable, but the company will not license the design to anyone. An attractive product, the internationally recognized brand name and a good global marketing network add a premium to its selling price and make an in-house strategy much more profitable than licensing.

The last example also illustrates the company's policy on licensing their trademark to unaffiliated parties. They will not. The corporate logo is seen as too precious an asset to risk with a licensee's possible quality shortfalls. However, minor brands associated with specific industrial products may be selectively transferred. But since 80 percent of the company's international licensing involves industrial products, trademarks are not so important a matter anyway as in consumer items. Industrial buyers, it is surmised, would in any event know or be told who the technology has been licensed from.

Yet another reason for a reluctance to license may simply be the feeling that a licensee will not succeed. The company regularly turns away scores of prospective licensees. In a few cases, the conclusion is reached that in some markets no licensee is likely to succeed. For instance, the company is unlikely to license gas turbine technology in Europe, despite some eager prospects, because they feel the market is saturated with enough firms already. Or take the case of steam turbines in nations like India: they do not believe the size of the market or a licensee's quality control would be adequate. But what if a country like India insists it wants the technology, for whatever long-term considerations, even if simply importing the equipment is cheaper in the short term? After all, the Indians did acquire this technology from the Czechs and from Siemens. This question was debated in the company. Some executives believed that perhaps they should be less scrupulous and supply the technology in such cases, regardless of whether it is best for the nation.

An example of environmental laws influencing licensing strategy is provided by capacitors which contain dielectric fluids with PCBs to stabilize the oils. This was a technical breakthrough when introduced but can be an environmental hazard if not handled properly. The company will license if the country's laws permit. Laws on this score vary widely from nation to nation. The item is not transportable and sub-licensing is prohibited except to controlled subsidiaries of the licensee. With effective territorial segmentation, there are thus several licensees worldwide.

Returning to the larger strategic contribution of the licensing program, income other than direct royalties and fees has been mentioned; there are other benefits as well. Licensees have often become joint venture partners later on. The license is thus used as a market entry wedge to test viability without a significant commitment by the firm. An investment can be made if the licensee is successful. Using licensees as contract manufacturers has also been mentioned above. The company has a useful phrase to describe many such arrangements as "technology led" deals, where the technology transfer is only the centerpiece of larger, more complex linkages with the other firm. Last, another occasionally important benefit is improvements or designs granted back by the licensee. In the overwhelming majority of cases, there is no prospect at all of the licensee further improving the company's technology. There are exceptions: an Italian licensee for electrical motors adapted the design and scale of production to European specifications which are more suitable for the Latin American market for motors. In the case of vacuum interruptors (for electricity transmission), a licensee made a very valuable contribution.

Some twenty-odd licensing executives in this company employing half a million people thus play a small but vital role in profits and strategy.

NOTES

1. U.S. Department of Commerce, *U.S. Direct Investment Abroad, 1977* (Washington, D.C.: U.S. Government Printing Office, 1981), pp. 20, 190, 191, 372. Affiliates are defined as foreign enterprises in which the U.S. firm has over 10 percent equity interest. About 7,000 of the 29,000 total is technology transferred by the foreign affiliates in turn to other unaffiliated foreign licensees, 22,000 being directly licensed by the U.S. firms.

2. Estimates made by the author from U.S. Commerce Department data in issues of *Survey of Current Business* and their latest Benchmark Survey, *U.S. Direct Investment Abroad, 1977*. Of the licensing income $6.1 billion is from U.S. firms' own majority affiliates, and $2.5 billion from independent and minority joint venture licensees. Licensing one's own affiliate not only creates an auxiliary channel for income extraction, it lowers political and convertibility risk somewhat. It may also lower the effective total tax on affiliate income repatriated to the United States.

3. Ford, D., and Ryan, C., "Taking Technology to Market," *Harvard Business Review,* March–April 1981, pp. 117–126.

4. Contractor, F., "The Role of Licensing in International Strategy," *Columbia Journal of World Business,* Winter 1981, pp. 73–81.

5. For Japanese technology import policies, a model for many other nations, see Ozawa, T., *Japan's Technological Challenge to the West, 1950–1974: Motivation and Accomplishment* (Cambridge, Mass.: MIT Press, 1974). For a useful summary of current LDC policies, see the series of articles, UNIDO, "Systems Affecting Technology," *Les Nouvelles: Journal of the Licensing Executives Society,* March 1982, June 1982, and December 1982, especially written by the UNIDO Secretariat for the Society.

6. UNIDO, "Systems Affecting Technology." Mexico is a good example of the regulation of technology transfer in LDCs. See, for instance, Delgado, J., "Comment on Mexico's Amended Law," *Les Nouvelles: Journal of the Licensing Executives Society,* September 1982, pp. 202–203.

7. With a strong dollar, licensing partially substitutes for exports from the United States but reduces employment in the short run.

8. A summary of the Nairobi round of the WIPO conference may be found in "LDCs Win Some Worrysome Points at Patent Talks," *Chemical Week,* November 18, 1981, pp. 18–19; or Mandros, P., "WIPO Conference on the Revision of the Paris Convention," *Les Nouvelles: Journal of the Licensing Executives Society*, December, 1981, pp. 6–7.

9. Revisions proposed in 1982 by the Senate Finance Committee.

10. For example, see pages 96, 102, 190, and 426 in *U.S. Direct Investment Abroad, 1977*. Moreover, information on non-affiliate licensing is sketchier, being available in only a two-digit classification and is less reliable, there being a fear of considerable underreporting to the Commerce Department despite a "mandatory" filing requirement.

11. Caves, R.; Crookell, H.; and Killing, J., "The Imperfect Market for Technology Licenses," *Oxford Bulletin of Economics and Statistics*, August 1983, pp. 249–267.

12. Root, F., *Foreign Market Entry Strategies* (New York: AMACOM, 1982). For further details and examples of the kinds of managerial and financial constraints faced by small firms attempting direct investments overseas, see Newbould, G., Thurwell, J.; and Buckley, P., *Going International: The Experience of Smaller Companies Overseas* (New York: Wiley, 1978).

13. National Science Foundation, *Science Indicators 1980* (Washington, D.C.: National Science Board, 1981).

14. Under a classical economics framework, in fact, patents are imperfections that lower global welfare. See Johnson, H., "The Efficiency and Welfare Implications of the International Corporation," in Kindleberger, C. (ed.), *The International Corporation* (Cambridge, Mass.: MIT Press, 1970), pp. 35–56.

15. See Business International, *Doing Business with Eastern Europe,* (Geneva: Business International Corp., 1972).

16. UNCTAD, *Major Issues in the Transfer of Technology to Developing Countries: A Case Study of Chile* (New York: United Nations, 1974).

17. Patel, S., "Trademarks and the Third World," *World Development* Vol. 7 (7), 1979, pp. 653–662.

18. In the theory of the discriminating monopolist, the monopolist's revenues increase asbuyer segmentation is increased. The firm's strategy should accordingly treat each nation separately if transport costs, tariffs, branding, or any other factors effectively segment one country from another as national markets, charging in each country as high a technology margin as that market can bear or at least as much as is extractable under the foreign investment laws or foreign exchange regime of the country.

19. Please see Chapter 5 and Table 20 for a fuller ᴜ ᵖlanation. I am summarizing these variables here because Table 32 later in this chapter lists companies' responses to these factors.

20. The next chapter discusses the organization of the licensing function. Even in very diversified firms where each product division may handle its own international operations, there often is a headquarters legal or accounting department that monitors licensing agreements and records receipts.

21. This will introduce biases since the overseas profit-to-sales ratio is not going to be the same from one industry or company to another. On the other hand, we can assert that the ratios LIMP1 and LIMP4 are conceptually acceptable since both numerator and denominator correlate with sales activity—the denominator directly, and the numerator because most royalties are expressed as a percentage of sales by the licensee.

22. A positive sign is expected also for the ratios LIMP1 and LIMP4 although an opposite hypothesis can also be made, *a priori*. Data for the variables COMPETE, SUPPLY, and other independent variables in the forty-four-company sample were collected specifically for the firm's licensed technology.

23. See the Commerce Department's *U.S. Direct Investment Abroad, 1977*. The chemical, petroleum, and pharmaceutical sectors are slightly overrepresented in this sample compared to the statistical universe.

24. See Contractor, F., *International Technology Licensing: Compensation, Costs and Negotiation* (Lexington, Mass.: D.C. Heath & Co., 1981).

25. The author is sometimes asked why in his empirical studies so far the sample is not focused on one industry but is rather an all-industry sample reflecting aggregate U.S. data. A one-industry focus would certainly be more incisive for that industry, at any rate, and reduce the "unexplained variance," i.e., variance not captured by the variables measured. However, a narrow, one-industry focus would not address larger policy issues that concern U.S. companies as a whole. Second, in an initial study such as this one, breaking new ground, one tries to get a sense of which of many hypotheses and variables are important and then may refine them later in an industry study. Third, as a pragmatic matter, it is extremely difficult in a one-industry study to get data from enough companies to assemble a sample large enough to obtain statistical significance in the analysis. Last, should one get strong statistical significance associated with non-industry-specific variables such as "sales" and it explains a reasonably large percentage of the sample variance despite there being several industries in the sample, as in our analysis, then one can draw general conclusions with a greater degree of assurance than warranted by equally strong statistics in a narrow sample.

26. Several studies indicate this, for example, Contractor, *International Technology Licensing*, p. 108. Also see Caves, et al., "The Imperfect Market for Technology Licenses."

27. Rugman, A., "A New Theory of the Multinational Enterprise: Internationalization versus Internalization," *Columbia Journal of World Business*, Spring 1980, pp. 23–29.

28. The statement is deliberately left vague for confidentiality reasons.

29. For trends in the electronics sector, see, for instance, Conrads, R., "Strategic Partnering: A New Formula to Crack Markets in the '80s," *Electronic Business*, March 1983.

30. A non-legal reader seeking a summary is referred to Antitrust Division, U.S. Department of Justice, *Anti-Trust Guide for International Operations* (Washington, D.C.: U.S. Government Printing Office, 1977). For British law, see Bloxam, G., *Licensing Rights in Technology: A Legal Guide to Managers in Negotiation* (London: Gower Press, 1972).

31. Hull, C., et al., *Statistical Package for the Social Sciences* (Chicago: SPSS Inc., 1981). The SPSS default rejection limits are rather broad. Some discretion was used by the author's research assistant.

32. The signs of coefficients were virtually identical whether the list-wise or the pair-wise deletion option in SPSS was used.

7

Organizing the Licensing Function

Considering the growing importance of foreign licensing as an income source—gross licensing income from abroad will likely cross the $10 billion mark by 1984—the organization of this function and its strategy role remain surprisingly variegated to the point of being treated *ad hoc* in some firms. Some examples from the author's research will serve to illustrate the diversity in the backgrounds of licensing staff and the degree of central corporate attention paid to this function. To the corporate planner at the Chicago headquarters of an industrial equipment manufacturer, the place of licensing in the company's international operations appeared quite minor. He used the familiar phrase "found money" to describe how top management viewed licensing income. A few miles away, however, in the consumer electronics division of a large conglomerate, licensing was described as the dominant, if not the only viable international strategy. This time it was their international marketing manager who, in fact, handled all overseas business, including licensing. Later, a patent attorney at one of Detroit's big three automobile makers lamented his organization's neglect of salable technologies and overseas licensing opportunities. "We could easily generate a couple of million dollars extra income on technologies already available in the company," he averred. Indeed, every few years there would be drives to take stock of the inventory of technical assets to see what could be done with them outside the firm; but the organization was too large, with top management attention elsewhere, and the idea was described as usually "falling between the cracks."

What accounts for the differences between companies as to the location, size, strategy role, and income contribution of the licensing function in international operations? Licensing executives appear to come to that job from a variety of backgrounds. One finds former line executives or engineers from a product division, patent attorneys, international marketing executives, and corporate planners, to name a few. Is this merely accidental, a point organization theorists will grant readily? Is this because, at least in some companies, licensing is a niche any senior, experienced executive is expected to fill? Or is the licensing executive's role a function of the industry, international development, and size of his company, and the perceived place of licensing in overall strategy? The objective of this chapter is to develop some of these normative propositions and compare them with a look at actual practice in firms. First we will look at an important theme in organization structure research, namely, the authority, influence, and mandate of headquarters staff departments such as the work done by W. French and D. Henning on headquarters personnel departments.[1] Here the staff department will be exemplified by the licensing department in an international company. Specifically, we are interested in the degree of centralization of the licensing activity as a function of company size, the international strategic role of licensing, and other environmental factors faced by the firm, as in studies by P. Blau or J. Child.[2] This will be examined empirically with data from the forty-four-company sample, augmented by detailed interviews in a dozen companies.

AN ORGANIZATIONAL TYPOLOGY

The organization of the licensing function ought to reflect its role in international strategy and characteristics of the firm. A simple typology is summarized in Table 41. The four types shown may be viewed as falling on a continuous spectrum ranging from licensing treated in a decentralized fashion at the divisional level in Type I, to a central headquarters licensing department designated as a profit center at the opposite extreme in Type IV. An examination of actual practice in companies, treated later, reveals unsurprisingly that most firms fall somewhere in the middle, with considerable overlaps on some of the subordinate considerations. Before that, however, let us examine some of the theoretical considerations in more detail.

The key questions to be decided by top management in each firm are the degree of authority shared by the divisions with the licensing department, i.e., the degree of central control, the speed and effectiveness of decision making, and the locus of responsibility for seeking new licensing opportunities.

Complete Decentralization

One pattern is to have each product (or regional) division handle its own licensing without any central supervision, as it seems best in the light of the division's strategic imperatives. This is commonly found in conglomerates whose product types have few synergies possible.[3] Decentralized licensing may then simply reflect the autonomous nature of the company's constituent parts. The advantages of Type I are the absence of central overhead and the more effective

Table 41
Types of Central Licensing Departments

	Type I — Entirely Decentralized; Handled by Product Divisions	Type II — Decentralized; Small H.Q. licensing Service and/or Legal Department	Type III — Centralized Licensing Department	Type IV — Central Licensing Department as a Profit Center
Headquarters Function	None	Providing negotiations and legal advice; monitoring payments and patent compliance; receiving income and keeping accounts.	All the functions shown left; in addition defining and coordinating licensing and coordinating licensing's role in overall strategy.	All the functions shown under Type III; in addition allocating licensing income to divisions according to a formula negotiated with them, after deducting department expenses.
Authority over Divisions?	N.A.	None; advisory role. Voluntary consultation by divisions.	Some shared authority in defining strategic role of licensing. Compulsory consultation by divisions.	Concurring authority, or in extreme cases, even functional authority for licensing.
Responsibility for Seeking Licensing Opportunities	N.A.	None to incidental.	Significant, shared with divisions.	High.
Costs of Negotiating, Technology Transfer and Licensee Service	Borne by each division.	Borne mostly by divisions; costs at H.Q. minor and typically not quantified nor broken down by division.	Significant negotiations, technical and legal costs at H.Q. department often allocated to each division.	Licensing costs and income are tracked and carefully accounted for by division, or even by agreement.
Accounting Description of Central Dept.	N.A.	Service Center.	Cost Center.	(Quasi) Profit Center.
Company Profile				
—International Penetration	Small or Nascent ───→			Large % of international in total profits.
—Diversification	Great Product Diversity; Conglomerate ──────────────────────→			Single Product-Type or Narrow Product Line.
—Percent of Bus. in LDC's or Socialist Bloc	Low ───→			High
—Political Risk or Sensitivity of Industry	Low ───→			High
Transport Cost or Tariff Impediment to Trade in Product	Low ───→			High

and rapid formulation of decisions at the divisional level. It is proper to view licensing as a strategic alternative to direct sales or exports and foreign equity investment as alternative ways of serving overseas markets. The choice between these has to be made somewhere in the company. Thus, in a very diversified company, the act of choosing between exporting, licensing, or capital investment had best be decentralized because, as we saw in Chapter 4, the choice partially depends on the product involved. The disadvantages, on the other hand, are the possible duplication and lack of coordination at the country level. Increasingly, with more legislation and regulation in many countries aimed at controlling foreign business, there is a need to coordinate the activities of various divisions of a multinational company in a particular nation. Even if there are no product synergies, once there are two or more licensees in a region, there may be definite advantages in coordinating or combining some functions. This may range from a simple requirement that all divisions retain the same law firm in a nation to forming a team of country specialists to advise the product divisions on the country's laws, environmental constraints, and business opportunities. This is, in fact, the next type on our organizational spectrum shown in Table 41.

A "Service Center" Department

In Type II, a small licensing service and/or international legal department performs only an advisory and monitoring role. The responsibility for seeking licensing opportunities and conducting negotiations remains with the divisions. The headquarters department has no authority over divisional licensing, although in several instances, after concluding an agreement, they have the responsibility for monitoring licensee compliance, protecting patents, and collecting royalty and other payments on behalf of the concerned division. Usually, in Type II, there is no attempt to calculate a breakdown of the central department's costs according to the service rendered each division. Rather, the department's costs are treated as part of general headquarters overheads. The Type II department is best described as a service center.

Shared Authority through Mandatory Consultation

In Type III, the licensing department shares in authority. Particularly on questions such as the effect of a proposed agreement on overall corporate strategy or legal and corporate tax issues, this may be achieved through a requirement mandating compulsory consultation between the division and corporate department. This is handled differently in different corporations. Some mandate that the division simply "touch base" with the licensing staff whose recommendation is not binding. Others require actual concurrence by the licensing department before the proposal can move further up for approval. This may give the department effective veto power in some cases.

A Quasi-Profit Center Department

Centralization is carried to its ultimate extent in Type IV, where the licensing department has effective functional authority by a rule requiring its concurrence with all key decisions, except those of a technical nature where the expertise still resides with the product division. Moreover, in Type IV, the department is charged with the responsibility for analyzing the company's technical assets and "marketing" these technologies worldwide. Thus, the prescription for Type IV that the responsibility for seeking international licensing opportunities primarily reside with the central department is congruent with the idea that responsibility correlate with authority. By contrast, in Type II, the department plays only an advisory or consultative role with no other responsibility for "marketing" the firm's technologies.

In Type IV, the central licensing department is usually designated a "profit center." While this is a good idea for management control and accounting purposes, the difficulties it can present highlight the inescapable tension between product divisions and central departments and illustrate why we cannot comfortably describe licensing as either a purely line or purely staff function.[4] In Type I, to have licensing completely decentralized carries the danger of duplication, lack of global coordination, and missed licensing opportunities. While these are minimized in Type IV, on the other hand, it carries the dangers of headquarters executives getting too divorced from the division's technologies. Worse, under the pressure of profit center accountability, they may initiate more agreements than is optimal for global strategy or undertake licensing arrangements that conflict with a division's plans for a product or plans in a particular country. Most agreements are made on an exclusive basis. Even on a non-exclusive basis, a license is tantamount to a partial or complete abdication of a market by the licensor company for the duration of the agreement. It may sometimes be worse if, even after agreement expiry, the licensee is still competitive with the licensor. Therefore, going all out and maximizing the number of global agreements is sub-optimal (in much the same way as maximizing revenue is sub-optimal in micro-economic theory). Rather, the number and extent of the company's licensees need to be optimized, that is to say, put in the context of overall global strategy, which in many countries will dictate alternatives such as direct sales or equity investment as superior alternatives. Type IV carries the danger of going beyond the optimum.

The difficulties of designating licensing as a profit center arise also because, while revenues from agreements would be received by the central licensing department in Type IV, costs of each agreement are borne by both the department and the divisions. Particularly with many product types in a company, it is uneconomical even for the largest licensing departments to have their own engineers for every product line. Thus, the majority of the negotiations, travel, technical documentation, and other engineering costs may well be borne by the product divisions even though revenues from licensees are collected by the licensing department. Certainly, the headquarters department also incurs costs, but it is tedious or even perhaps impossible to allocate these to each agreement or each negotiation with a prospective licensee. To avoid these difficulties, some artificial formula is usually devised whereby divisional costs are charged to the central department. Or at the end of each year, "profits" of the central department are credited to each division *pro rata*, according to its contribution in that year's licensing revenues. That is why it is best to describe Type IV as the "quasi" profit center type.

Type IV has a strong advantage, however. It usually focuses the responsibility for seeking new licensing business narrowly in the company, in the hands of technology transfer and legal specialists. By contrast, divisional line managers may not only be too busy, but they may have a bias in favor of in-house production. On the other hand, we saw that with profit center accountability pressures in a central licensing department, too much licensing also may be sub-optimal for the company as a whole if, as occasionally happens, more lucrative business opportunities in a country exist and are preempted by a licensing agreement made heedless of the overall strategic context. Whether to adopt Type IV will depend on which side of the optimum the firm presently lies.

What kind of international company will opt for each organization type? As one moves from Type I to IV on the spectrum of organizational alternatives summarized in Table 41, one moves toward greater centralization and head-quarters participation in international licensing. Past studies in organization de-sign suggest the following independent or underlying variables are involved:

- Degree of product diversification (see Child or N. Berg[5])
- Extent of international involvement of the company (see H. Schollhammer[6])
- Product cycle or technology maturity
- Degree of environmental sensitivity, complexity, or regulation associated with the industry in foreign markets (see P. Khandwala[7]).

Companies that are diversified and have no product synergies will likely opt for a position closer to the decentralized Type I. Conversely, it is only in a single-product or narrow-product-line firm that the advantages of the quasi-profit center mode in Type IV would overcome its drawbacks. Greater centralization, on the other hand, may be simply a reflection of the greater internationalization of the company, accompanied by the growing use of several central functional spe-cializations, such as licensing, superimposed on product or regional divisions, as Schollhammer posits.[8] The direct relationship between product or technolog-ical maturity and the degree of centralization is not certain, although some work seems to imply that central controls will increase as the firm moves along its learning curve, to take advantage of its economies and, in some industries, the economies of vertical integration.

Table 42 illustrates the hypothesized connections between variables. The key

Table 42
Hypothesized Relationships between Licensing Centralization and Other Variables

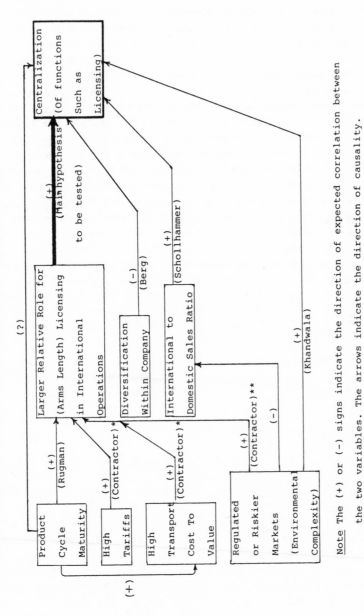

Note The (+) or (−) signs indicate the direction of expected correlation between the two variables. The arrows indicate the direction of causality.

  * In Chapter 6.

  ** In Chapters 4 & 6.

dependent variable is the degree of centralization of the licensing function. We proposed above a negative correlation between it and diversification in the company and a positive correlation between it and the ratio of international to domestic sales. We are also not certain about the direct relationship between product-cycle maturity and centralization of staff functions. However, indirectly, we can propose a relationship. A. Rugman theorized a greater role for arm's-length licensing in the overseas strategies of a company when the product is in its mature stage.[9] In Chapter 6 we found this to be true (with declining real prices over the product cycle as a possible underlying explanation). However, there were several other factors such as high tariffs, a high transport cost to volume ratio, and environmental complexity or risk that also contributed to a greater role for international licensing. Our central hypothesis is that, the larger the strategic role of licensing in international operations, the greater the degree of centralization of this function in the firm.

Khandwala found that environmental uncertainty contributed to functional departmentalization and staff support, regardless of whether the firm is international or domestic.[10] Last, with possibly declining prices as the product cycle matures, transport costs (as a percentage of value of the product) may become a barrier to trade in the same way as high tariffs, thus favoring on balance the use of licensing as an alternative strategy.

PRACTICE IN FORTY-FOUR U.S. COMPANIES: SOME STATISTICAL MEASURES

The organization of the licensing function in U.S. companies was measured as part of the forty-four-firm sample discussed in the last chapter. Also presented later are a dozen detailed mini-cases, based on interviews. Since there is no empirical work extant on this topic, this is a first step toward investigating these hypotheses.

The degree of centralization of licensing was measured on two different scales, as shown in Table 43. CENT1 on a five-point scale measures authority of the headquarters licensing department, whereas CENT2 measures the respondent's perception of the role of the department. (The two measures were also intended as a check on one another to catch any hasty or anomalous responses. And indeed, we see in Table 44 that there is a strong positive correlation between the two. This also fulfills the dictum that authority should go hand in hand with responsibility or role.)

Table 44 shows correlation coefficients and their significance for associations with CENT1 and CENT2. There is no significant association with the size of the company as measured by total SALES. We see that absolute licensing INCOME correlates negatively with centralization of the function, although with rather weak statistics. While this was unexpected, it does not violate any of the a priori hypotheses. Our central hypothesis claims that, as the relative importance of licensing increases over other international strategies, we would have increased

Table 43
Degree of Centralization of Licensing Function

(44 Company Sample)

CENT1 Code	Perceived Authority of Headquarters Licensing Department (CENT1)	Number of Companies
1.	Licensing handled by divisions; no headquarters department	2
2.	Headquarters licensing department will advise divisions if asked	3
3.	Divisions must keep headquarters department appraised	14
4.	Divisions must obtain specific headquarters approval for each license	17
5.	A headquarters department has independent authority to conclude agreements	8
9.	No response	0
	(CENT1 Mean = 3.5909)[a]	44 TOTAL

CENT2 Code	Primary Role of Headquarters Licensing Department (CENT2)	Number of Companies
1.	Purely advisory	3
2.	Performing a licensee monitoring role on payments, violations, etc.	6
3.	As jointly responsible for licensing with the divisions	20
4.	As independently responsible in a profit center sense	12
9.	No response	3
	(CENT2 Mean = 3.00)[a]	44 TOTAL

Notes a. The mean is calculated only on the responding companies.

   b. These questions are from Part III of the questionnaire. Please refer to Appendix B in Chapter 6.

Table 44
Correlations between Licensing Centralization and Other Company Variables

(44 Company Sample)

Variable	CENT1	CENT2	
INCOME	-0.25	-0.26	Pearson Correlation
	$(0.07)^+$	$(0.07)^+$	Coefficients Shown
SALES	0.14	-0.11	At Left
	(0.22)	(0.28)	Significance Levels
LINC2	0.53	0.35	Shown in Parentheses
	$(0.03)^*$	(0.13)	
ROLE	0.38	0.36	** Better than 0.025
	$(0.01)^{**}$	$(0.01)^{**}$	* Better than 0.05
REGRAT	0.25	0.08	+ Better then 0.10
	$(0.10)^+$	(0.34)	
TRANSP	-0.18	-0.13	
	(0.15)	(0.23)	
TARIFF	0.28	0.07	
	$(0.04)^*$	(0.34)	
PRICE	-0.58	-0.18	
	$(0.01)^{**}$	(0.32)	
CENT2	0.67	1.00	
	$(0.00)^{**}$	$(0.00)^{**}$	

Variable Definitions

INCOME: Licensing Income in $ millions from abroad

SALES: Total Sales of company

LINC2: Ratio of Licensing Income <u>Over</u> Exports and Sales
of Foreign Majority Affiliates

ROLE: Value of $\sum_{i=1}^{i=15} ROL_i$ for the company (See Table 32).
This is the summation of the strategy role scores
for the company.

Table 44 *(continued)*

REGRAT: Ratio of Number of Agreements in Developing Nations

over Number of Agreements in Developed Nations.

TRANSP: Transport Cost Impediment to Trade - 1: Yes;

2: Only Short Distances;3: Distance is no Problem

TARIFF:Tariff Impediment to Trade - 1: No; 2: In Some

Nations; 3: In Most Nations

PRICE: Inflation-adjusted price over the years has -

1: Dropped; 2: Same; 3: Risen

centralization. And indeed, the variable LINC2 (which is a surrogate for the relative importance of licensing in overseas operations) does have a strong positive correlation with CENT1. While the CENT2 sign is positive as expected, the statistics are not significant; therein lies a story. As we see in Table 43, only twelve of the licensing departments have an independent profit center role. We saw earlier that this organization type has drawbacks that increase in severity as products and divisions increase—only in a narrow- or one-product company do the advantages of a quasi-profit center department overcome its disadvantages. Hence, in many multiproduct companies, even though the relative use of licensing abroad is high and the authority of the licensing department (CENT1) is high, the department cannot play a profit center role. It is not surprising, therefore, that CENT2 lags CENT1 in the strength of its correlation with LINC2.

Another way to measure the relative importance of licensing in overseas strategy is to calculate (from Table 32 in Chapter 6) the sum of the scores given by companies to the fifteen strategic factors favoring the use of international licensing. The reader will recall that fifteen factors were supplied to respondents who first checked only those factors that were relevant to their company, and then they scored the checked items thus: fifteen = most important, fourteen = next in importance, and so on, down until the last checked factor. Only a minority of the fifteen factors were actually ever checked by a company typically, and the unchecked factors were allocated a score of zero. We have thus created an index for each company j:

$$ROLE_j = \sum_{i=0}^{i=15} ROL_{ij}, \text{ where } ROL_{ij} \text{ is the rank for the}$$

ith factor in company j
$(j = 1, \ldots, 44)$

ROLE is an index that varies from a theoretical minimum of 0 to a theoretical maximum of 120. The actual value of ROLE for each firm falls in between and measures, on *a priori* strategic considerations, the likelihood of its choosing licensing over other international strategies such as exporting or direct investment.[11]

As we expected, ROLE correlates positively with both CENT1 and CENT2, with high significance, further buttressing our principal hypothesis that centralization of the licensing function accompanies its relative importance in international operations.

Data limitations prevent us from examining other hypotheses such as the effect of product diversification on centralization. We have, however, some impressionistic measures for the effects of tariffs, transport costs, and product-cycle maturity. We find that high tariffs or transport costs do enlarge the international role of licensing (presumably by depressing trade in the item and creating appropriable profits in sheltered foreign markets), and that these are associated with higher centralization of licensing. (The negative sign for TRANSP is in fact as expected because of the way that variable is structured. See Table 44.) The coefficient is significant in only one case, but the signs are as expected, *a priori*. Product cycle maturity is a difficult thing to measure in the best of circumstances. With caveats and reservations discussed in Chapter 6, let us take the tangible measure of PRICE which may decline (although not necessarily) with product-cycle maturity. Thus, if product-cycle maturity is associated with greater centralization (with either direct or indirect causality as shown in Table 42) we should expect to find a negative correlation between PRICE and CENT1 or CENT2. (Refer to Table 44 for a definition of PRICE.) Indeed that is what we find, although the relationship is significant only with CENT1, which for reasons discussed above is a better measure of licensing centralization.[12]

Overseas market risk or complexity was not accurately defined in this sample. We can, however, from the questionnaire construct a ratio (REGRAT) of the number of agreements in developing over developed countries as an index of environmental risk or regulation faced by the company. The higher this ratio, the higher we expect the degree of centralization of that activity to be, i.e., the more headquarters attention paid to risk and foreign country rules and regulations. While the sign of both correlation coefficients for REGRAT are positive as expected, there is weak significance to only one of them.

Table 45 gives other information on the length of overseas licensing experience in the companies and characteristics of the responding executives.

CASE HISTORIES OF A DOZEN COMPANIES

Licensing and international executives were interviewed to develop case histories of organization for licensing in twelve companies. These are summarized in Table 46. There is a wide industry coverage, even though the sample possibly overrepresents larger U.S. licensor firms.[13] Nevertheless, interesting conclusions are derived.

A brief overview of strategy in each company will help understand why licensing is organized the way it is and its role in international operations. Let

Table 45
Other Information on Company and Licensing Staff

(44 Company Sample)

I. First licensing to independent parties overseas:

	No. of Companies
- Over 20 years ago	34
- Over 15 years ago	2
- Over 10 years ago	4
- Over 5 years ago	1
- Under 5 years ago	0
- No response	3
	44 TOTAL

II. Number of Full-Time Licensing Executives:

	Non-Legal	Legal
Mean	3.39	1.12
Std. Dev.	3.86	1.47
Range	0 - 15	0 - 7

III. Type of Responding Executive:

- Attorney	8
- Non-legal licensing executive	23
- Line executive	7
- Other	5
- No response	1
	44 TOTAL

IV. Respondent is member of:

- Central headquarters licensing department	25
- Division, or a part of the company	14
- No response	5
	44 TOTAL

Table 46

Organization of Licensing Activity in Twelve Companies

(a) Is Licensing A Profit Center?

(b) Is Licensing A Department?

Firm A	Firm B	Firm C	Firm D	Firm E	Firm F
Functionally centralized under corporate Development, but global market entry strategy left to each product group.	In Marketing Department, since licensing integrated with component and product exports. Full time licensee service group: 3 buyers for component and equipment purchases of licensees; 15 appliance engineers; one electronics engineer. Part-time use of R&D, accounting and traffic personnel.	Strategic direction and supervision by "Technology Transfer Review Board" a committee of senior Managers. Important distinction between patent and know-how licensing is reflected in a separate patent department, which handles patent licenses. "Know-how" licenses negotiated jointly by division staff and patent lawyers, subject to the Board's review. Thereafter licensee service and relations handled by product divisions; financial and legal monitoring by patent dept.	A separate subsidiary formed to handle licensing (and construction projects for licensees); has its own lawyer, accountants and executives. The separate subsidiary gets know-how from the divisions at no cost, and engineering and other services at cost. In turn, the net earnings of the subsidiary are divided up and "credited" to each division based on its share in the licensing activity.	A "Technology Marketing Division", negotiates, facilitates and services agreements for the operating divisions in the basic aluminum processes. For peripheral products and processes, they handle global licensing, independently of the divisions.	Product types, subsidiaries deemed too diverse to centralize licensing. One senior executive in each subsidiary or group assigned licensing when it occurs. One executive at HQ (V.P. Corporate Licensing) monitors, checks legal aspects, congruence with corporate policy and arranges once a year for a licensing review meeting attended by group executives.
a) No b) No, but within Corporate Development	a) No, but Marketing is b) No	a) No b) Yes, Patents & Licensing	a) Yes, see above b) Yes, see above	a) No b) Yes	a) No b) Yes

Firm G	Firm H	Firm I	Firm J	Firm K	Firm L
Handled by each industrial division, but coordinated at HQ by a company wide "Patent Board" and a central licensing department which monitors all agreements and records revenues and costs. The "Patent Board", which is an occasional panel, meets to set policy or resolve conflicts between divisions as to technology licensing. Both the Board and licensing department report to an Executive Committee which has V.P.'s from each industrial division, and comprises the governing body for the entire company.	Entirely decentralized with no company-wide links, in keeping with diversified nature of firm. Only links with other groups are informational (eg: In exploring a new market, see if other groups have contacts). Just before an agreement is finalized, it is run past the HQ lawyers and tax specialists.	Licensing agreements are the responsibility of each operating product group and subsidiary. The New Technology and Licensing (NTL) department, which is part of the "International and Diversified Technologies Group", handles legal aspects, negotiates and monitors agreements, and maintains a computerized record of the entire firms' patents in each nation. NTL has 9 professionals (lawyers and engineers).	Decentralized completely to the product divisions, except that ideas of licensing proposals must pass through V.P. International and HQ lawyers for compatibility with overall global strategy in the context of global planning, done with a computerized product/country strategy matrix. The Firm is basically organized on product lines with product lines with regional overlay (dotted lines).	No organization for licensing per se. Basic assembly cum licensing arrangements handled by world regional groups with legal and technical coordination at HQ. For peripheral products and technologies, handled by product subsidiaries, with legal coordination in International. Periodically, task forces or committees are set up to take a technology inventory and identify licensing opportunities.	Centralized international licensing department which handles all non-affiliate licensing. Over 380 licensees in 47 nations. Affiliate licensing under the purviews of divisions. There is a separate central legal department.
a) No b) Yes	a) No b) Yes	a) No b) Yes	a) No b) No	a) No b) No	a) Yes, in an artificial sense. Keeping 10% of licensing revenues, 90% are passed on to divisions. b) Yes

Source: Contractor, F., *International Technology Licensing: Compensation, Costs and Negotiation* (Lexington, Mass.: Lexington Books, D. C. Heath, 1981). Used with permission.

us look at individual companies before we draw general conclusions for organizational design. The reader is requested to read the company descriptions simultaneously with Table 46.

Firm A is a Chicago-based heavy industrial equipment manufacturer with several divisions and overseas equity affiliates. Licensing to independent foreign firms is viewed with circumspection and done for older standardized technologies or in areas such as Eastern Europe where the strategy alternatives of equity investment or selling via exports are precluded. This being decided on a case-by-case basis, licensing is therefore handled under the corporate planning department, which can take an overall global view.

Firm B, by comparison, relies almost entirely on licensing as the dominant international strategy. Transport and tariff barriers make direct exporting of the company's single product (a consumer electronics item) difficult in developing nations, their principal overseas market. They are not that big a company to muster the financial and managerial resources to make equity investments and compete on their own. That leaves licensing, which, coupled with the much lower duties on components or sub-assemblies supplied to licensees, makes licensing tantamount to component exports. Margins on parts plus royalties add up to a very attractive business. Moreover, licensees crave their internationally known trademark. This is encouraged to lock in the licensee. An international "marketing" department thus handles both licensing, component exports, and technical service functions.

Firm C, a high-technology defense and consumer electronics company, does not license independent overseas firms except in older models or consumer products, for fear of licensee competition. This has to be examined very carefully on a division-by-division basis, a function performed by a review board of senior managers at headquarters. Patent and know-how licensing are separated; the former is much more the province of a headquarters patent department, whereas for know-how, there is shared responsibility with the appropriate division.

Firm D, a Pennsylvania-based steel company, is typical of the industry in that there is essentially one product and standardized processes in a mature industry. Investment costs and political sensitivity preclude foreign investment, just as protectionism abroad precludes exports. However, licensing of specialized applications of steel, as well as peripheral processes involved in steel making, such as galvanizing, becomes a significant overseas income source to be maximized. Profit center organization of the licensing function is, therefore, correct and desirable, since licensing maximization will not intrude upon other strategic alternatives under these circumstances.

Firm E is a globally integrated aluminum giant to whom licensing (except as part of much larger equity ventures) is a trivial business. That is to say, licensing agreements as part of overseas turnkey or joint venture operations comprise an important income channel auxiliary and subordinate to dividends. However, peripheral process technologies, such as pull-top cans, anodization, or fume control, while minor or trivial by comparison, yet constitute in the aggregate throughout the firm sufficient justification for a separate headquarters "technology sales division" to pool and offer such technologies for licensing worldwide.

Firm F, typical of the pharmaceutical industry, only infrequently licenses for cash generation as the dominant motivation. (More often, cross-licensing or reciprocal technology exchange is the factor.) This is because, in most nations, direct investment and exports of the drug or active ingredient are both available and usually preferred options, these being seen as providing superior or more easily extractable returns compared with royalties and licensing fees.

Firm G is a large chemicals manufacturer. With many technically sophisticated products, many of which are easily transportable, equity investment and exporting are usually preferred over licensing, except in low and obsolescent technologies or regions such as socialist countries. Yet there are so many licensing opportunities (their licensees being already over four times the number of their equity affiliates globally) that a large central licensing department is needed to play a monitoring and coordinating role, supervised by a "patent board" of senior executives for interdivisional and regional strategy coordination.

Firm H, actually a division of a very diversified company, had a policy a decade ago not to license. But since then, several firms abroad have caught up with their technology. Equity investment or supply of components are both infeasible because of the military application of the end products. Thus, they may as well license the process technologies. This now comprises a substantial proportion of total profits.

Firm I is an energy and natural resources conglomerate. Their top management views licensing as the third-best overseas option but allows their new technology and licensing department to develop international agreements selectively. In this they have to "compete" with their export and international people to determine what items may be licensed.

Firm J is a conglomerate with high-technology defense and aerospace items, as well as automobile parts and consumer electronics products. While its licensing is decentralized, it was the only company interviewed to subject, formally and routinely, every combination on its product/country matrix to a case-by-case analysis of the preferred strategy at headquarters. Licensing often wins out over alternatives when the technology lead is slim, where licensing is the only way to do business in a country, where a technology is viable but not of interest to the firm or compatible with existing product lines, or where very quick entry is desired into the foreign nation.

Firm K is one of Detroit's auto makers and has several large assembly-cum-licensing agreements internationally, some of which are tantamount to component supply operations, similar to Firm B. There is no strategy for the great many peripheral technologies, such as special paints, body coatings, and patented improvements in mechanical design, which, if exploited, could significantly add to income without increasing competition. This idea was described, however, as "falling between the cracks" of the giant corporation.

Firm L, a conglomerate, is one of the biggest companies in the world. A large central department supervises over 400 licensing agreements, which vastly exceed the number of equity affiliates globally. If maximized, the number of licensees could be thousands, but this would be sub-optimal as licensing may then intrude upon the presumably more profitable options of exports and equity investment. Thus, despite being designated a profit center, the department executives do not maximize licensing; rather, they behave "optimally" for the company as a whole. This does not imply wise self-restraint on the part of the headquarters licensing executives. Since senior management in this case recognizes the artificiality of the profit center accounting, measurement of managerial performance of the licensing staff is done in fact by using criteria other than the department's "profits." Indeed, intra-corporate charges (i.e., between the divisions and the licensing department) are fixed artificially, rather than on actual costs, so as to show a certain predetermined level of profit each year for the headquarters licensing department.

CONCLUSIONS

Several important conclusions emerge for organization design:

1. It is only in an extremely diversified company that licensing may be decentralized, a case found only in Firm H. In six firms (A, C, G, I, J, and L), despite significant product diversity, the need for coordination of legal aspects, coordination of various operations at the country level, and coordination of strategy required some form of centralization.

2. As companies become more international and enjoy more strategic options for entering foreign markets, so also does the need for coordination of licensing into overall strategy. Licensing can no longer be *ad hoc* or heedless of the other strategic options it may preempt or future competition it may create. Statistically speaking, we demonstrated that the degree of centralization of licensing at headquarters depends not on the absolute licensing income it earns so much as the relative importance of licensing over other international strategies.

3. The means for senior management review of strategy coordination are diverse. (See Table 46.) In Firm C, a "technology transfer review board" comprising senior executives from product divisions, licensing executives, and the vice president international oversee international licensing, deciding if and when it is appropriate. At Firm G, a company-wide "patent board" performs the same role. At Firm A, coordination is achieved by placing licensing under corporate planning. In Firm J, international licensing proposals must pass through the vice president, international, and be analyzed in the context of a computerized planning process that prescribes preferred strategies for each product-nation combination.

4. Just as decentralization may mean neglected licensing opportunities (as in Firm K), licensing responsibility should not be completely taken from divisions and centralized either, without there arising the danger that an all-out mandate to maximize licensing revenue would be sub-optimal for the firm as a whole. Firm L knows this, and the idea of making licensing a "profit center" (Type IV) is more for management reporting

purposes than anything else. In fact, the headquarters staff are judged by non-financial criteria.

5. However, there are three examples (Firms B, D, and H) where licensing is quite properly maximized. Why? Because, with investing overseas or exporting unlikely, licensing becomes the dominant overseas strategy. Then, Type IV organization is appropriate. (Of these three firms, it was actually found only in Firm D, however. See Table 46.)

6. Licensing is likelier to be the firm's dominant overseas strategy, and organization likely to be closer to Type IV, if:

   a. Products are mature and the technical lead is slim, and

   b. The product range is narrow or there is one product type, i.e., the complexities are fewer and the licensing department has a clear mandate.

7. In general, most firms will opt for Type II or Type III organization. What does this augur for the background of licensing executives? They must tolerate shared authority and responsibility and reconcile themselves to very imperfect measures for managerial effectiveness by which they will be judged. But far more importantly, the licensing executive must be able to appreciate the strategic alternatives to licensing (which lie outside his domain) and take a top management view. Some scholars see licensing growing in relative importance in the coming decades compared to its hitherto minor role in international operations. Hence, the need for greater discrimination on a case-by-case basis (only done explicitly in one company above, Firm J). This means, for the licensing executive, a need to superimpose on the nitty-gritty of negotiating agreements, reading foreign laws or collecting royalties, the larger view of licensing's place in the overseas expansion of the company.

NOTES

1. French, W., and Henning, D., "The Authority-Influence Role of the Functional Specialist in Management," *Academy of Management Journal*, September 1966, pp. 187–203.

2. Blau, P., "A Formal Theory of Differentiation in Organizations," *American Sociological Review*, April 1970, pp. 200–218. Child, J., "Predicting and Understanding Organization Structure," *Administrative Science Quarterly*, Vol. 18 (2), 1973, pp. 168–185.

3. See, for instance, Berg, N., "What's Different about Conglomerate Management?" *Harvard Business Review*, November-December 1969, pp. 112–120.

4. The advantages and drawbacks of centralized control are usefully summarized in Vancil, R., "What Kind of Management Control Do You Need?" *Harvard Business Review*, March 1973, pp. 75–86.

5. Child, "Predicting and Understanding Organization Structure"; Berg, N., "Strategic Planning in Conglomerate Companies," *Harvard Business Review*, May-June 1965, pp. 79–91.

6. Schollhammer, H., "Organization Structures of Multinational Corporations," *Academy of Management Journal*, September 1971, pp. 345–365.

7. Khandwala, P., "Viable and Effective Organizational Designs of Firms," *Academy of Management Journal*, September 1973, pp. 481–495.

8. Schollhammer, "Organization Structures."

9. Rugman, A., "A New Theory of the Multinational Enterprise: Internationalization versus Internalization," *Columbia Journal of World Business*, Spring 1980, pp. 23–29.

10. Khandwala, "Viable and Effective Organizational Designs."

11. The score for ROLE is never zero since all respondents checked at least one factor. Nor would the value for ROLE be at its maximum of $120 = 1 + 2 + 3 \ldots + 14 + 15$, either, because none of the respondents checked all the factors.

12. Since the use of the variable PRICE is an at best a tenuous description of the product-cycle stage, all we can say is that if we had found a relationship contrary to *a priori* expectation, that might have been cause for concern—even if we cannot place too much weight on our finding which is congruent with expectations.

13. The sample of twelve firms may not be statistically valid, but it is representative of almost all product types in the Department of Commerce breakdown for U.S. licensing receipts. See U.S. Department of Commerce, *U.S. Direct Investment Abroad, 1977* (Washington, D.C.: U.S. Government Printing Office, 1981), p. 400.

8

Negotiation Strategies and Tactics

The key to successful negotiation of a license is planning. This chapter presents a negotiation planning procedure. It starts with the international strategic context within which the licensing agreement is contemplated and takes the reader through to the specific details of designing royalty fees and other compensation.

All too often companies regrettably follow the reverse procedure. They begin by discussing the details of royalty rates, front-end, and technical fees with the prospective licensee, and then compute the cash flow to see if it is acceptable according to conventional financial criteria. It often is acceptable, because the costs of implementing an agreement and transferring the technology may be small compared to the incremental licensing revenues that will start flowing from the agreement. A high return on investment may result. That does not mean the agreement should be undertaken. In the larger strategic context it may be sub-optimal. We have seen in earlier chapters how the licensee may become a competitor, how an alternative strategy such as equity investment may be better, how a high ROI figure may mean a rather poor net present value, and so on. To put a proposed license into proper perspective and to incorporate these external strategic factors into decision making, a company must begin by estimating the value of its technology and later work its way down to the specifics of compensation types. After all, the essence of a license is the transfer of a technology or a proprietary advantage from one firm to another. The firm possessing this advantage should estimate its value to the recipient before beginning negotiations. The technology recipient firm's strategy and market position need to be evaluated also.

The valuation of proprietary technology when transferred from one entity to another has been a vexing issue since modern science began. Leo Baekeland (of Bakelite fame) was a relatively young scientist when he invented Velox, the first photo paper that could be printed using artificial light. George Eastman, the maker of Kodak cameras, immediately invited Baekeland to Rochester to discuss buying the rights to the process. Baekeland fancied himself as a hard-headed businessman and after some thought decided to ask for $50,000, and settle for no less than $25,000, reasonably large sums of money in those days.

Eastman offered him a million. Baekeland may have been thinking in terms of the costs of developing his process, but in this case the value of the technology was related more to its market application. In general, both costs and potential market revenues need to be calculated. A salient fact of modern business, especially if "high" technology is involved, is that there is usually a significant gap or margin between market revenues, and production and distribution costs. This "margin" makes a contribution toward overhead and covers ongoing and past R&D efforts. When the technology stays within a firm there is no problem (unless it turns out later that revenues are below expectation and do not cover all costs). A license, *ipso facto*, involves two companies, and the agreement is a negotiated formula by means of which the licensor shares in the profit margin of the licensee. And the licensee's margin obviously has to come from the difference between their revenues and costs. This is why the act of negotiating a licensor's compensation cannot be divorced from an examination of the licensee's market and their costs.

A PROCEDURE FOR PLANNING NEGOTIATIONS

The executive in the licensor company planning negotiations should go through the following sequence of questions, also outlined in Figure 4:

a. How does a licensing arrangement in this country fit into the global strategy context for our firm? (Step 1)

b. What is the value of our technology and expertise to the country's market and to our prospective licensee? How do we quantify this value? (Step 2)

c. What is an appropriate share of the above or a reasonable amount of return we should extract from this nation as compensation for having parted with our technology and having contributed our expertise? (Step 3)

d. By what combination of compensation types should we earn this desired amount? (Step 4) This can be a combination of royalties, lump-sum fees, technical fees, or other contracted payments. However, these may not add up to an adequate total compensation for the licensor. Or perhaps the total compensation desired by the licensor necessitates a royalty rate and an agreement length greater than the local government rules permit. In such a case, it may be necessary to consider negotiating for additional forms of compensation such as a stake in the equity of the licensee company or supply of components to them on which additional profit can be made by the licensor.

Let us first review the whole negotiations planning exercise and its rationale before examining the mechanics of each part later in the chapter.

Figure 4 outlines this decision process, which may require several iterations

Figure 4
Steps in Planning For Negotiations

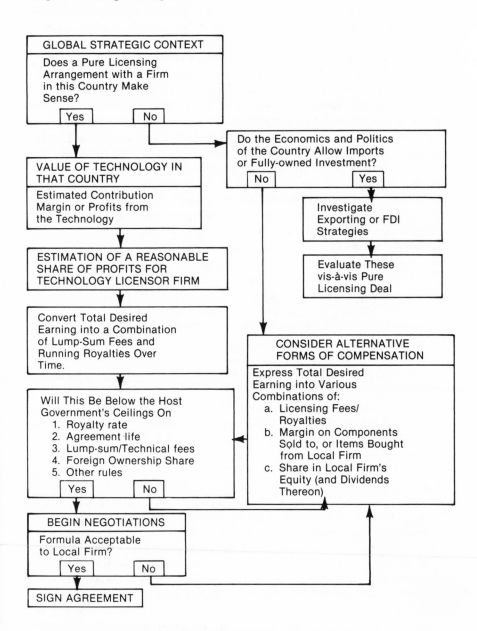

GLOBAL STRATEGIC CONTEXT

Does a Pure Licensing Arrangement with a Firm in this Country Make Sense?

Yes | No

VALUE OF TECHNOLOGY IN THAT COUNTRY

Estimated Contribution Margin or Profits from the Technology

ESTIMATION OF A REASONABLE SHARE OF PROFITS FOR TECHNOLOGY LICENSOR FIRM

Convert Total Desired Earning into a Combination of Lump-Sum Fees and Running Royalties Over Time.

Will This Be Below the Host Government's Ceilings On
1. Royalty rate
2. Agreement life
3. Lump-sum/Technical fees
4. Foreign Ownership Share
5. Other rules

Yes | No

BEGIN NEGOTIATIONS

Formula Acceptable to Local Firm?

Yes | No

SIGN AGREEMENT

Do the Economics and Politics of the Country Allow Imports or Fully-owned Investment?

No | Yes

Investigate Exporting or FDI Strategies

Evaluate These vis-à-vis Pure Licensing Deal

CONSIDER ALTERNATIVE FORMS OF COMPENSATION

Express Total Desired Earning into Various Combinations of:
a. Licensing Fees/ Royalties
b. Margin on Components Sold to, or Items Bought from Local Firm
c. Share in Local Firm's Equity (and Dividends Thereon)

and rounds of negotiation (involving the government in some nations) before an acceptable formula is devised for compensating the technology supplier company. The planning procedure moves from the broad to the particular. First, it focuses attention on the larger question of the value of the technology to the country, which creates a benefit or a profit there. The next question is what portion of the profit created should accrue to the firm that supplied the technology. Last, we ask by what means is the technology supplier to be compensated.

By broadening the number of possible ways for compensating the licensor, not only is the likelihood of negotiation success increased, but there are other strategic advantages realized. All too frequently, licensing negotiations are abandoned because the royalties and fees the prospective licensee is willing to offer or government rules allow do not add up to a sufficient total to interest the licensor. Adding to the core license, additional arrangements such as the licensor buying a partial (usually small) share in the licensee company will often make the difference. Additional compensation to the licensor may also be available in the markups they earn on parts sold to the licensee or finished products bought back for sale in international markets.

I strongly believe that such mixed arrangements involving more than a simple license are becoming more important in international business. This chapter looks at the larger strategic options of licensing involving some equity stake in the licensee, and trade between licensor and licensee combined into one contractual package. Nevertheless, the corporate reader interested merely in a pure licensing agreement will still be interested in the overall negotiations planning approach, which remains valid.

Besides raising the total value of the agreement, a licensor would gain from a closer association with the local firm that a shareholding brings. Moreover, their profit margin on items traded with the licensee is income earned outside the tax jurisdiction of that country. Should the local operation be very successful, the licensor can at least have some share in success via increased dividends, as opposed to royalties, which are usually constrained to a fixed percentage of turnover.[1]

Licensees may welcome such arrangements. A small equity stake by the licensor is normally not a critical infusion of capital. However, it symbolizes a long-term interest and a closer association than an arm's-length license. As for the purchase of components, licensees welcome it if the cost is lower than or comparable to local procurement. In the case of a sophisticated or high-technology item, this is likely to be true (unless the country has prohibitively high tariffs); and a part supplied by the licensor carries a higher quality assurance. The viability of the licensee exporting some of their finished product is more doubtful as a general rule.[2] Where this is possible, however, it may add to the profit of the licensor acting as export agent. At the least such an arrangement sweetens the deal in the eyes of a government seeking foreign currencies for their balance of payments or facilitates the import of components (in a back-to-back agreement linking the import with an equivalent export).

We should not forget that today there may be some seventy-odd countries with significant to serious, chronic balance-of-payments headaches and government controls on foreign exchange. Rather than not do business in such an environment, all that may be called for is a little more flexibility on the part of licensor executives.

The reader will think that what is being proposed here sounds like a combination of licensing, joint venture, and counter-trade. That is the intention. The licensing agreement, transferring a patent, trademark, technical information, or know-how still remains the centerpiece of the arrangements. But in today's international business environment, a pure licensing agreement will often not provide sufficient total compensation for the licensor, for the technology or expertise given up. Hence, the need for auxiliary arrangements.

This chapter gives two detailed numerical negotiation cases. The first details a situation where there is to be a license cum joint venture. The second case considers a pure license versus a pure joint venture. Let us first detail the planning procedures outlined above and in Figure 4.

THE GLOBAL STRATEGIC CONTEXT (STEP 1)

Ideally speaking, a company will have a global plan under which each combination of its products and (potential or actual) markets is periodically reviewed. For each global product/market combination, the planners should have some sense, and a written justification in a few pages, of the preferred business strategy. For many cells in the product/market matrix the recommendation may well be to do nothing at present. For others, importing the product or establishing controlled affiliates may be prescribed. For some, a licensing strategy would be best.

When considering licensing in a nation, it is very useful to begin the negotiations planning with an internal review in the licensor company that identifies the strategic intent of both licensor and licensee. The end product would be a short list of objectives such as shown in Table 47. In Chapters 5 and 6 we made a comprehensive assessment of the strategic uses of licensing. The reader will realize that Table 47 is only an example.

This product of the initial "brainstorming" meeting reminds negotiators during the heat of the bargaining process about their company's overriding objectives in the proposed arrangements. This may sound obvious but there are many instances where inexperienced negotiators get so swept up in the details or in the foreign environment as to lose sight of their company's primary objectives.[3]

Perhaps more importantly, the initial strategy review serves to bind the licensor company negotiating team more closely. We saw in the last chapter that international licensing involves the overlap of several constituencies in the licensor firm:

Table 47
Some Examples of a Strategy Checklist as Part of Negotiations Preparation

Possible Reasons For Licensing In This Nation

(In Random Order)

Licensor	Licensee
-Income	-Avoid R&D costs
-Licensee Technology	-Upgrade technology
-To sell components/	-Incremental Income
product	-Receive valuable
-To avoid lapse of patent	brand names
-To test market	-Sell internationally
-Lower taxes	via licensor
-Too small a market for	-To pre-empt licensor
FDI	competition
-Licensing only feasible	-Reproduce proven
method under government	manufacturing techniques
rules	-Future links/other
	business with licensor
	-To receive future
	technology from licensor
	-Prestige effect of
	associating with
	international company

- Product division personnel may have a bias for exporting from home-country plants.
- International division executives may have a preference for majority or fully owned subsidiaries as a market entry method. (They may, moreover, resent having to sell some of the licensee's output in third countries.)
- The full-time licensing executives may have a bias in favor of increasing the number of agreements (especially if the licensing department is a profit center).
- Patent attornies may have a strict or conservative interpretation of intellectual property laws and the effect of the license on the legal standing of the company's patents and trademarks.

The initial internal review serves to reconcile the various interests within the company and give advance notice of the effects of the license, when implemented, on other parts of the corporation.

VALUE OF THE TECHNOLOGY IN THE COUNTRY AND A TARGET COMPENSATION FOR THE LICENSOR (STEPS 2 AND 3)

The next steps in the planning procedure call for estimating a value for the technology in the nation and targeting a reasonable compensation for the licensor. We will call the amount of money to be repatriated from the licensee country and paid to the foreign licensor not a profit, but a "repatriable margin." This serves to remind us that what is extracted from a country by foreign technology suppliers is not pure profit. In a global strategic sense, that income stream has to first contribute to research and development outlays and overhead in the technology supplier firm's headquarters before the remainder can be labeled pure profit.

How is the negotiator to estimate a target "repatriable margin"? As a minimum, the licensor firm must recover all the incremental costs of proceeding with the agreement. These include the technology transfer costs (C_4 in Table 48), the value of business foregone as a result of undertaking the license (C_5), and the cost of purchasing stock in the licensee company, if that is to be done with cash (C_3). See Table 48. Since we are computing the incremental outlays of the licensor firm as a bare minimum value that must be recovered from the license, we need to include in C_3 only contributions in cash or kind and not the value of already created intangible assets, such as patents or trademarks, if any.[4] Technology transfer costs (C_4) may be defined as the direct incremental costs to the company of transferring the technology to that country, such as training, personnel, engineering, travel, legal, etc., as the costs of establishing viable production.[5] These are usually incurred in the first year or so of the agreement, although even after the license is operational, there may be recurrent licensor headquarters costs of quality control, engineering, or administrative assistance that the firm is obligated to bear. All of these (discounted to present value) comprise the C_4 category. Third, we have the cost of direct business foregone by the licensor firm due to the formation of the venture (C_5). For instance, the firm may have been selling products already in that country, and in neighboring markets. The company can estimate the future sales that might have occurred under the existing arrangements, which will now be terminated in favor of the licensee. The present value of the foregone profit stream gives us the calculation for C_5. The sum of $[C_3 + C_4 + C_5]$ gives us the absolute minimum for the repatriable margin the licensor must recover from the venture.

But this is not enough. Margins repatriated from foreign affiliates and licensees should, in addition, contribute to headquarters overheads and to research and development. But how much? Again, theory cannot help us, except to indicate that there need not be a uniform spreading of such central expenditures over various overseas operations proportional to the sales of the product in each territory. Indeed, some foreign operations will contribute more than average, others less. Nevertheless, as a useful benchmark for planning and negotiations, a company may calculate a weighted average figure. The sum of $[C_1 + C_2 + C_3 + C_4 + C_5]$ in Table 48 gives us an indication of a desired minimum margin from the country.

The maximum cannot be greater than the entire gross margin earned by the licensee company. Actually, the licensor will only try for some share, rather than try to secure the entire gross margin for itself. A license is a sharing mechanism whereby the net value created by the technology is to be shared between two companies. Therefore, for negotiation purposes it is important to get some idea, however vague, of the total gross margin, M in Table 48, to be shared by the two companies. (The reader should note that the gross margin M defined in Table 48 is not a contribution margin in conventional micro-economic terms, since we are specifically excluding royalties and assuming imported component, if any, is supplied at licensor cost.) What we want to estimate is the total economic rent that is to be shared by the two companies. That is defined thus: the gross margin M as defined in Table 48, plus any additional profit on components or products traded, comprises the maximum that can be earned by the two firms jointly. (We will see later that when the licensor buys some equity in the licensee company a complication arises whereby the revenues, and hence the margin itself, are determined by the mix of arrangements used to compensate the technology supplier. Nevertheless, we can calculate an initial figure, refining it later, in iterative steps, as changes in the arrangements are negotiated.)

The reason for making these estimates before entering negotiations is that they can serve as benchmarks and define a bargaining range, although they cannot prescribe an exact division between the two companies. *The difference between the (hypothetical) maximum and the desired minimum thus constitutes the licensor firm's bargaining range.* Moreover, such calculations help to avoid the kinds of surprises Baekeland suffered, or its opposite where, for instance, U.S. firms have begun negotiations with licensees abroad only to discover after several hundred executive hours and travel that the proposal is infeasible, with the best of intentions on both sides, because the "maximum" is below the desired, or even the absolute "minimum," as we have defined them. (*A priori* there is no

Table 48
Some Criteria for Setting a Target Compensation

COST-BASED CRITERIA	OTHER CRITERIA	MARKET-BASED CRITERIA
—Share of Global R&D $[C_1]$	—Local Development Cost (for similar technology) $[C_6]$	Revenues from Market based on:
—Share of Central Overheads $[C_2]$		Value of new product in marketplace (finished product)
—Equity share in Licensee firm $[C_3]$	—Other offers (from international companies) $[C_7]$	less
—Technology Transfer costs $[C_4]$	—Cost-saving via efficiency improvements (on existing product) $[C_8]$	Production and distribution costs**
—Value of Foregone Business $[C_5]$		=Gross Margin $[M]$
		** Not including royalties, and assuming imported component supplied at cost

Costs Incurred in: Licensor's country / Local

"REPATRIABLE MARGIN" FOR FIRM SUPPLYING TECHNOLOGY

—Absolute minimum : $[C_3 + C_4 + C_5]$

—Desired minimum : $[C_3 + C_4 + C_5 + C_1 + C_2]$

—Hypothetical Maximum: $[M + \text{profit on traded items}]$

—Conditioning Criteria

$[C_6]$ or $[C_7]$ or $[C_8]$

Note: All should be computed on Present Value basis

reason why this cannot occur. Such an eventuality is possible where the market value of a product is low, where the licensor company is already doing some business directly, and where technology transfer and capital investment costs are high.)

Three other conditioning criteria may further reduce the licensor's bargaining range, in some cases. Comparable offers to the local company from other international firms (C_7) may force the licensor to accept a lower repatriable margin. Similarly, the local firm may compute the cost of their own development of a comparable product or technology (C_6) and would be consequently unwilling to allow the licensor to extract a margin exceeding that cost—although going with the licensor's already developed technology may be faster and more certain. If we are talking of an existing product, already being made by the licensee, they would be unwilling to offer more than the cost saving derived from more efficient production technology offered by the licensor (C_8).

In brief, after estimating all these benchmarks, the licensor firm obtains a bargaining range for their repatriable margin. This is defined by the desired or absolute minimum as a floor, and with the maximum only as a hypothetical upper limit that they never hope to actually reach, since some or most of the profit has to be left for the local licensee. More practical upper limits for the licensor are defined by other conditioning criteria such as other companies' offers and the willingness of the local firm to go it alone.

A later section in the chapter also provides a checklist of variables that influence the compensation amount. It is useful for negotiators to go over such a checklist as a routine part of planning for negotiations.

DESIGNING THE COMPENSATION FORMULA (STEP 4)

Having determined by the above process a target repatriable margin desired by the licensor firm as an appropriate amount to be extracted from that country, the next question is what combination of royalties, perhaps an equity share in the licensee company, and markup on component supplied (or product bought back) will make up the desired total. The subject is best explained in a numerical example, with the algebra treated in Appendix A. Our example treats the most general case of a license cum joint venture, but the principles remain basically the same even in a pure licensing deal.

Let us suppose a U.S. firm has, after many years and a large expenditure on research and development in the U.S., developed a specialized machine. A potential market exists for this machine in another country where it is to be manufactured in a license cum joint venture with a local company. After going through a valuation process according to the above planning criteria, the American firm has decided that a repatriable margin of $16 million per year would comprise an appropriate return from that country, for having given up their technology and abdicated the market in favor of the licensee. (The label ''repatriable margin'' reminds us that it first has to contribute toward U.S. overheads and R&D expenses before we can label the remainder as pure profit as we see in Figure 5.) Patents, knowledge, and trademarks are to be transferred to the local firm under license. Because of the strategy considerations discussed earlier, the U.S. company will buy a small share in the licensee firm.

Market research shows that, within a small range at least, the demand for this machine in the country can be modeled by the expression $ price per machine = 100,000 − 25 (number of machines sold). (For calculations either the local currency or the dollar can be used.) The variable cost of producing and distributing the machine in the country is $15,000 each.[6] In addition, a special component will be bought from the U.S. company and assembled into the machine. This component costs the U.S. company $10,000 each but it is understood that they will mark up the price and sell it to the licensee at [$(1 + m)$ 10,000] where m is the markup. Incidentally, there are many situations where licensees and local partners are perfectly agreeable to this. There are several reasons. Perhaps the venture is inherently profitable anyway, and they want the association with the U.S. firm. Perhaps they realize there may be additional costs to the U.S. firm, such as warehousing the components. Local firms may realize that their country's rules on the remittance of dividends or royalties are so stringent that the only prospect for reasonable compensation to the U.S. firm is through such a transfer-price understanding.

Last, the fixed costs of the local firm are estimated to be $26 million. In addition, the U.S. company will bear, on its own, additional fixed charges in the country, of $1.2 million for warehousing the components, legal, personnel, and other costs that are not borne by the local firm. This often occurs.

The negotiators in the U.S. company should ask: "What combination of a share in the equity of the licensee firm (α) plus royalty rate (r) plus markup on component (m), will yield a total of $16 million?" There are a great many algebraic solutions to this question. Some of them are shown later in Table 49. For the moment let us examine just one solution: $\alpha = 0.30$, $r = 0.098$, and $m = 0.20$ (i.e., the U.S. company owns 30 percent of the shares, charges a 9.8 percent royalty on sales, and marks up the component by 20 percent). This solution is shown in Figure 5.

The objective for the U.S. company is to earn a repatriable margin of $16 million. Since their actual outlay or contribution toward local overhead and fixed costs is to be $9 million (we will see why shortly) this is equivalent to their targeting their share of gross margin at $16 + $9 = $25 million. The U.S. partner's share of the gross margin is defined (in Figure 5) as the sum of:

1. Royalties (in this example at 9.8 percent on sales)	$8,922,698
2. Markup on component (in this case 20 percent)	$2,803,200
3. Pro rata share of the local firm's total contribution margin (proportional to the shareholding of the U.S. firm; in this example 30 percent)	$13,284,611
	$25,000,000 (Total)

Figure 5
Schematic Diagram of Income and Cost Flows in
International License-Cum-Joint Venture Agreements

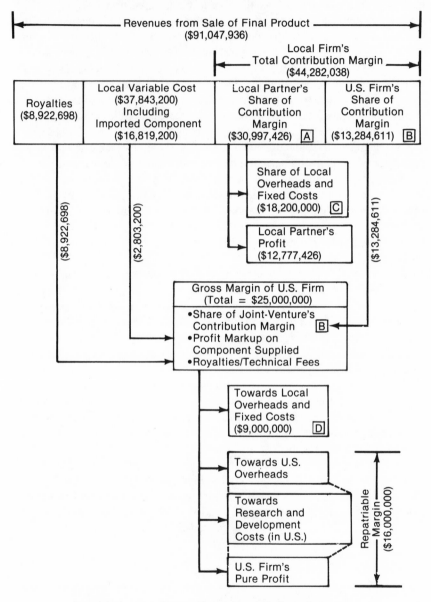

Amounts in parentheses illustrate a solution where

- Equity Share of U.S. Firm   = 30%
- Royalty Rate   = 9.8%
- Markup on Component   = 20%

The three income flows add up to $25 million as desired.[7] From this, subtracting the U.S. company's actual contribution of $9 million toward local overheads and fixed costs, leaves a repatriable margin of $16 million. (Or if the reader prefers, we can say that royalties + component markup = $11,725,898 is a "clean" unencumbered return, whereas out of the $13,284,611 contribution margin share, the U.S. company makes an actual outlay of $9 million.)

Under this particular solution, the selling price for each machine works out to be $64,960, at which price 1,402 machines are sold, to give a revenue of $91,047,936. The local partner or local investor's profit computes to $12,777,426 as shown in Figure 5.

Notice that a seventy-thirty split of the $26 million fixed costs, proportionally to the shareholding of the local and U.S. partners in the company, would be a ratio of 18.2 to 7.8. The local partner does contribute $18.2 million toward fixed costs, leaving them a profit of $12.78 million. However, the $1.2 million in additional fixed costs the U.S. firm bears brings its total contribution to $7.8 + $1.2 = $9.0 million. Thus, in effect, in many such situations, the foreign partner or technology supplier ends up with a disproportionate burden of all local fixed costs. But then, they also end up with more than a proportional share of earnings, in the form of royalties and component margins. We see in Figure 5 that

$$\frac{D}{C} = \frac{9.0}{18.2} \text{ is a higher ratio than } \frac{30\% \text{ equity share}}{70\% \text{ equity share}} = \frac{B}{A}$$

In practice, all calculations should ideally be done on a present value basis, taking figures for each year of the project. Since we are laying out a set of principles here, computing present values would be a needless complication. Of course it should be done.

Before examining some alternative solutions let us conclude by relating this example to the bargaining range in Table 48. We find that [(revenues) − (total variable costs) − (all local overhead fixed costs)] + [profit on traded components] = $28,777,426 (neglecting some rounding errors) gives an approximate idea of the hypothetical maximum economic rent to be shared between the U.S. technology supplier and local investor. In our example, the amount was split into $12,777,426 for the local partner, and $16 million for the U.S. firm. Without the additional arrangements beyond the core technology license there would have been little chance of extracting the desired $16 million on a royalty basis alone. This is only an example, but it has general lessons.

ALTERNATE SOLUTIONS FOR COMPENSATION DESIGN

To generate a number of alternate solutions, a small computer program is needed based on the algebra outlined in Appendix A. In essence we have three variables: α, the U.S. firm or foreign technology supplier's equity share; r, the royalty rate on sales; and m, the markup on the component. For simplicity of presentation, the way in which the algebra is written in the appendix targets the

U.S. firm's gross margin (π_2), from which we easily compute their repatriable margin by subtracting their actual contribution toward local fixed costs and overheads.[8]

The computer is asked to plot a graph showing all possible α, r, m combinations which produce a constant targeted gross margin for the U.S. technology supplier. This produces a leftward-bending U-shaped curve whose general form is shown in Figure 6. The corporate negotiator can read off different values of α, r, and m from the graph. Of course, for a different level of U.S. firm gross margin (π_2), a different graph would have to be plotted (by simply specifying the new value for π_2 and running the program again).

To continue our illustration, some of an infinite number of alternate solutions to our example are shown in Table 49. A computer plot for a U.S. firm gross margin constant level of π_2 = \$25 million is depicted in Figure 7. The five solutions (a) through (e) in Table 49 are also plotted in Figure 7. The horizontal axis in Figures 6 or 7 measure various possible royalty rates (r) ranging from zero to a maximum value of 27 percent, in this case. The vertical axis measures the markup on the component (m). The third variable, α, namely, the share of the U.S. firm in the local company's equity, is shown by a series of solid contour lines. In this case, the computer was asked to plot 10 percent increments of equity, i.e., α = 0, 0.1, 0.2, etc., but any interval can be specified. Notice that when α = 0 it is a pure licensing arrangement.

The interesting fact is that while the U.S. company's margin is algebraically constant, by definition, over the whole graph, the local licensee or joint venture partner's contribution margin (π_1) shown in broken lines, varies over the graph. The contribution margin of the local partner, π_1, increases in a "southwestward" direction and is maximum at the origin itself (where r = 0, m = 0).

What we have is a computerized procedure that gives the negotiators a great many combinations of royalty rates, component markups, and equity share, all of which generate the same contribution margin for the technology supplier company. That is the basic purpose. Thus, while the technology supplier is indifferent, since their compensation is constant (under this scenario—there are others), the licensee or local partner and the product consumer are not indifferent to the compensation mix used, as we see below.

Let us explore some negotiation dynamics resulting from the above. In Figure 7, let us suppose as an example that the two parties are initially negotiating on the assumption of a U.S. firm equity level of 30 percent, i.e., α = 0.30. The 30 percent equity level is arbitrary, as an example. The same principle holds for any α, including α = 0. We see it is in the local licensee's own interest to allow a higher royalty rate to the technology supplier. To illustrate, let us compare solutions (a) and (b) in Figure 7 and in Table 49. A 9.8 instead of a 2.0 percent royalty rate not only allows the markup on the component to drop from 76 percent to 20 percent, but the overall result is to raise the licensee's own profit from \$12.37 million to \$12.79 million. We see this in Table 49, (a) versus (b).

Figure 6
The General Shape of the Negotiation Curves
for a Constant Foreign Firm Gross Margin

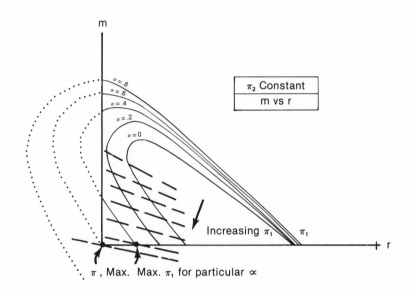

Further increases in the local party's margin π_1 are possible by the licensee conceding a higher equity participation to the foreign technology supplier. This apparently surprising and counter-intuitive result is illustrated with solution (d) in Table 49. With $\alpha = 0.40$, the local firm's margin rises to $31.2 million, and profit to $15.6 million. How do we account for this seemingly odd result? Comparing solutions (d) and (a), which have the same royalty rate, we find that the willingness of the licensor firm to accept a lower component margin m is only a small part of the explanation. The more important part is that as the licensor firm increases its equity share in the local operation, the market is expanded for the end product because of a lower (optimum) price for the end product. This is shown in the bottom row of Table 49. (The algebra in Appendix A explains how the licensor prefers a lower optimum price and hence larger sales volume than the local licensee.)

Allowing equity participation by the licensor, with corresponding reductions in component margins and royalties, of course, is thus good for the local investors in raising their profits. It is also good for consumers of the end product, a point we will elaborate upon in the next chapter, which looks at the impact on the nation and economy.

Extending this logic to its ultimate extent, we see that the optimal solution for local investors as well as consumers is at the origin in Figures 6 and 7, where

Figure 7
α, r, m Combinations for a Constant U.S. Firm Gross Margin of $25 Million

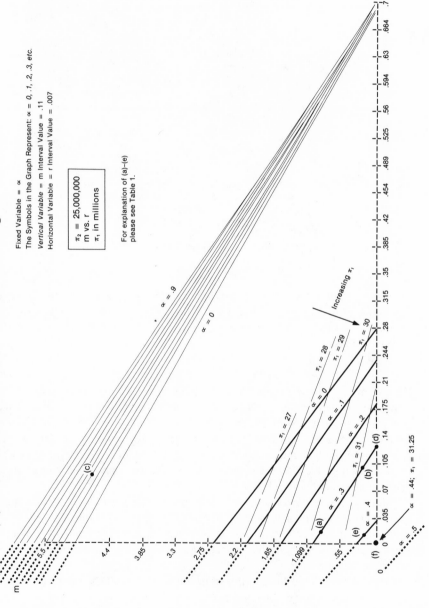

Fixed Variable = α
The Symbols in the Graph Represent: α = 0, .1, .2, .3, etc.

Vertical Variable = m Interval Value = .11
Horizontal Variable = r Interval Value = .007

π_2 = 25,000,000
m vs. r
π_1 in millions

For explanation of (a)–(e)
please see Table 1.

Table 49
Some Alternative Designs for Structuring the Joint Venture

		(a)	(b) Solution in Figure5	(c)	(d)	(e)	(f)	(g)
				SOLUTIONS MARKED ON FIGURE 7			OTHER SOLUTIONS	
U.S. Firm's Equity Share	(α)	0.30	0.30	0.30	0.40	0.44	0.40	0.57
Royalty Rate	(r)	0.02	0.098	0.097	0.02	0	0.069	0
Component Margin	(m)	0.76	0.20	4.56	0.16	0	0.16	0
Local Partner's Share of Contribution Margin (π_1)		30.57	30.99	3.02	31.20	31.25	28.44	24.23
Local Partner's Actual Contribution		18.20	18.20	18.20	15.60	14.56	15.60	11.18
Local Partner Profit ($ millions)		12.37	12.79	-15.18	15.60	16.69	12.84	13.05
U.S. Firm's Gross Margin ($ millions) (π_2)		25.00	25.00	25.00	25.00	25.00	27.60	31.98
U.S. Firm's Actual Contribution *		9.00	9.00	9.00	11.60	12.64	11.60	15.98
U.S. Firm's Repatriable Margin ($ millions)		16.00	16.00	16.00	13.40	12.36	16.00	16.00
$ Product Price Per Unit		66,620	64,960	89,092	63,577	62,500	64,286	62,500

Notes * Assuming the U.S. firm's contribution towards local overheads and

fixed costs is [26.0 α + 1.20]million

See Figure 7 for graphical plot of solutions (a) – (e)

189

- Royalties and component margins are zero; $r = 0$, $m = 0$.
- The licensor has a 44 percent stake in the venture; $\alpha = .44$.
- The local partner gets a maximum margin of $31.25 million and maximum profit of $16.69 million
- Consumers get the product at the lowest price of $62,500 per machine.

In this model, local interests would appear to be best served by a technology transfer under a pure joint venture situation. (The technology supplier is supposed to be indifferent.) This is, of course, a theoretical possibility which may not be attainable or desired. This also has several implications for host government policies which we need not pursue here. In brief, host governments that arbitrarily place a cap on foreign equity percentages in local companies may be preventing the corporate negotiators from reaching optimal solutions for their shareholders and for consumers of the product, in some instances.

We may also observe in passing an extremely sub-optimal solution that the theory says is possible, a solution such as (c). The product price is set very high, selling a small quantity to a select market.[9] The foreign firm still makes a repatriable margin of $16 million but this is at the expense of consumers and the local partner's profit.

Last, with higher licensor firm equity levels in solutions (d) and (e), their repatriable margin falls below the target of $16 million, even though the gross margin stays constant at $25 million. This is because as the foreign firm increases its equity participation, their actual contribution toward local overhead and fixed costs also rises. The computer can, however, easily generate more solutions such as (f) and (g) in Table 49 where the repatriable margin is restored to $16 million by increasing the U.S. firm gross margin.[10] Similarly, more solutions can be generated for different levels of the gross margin.

All in all, what is shown here is a methodology that negotiators can use to generate alternative solutions for structuring an agreement. (There are, in fact, many other, more complex negotiation scenarios than the one outlined here. These can be obtained by writing to the author.)

THE NEGOTIATIONS PLANNING PROCEDURE SO FAR

It is useful at this stage in a detailed chapter to review the basic outline of the planning approach described so far. We began with the idea that a proprietary technology has a value, which depends not so much on the costs of creating it (research and development) or on the costs of recreating it in a foreign country (transfer costs), but rather its value should be determined by market or demand conditions in the foreign nation. Before plunging into negotiations, the firm possessing the technology may well conduct a strategy review of the exact role of the technology in the company's long-range global plans. This also serves to reconcile the divergent constituencies within a large, diversified, international company and have product divisions, international personnel, and licensing executives all agree on a common negotiations posture. We next provided several criteria or benchmarks that help the technology-possessing firm to estimate a total desired amount to be repatriated from the licensee as compensation for contributing technology and expertise to them.

The chapter next presented details on designing the compensation formula to make up the total amount of desired compensation. In keeping with the recommendation of the book that licensing agreements should be used as the centerpiece of broader arrangements, a mathematical model was presented for a licensing-cum-joint venture-cum-trading agreement. In the most general terms, the firm supplying technology can be compensated in three ways: by royalties, by earnings on a share in the equity of the licensee company, and by profit markups on components supplied to them (or product bought back, for that matter). The model assessed the trade-offs between the three compensation types. (While the model was presented in the broadest terms, it can be simply adapted to a pure licensing or a pure equity-sharing [joint venture] situation by making some variables equal to zero.)

LICENSING VERSUS A JOINT VENTURE

What if the strategic choice in a country is *between* a pure licensing agreement and a pure equity-sharing joint venture arrangement? We outline in this section some salient considerations determining the choice. The ''Bedford Products'' case in Appendix B describes such a situation, involving technology transfer to the United Kingdom. A U.S. company manufacturing small compressors for refrigeration and air-conditioning equipment has a patented design and engineering expertise, which it has exploited in the U.K. market by direct exports from its U.S. plant. With growing competition from European manufacturers making inroads into the British market, with a strengthening dollar, and with lower labor and material costs in the United Kingdom, the pressures are building either to lose business in that country eventually or to have local manufacturing of the compressors.

This is an acute situation, facing hundreds and perhaps thousands of American firms in the first half of the 1980s. Many of them were small or medium-sized companies that greatly expanded their exports from the United States in the late 1970s, only to find their foreign markets eroded by the mid 1980s by the dual squeeze of a stronger dollar on the one hand, and a declining technological edge over international competition, on the other. For several firms, a fully owned subsidiary is ruled out because of lack of international experience and the risk of going it alone in a foreign market.

The first question to be addressed is the availability of managerial and financial resources to sustain a foreign equity investment. In a pure licensing arrangement this commitment is much lower. The level of risk has to be assessed next. In the Bedford Products case the market was already established, and furthermore there could be attractive financial incentives given to a foreign investment in the United Kingdom. Another significant consideration is the possibility of an independent licensee turning into a competitor. This was not a realistic fear in this case.

Ultimately, however, the choice between a license and a joint venture often comes down to the planning time horizon and the rate used to discount future cash flows. The shorter the company's time horizon, the more likely it is that licensing will be chosen. The higher the discount rate used (reflecting perhaps higher environmental risk or higher cost of capital to the company), the more likely it is that licensing would be chosen, other things being equal.

Figure 8 shows the cumulative cash flows, over time, from licensing and a joint venture. Typically, in early years, a joint venture involves far heavier costs and consequently will have a significant negative cash flow that will not be overcome until a few years have passed. After that, however, the rate of positive cash flow accumulation is much higher than licensing (if all goes well with the project and it shows profits). The slope of the cumulative cash flow line for a joint venture is consequently steeper. Licensing by contrast involves modest transfer and other costs in early years, but the cash inflows to the licensor are also typically, though not necessarily, lower than in joint ventures. As a result, a cumulative cash flow line for licensing such as LL_1 does not dip for long into the negative zone, but it has a shallower slope.

Hence the net cumulative cash flow will typically remain higher for licensing, for some years, before being surpassed eventually by the cumulative cash flow for the joint venture alternative. On an undiscounted, simple addition basis this may happen in a few years. (The Bedford Products case shows this to occur in a little over three years.) In Figure 8, the crossover point for the two alternatives, on an undiscounted basis, is represented by point A; this occurs after a time span of $0A_1$ years.

But in fact, future cash flows are to be discounted. As we apply to the calculations a higher and higher discount rate, this causes the curves for both licensing and the joint venture option to have a shallower slope. This makes the crossover or breakeven point between the two options move further to the right (A to B to C in Figure 8), i.e., further out in time. That is to say, licensing remains a superior option for a longer period of time, as the discount rate is increased (from $0A_1$ years, to $0B_1$ years, to $0C_1$ years in Figure 8).

In an era of high interest rates worldwide, and when the country in question is "risky," companies will use higher discount rates, which favors the licensing alternative.

So far, we have prescribed applying the same discount rate (high or low, depending on the company and source of financing, etc.) to either option and comparing the two. But is that reasonable? After all, we have argued in earlier chapters that licensing is inherently less risky than joint ventures, in any country or market context. (The reasons are by now familiar: royalties are pegged to turnover, and not profit; they are more easily repatriated, taxed less, and so on.) The point, however, is that if we apply a lower discount rate to the licensing option, that tends to extend the breakeven point further yet out in time (represented in Figure 8 by the point D, occurring at time $0D_1$).

Figure 8
**Comparison of Cumulative Net Cash Flows under Licensing
versus Joint Venture under Various Discount Rates**

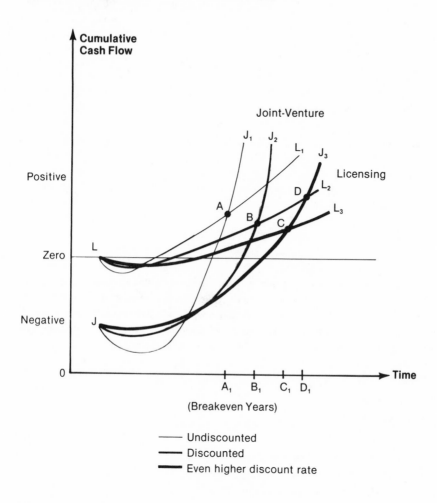

Thus, if a company's planning horizons are short, if quicker cash inflows are desired, if interest rates are high, and if the country or market in question is risky, the licensing option will be favored. The Bedford Products case detailed in Appendix B gives an example of the above calculations and plots the various curves. The case also illustrates other strategy considerations.

CAVEATS AND REMINDERS FOR WRITING AGREEMENTS

Writing an agreement is not something that should be left to lawyers, although they are indispensable. Even company attorneys tend not to be aware of every strategic issue of concern to operating divisions. Besides, good lawyers will bring to a negotiation their own checklist of points to be negotiated and written into the agreement. While conditions and requirements vary considerably from license to license, in my experience the following are some crucial items:

What Is Being Transferred?

- The agreement must define the technology exactly, and as narrowly as possible from the licensor's perspective.
- How do we define a "future improvement"? Will those be passed on to the licensee free of charge, or will there be additional payment; if so, how much or how will it be negotiated?

Types of Compensation

Some governments try to limit or scrutinize some categories of payment. Not all categories of payment may be deductible for taxes to the licensee, nor will the tax treatment be identical for the licensor. As a rule it is useful to be aware of alternative forms of payment and agree with the licensee on more than one or two channels of payment:

- Lump-sum fee (paid at signing, start-up, or later?)
- "Running" royalty
- Plant design and commissioning
- Technical assistance fee
- Per diem charges for technicians/personnel loaned
- Patent royalty (if treated separately)
- Trademark royalty (if treated separately)
- Management consultancy fee
- Sale of plant and equipment
- Sale of components
- Purchase of product from licensee
- Shares in licensee company stock and dividends thereon

With such a comprehensive list, if the licensee wants the technology seriously and will cooperate, there are always means to compensate the technology supplier adequately, even in the more restrictive LDCs and Socialist-bloc nations.

An up-front lump-sum fee is desirable because it may cover the licensor's transfer costs and is definite proof of the licensee's intention to go into production. Too large an amount, however, may be too large an early burden on the licensee (unless the lump-sum is financed by a bank). "Running" royalties, by contrast, mean a "pay as you earn" situation for the licensee. Sometimes, the lump-sum amount is applied as a credit against future royalties.

Royalties are usually a flat percentage of sales (or a flat amount related to physical output, tonnes or square feet, or gallons, etc.). However, royalties may decrease with volume—the licensor having taken a share of the earnings now leaves more of the further gains of expansion to the licensee. Or royalties may in rare cases increase with volume of output—the rationale here would be that this enables the licensor to share with the licensee in the cost economies of a large scale of production, if achieved.

Level of Compensation

By now, readers will have appreciated this chapter's contention that each technology transfer carries a unique value. Licensors should try to avoid mention of industry royalty norms or "most favored licensee" clauses that would tend to reduce compensation toward that paid by the lowest-paying licensee. (Licensees will, for these very reasons, try to mention these factors in negotiations and try to find out what other licensees are paying for the technology.[11])

As we saw earlier in this chapter, compensation is related to several benchmarks of cost and market value. The list below provides further detail and demonstrates the uniqueness of each situation. The $+$ or $-$ sign indicates whether the total licensing agreement compensation increases or decreases as a function of the following variables:

- Size of market or territory $(+)$
- Competition faced by licensee in the product market $(-)$
- Transfer Costs $(+)$
- Opportunity costs to licensor $(+)$
- Exclusivity granted to licensee $(+)$
- Years since the patent was registered $(-)$
- Age of technology in general $(-)$
- Exportability of product by licensee $(+)$
- Number of alternative sources for similar technology $(-)$
- Commercial proof of production viability, as opposed to pilot plant or unproven method $(+)$
- Strength of patent and its defensibility $(+)$
- Inclusion of internationally known trademark $(+)$
- Ubiquitous licensing of standardized process to many licensees $(-)$

- Agreement includes present and future technologies developed by licensor (+)
- Inclusion of performance guarantees (+)
- Agreement includes other income sources for licensor, such as supply of components (−)

Payment Definitions

- Most royalties are linked to licensee "sales," but how is "sales" defined? "FOB less returns less excise duties," for example? Are royalties to be paid monthly, quarterly, or annually?

- In the agreement, a licensor should prefer the words "payments received" versus "payments made." For example, a licensee may make the payment, but the remitting bank may fail (such a thing has happened); or the funds are deemed inconvertible. In such cases the licensee has "made" the payment, but the licensor has not "received" them. If the agreement merely says "payment made," the licensee is absolved of legal responsibility.

- The question of foreign exchange risk is linked to the issue of indexation. Many agreements make no mention of this, on the assumption that a devaluation of the licensee's currency will (in the long run, through Purchasing Power Parity theory) be offset by inflationary increases in local currency sales of the licensed product to which the royalties are pegged.[12] Since this economic adjustment occurs relatively freely in nations with floating currencies, this need not be a large worry in such countries. Nor is it a worry in countries where the government "manages" the foreign exchange rate; the overwhelming tendency is to "support" their currency, to prevent or forestall its devaluation, thus "overvaluing" it, despite domestic inflation. This benefits the licensor. When then are these foreign exchange factors of major concern? In two scenarios: (1) in the cases where the government is alleged to "undervalue" its currency, notably the Japanese yen, and (2) when the royalty is not expressed as a percentage of sales value, but linked to other criteria such as physical output measures. In such cases, from the licensor viewpoint, it is necessary to write specific escalator clauses linking royalties with a price index.[13]

- Who pays the withholding tax, or value added tax (VAT) if these are levied on royalties? Agreements may specify that the licensee does. However, when there is a tax treaty between the licensee's and licensor's countries, that gives the licensor a tax credit. If so, this question may have only minor significance.

Defining the Territory

Since one of the critical factors in determining compensation is the size of the market, defining the limits of the licensee's territory is important. Limiting territory is also crucial because the licensor may be doing business in neighboring countries or may wish to establish licensees there. This issue is a legal minefield because both U.S. antitrust law and the recipient country's regulations apply. Attorneys will want to concern themselves with whether it is legally permissible to specify place of manufacture and/or sales territory.

While of definite concern in industrial nations, particularly the European Economic Community (EEC), it is easy to overdo this point in other nations and hurt the negotiations process needlessly.[14] As a practical matter, many licensees have their hands full with their own country's market and the propensity to export is usually very low (although this is a matter to be carefully assessed by the licensor). At any rate, when an explicit prohibition cannot be written, the licensor may, with feigned generosity, offer themselves as the international marketing channel. That way, there may at least be some control (and a chance to earn additional profit).

The last territorial issue concerns sub-license rights. Should the licensee be given those rights and under what conditions?

Trademark Licensing

Among points to be specifically concerned about in trademark licensing:

• Should the trademark be licensed? A well-known trademark may have great economic value to the licensee (which incidentally will be shared with the licensor). However, it may also be tarnished by a poor quality item made by the licensee. More likely, with a widely licensed brand name there may arise a doubt in the minds of consumers as to whether the item is superior or "elite."

• If transferred to the licensee, the agreement should state its exact form, display methods, territory, the party that will hold registration (licensor or licensee), and who is responsible for defending it against third party infringement.

• A critical issue with trademarks is what happens on termination of an agreement. Extensive use of the trademark by the licensee is tantamount to them locking their company into its use. The wider the mark's recognition among consumers, the more the licensee becomes dependent on its continued use. When an agreement is to be renewed, this may reduce their bargaining leverage vis-à-vis the licensor if the latter still holds the rights to the trademark. Do the country's laws permit the licensor this privilege?

Cancellation of License

It is important for both parties to agree in advance on the conditions under which the agreement may be cancelled. Three principal licensor concerns are:

• Failure to develop or sell the licensed product or to use the licensed process. This can be handled by specifying either a minimum annual royalty amount or minimum turnover, failing which the agreement is void. (Of course, it is clear that when a licensee is making a large capital investment incorporating the technology, their intention of making a commercial success of the venture is strong. In such a case it may be overzealous to insist on such a clause.)

- Maintenance of quality standards, especially if a trademark is licensed. Besides the threat of cancellation as a last resort, the licensor may reserve the right of periodic inspection.
- Inconvertibility of royalty payments from licensee currency to hard currencies. It may be worth it, to make inconvertibility a reason for agreement cancellation. However, in practice that market may not be accessible to the licensor anyway.

Miscellaneous Significant Agreement Items

- For transfers of unpatented proprietary know-how, a secrecy or non-disclosure agreement from the licensee may be necessary.
- In some cases where licensees have already done in-house development of a similar technology, a specific admission of the validity of the licensor's patent reduces the likelihood of future litigation in the event that the present agreement is abrogated.
- In case a third party challenges the patent, who is obligated to bear the costs of conducting a defense? The licensor or licensee?
- Whether defensible under the licensee country's laws or not, it may be worth trying to include a clause that the licensee will not contravene the export control or licensing provisions of the U.S. government. This is of relevance to military or high-technology industries.
- If the licensee acquiesces to this, a provision may be included whereby the licensee is obligated to "grant back" to the licensor details on improvements made on the licensed technology. But will this be done *gratis*, or will a reverse license or payment be negotiated? This is another area where, under the urging of attorneys, licensors sometimes take too strong a stance, insisting on a grantback provision. My earlier survey shows that as an all-industry generalization (which will of course not apply to specific situations) in agreements between U.S. licensors and foreign licensees, 44 percent of them had grantback clauses—however, information of value was received back from licensees in only 12 percent of cases.[15] Thus, if the actual likelihood of receiving information from licensees is low, then insisting on it may only impede negotiations. Worse, it may make the licensee ask for "future improvements" from the licensor as a *quid pro quo*. This has to be evaluated on a case-by-case basis.
- The inception date of the agreement should be carefully negotiated. For example, an agreement may commence on signing or when the licensee factory produces the first item or when the first sales are recorded or when the government approves the agreement. The point is simply this: licensors will be eager to receive payments sooner; licensees will be eager to delay payment. (In extreme cases, a government may delay registration of an agreement for months or even years.)

The above points were intended as a necessary and useful checklist in negotiating an agreement. As a final matter, once a document is drafted, the two parties should agree on which language will be used in the final, operating, legally binding version. Usually it is highly illuminating to hire four completely new translators at this stage, two hired by the licensor and two by the licensee. Working independently, the draft document is translated (say from English to

Japanese); then it is retranslated into the original language (Japanese back to English). This relatively inexpensive process can reveal and forestall potential misunderstandings. Negotiators are sometimes very disconcerted to find that in comparing the original to the retranslated version, there can be glaring differences in interpretation arising from linguistic and cultural differences. It is better to reveal these in advance by this process.

A NEGOTIATION PHILOSOPHY IN LICENSING

In recent years there have been a number of publications and seminars purporting to teach the art of negotiating. They give pointers on matters such as timing, assertiveness, withholding versus disclosing information, and so on. To that extent they may have a degree of usefulness, but many of the tactics covered apply to "win-lose" situations or what are known as "zero sum" games.

Licensing is by its very nature a "win-win" or "positive sum" game. The licensor, by expanding the use of proprietary knowledge, increases wealth and value in the licensee's territory—the main problem is to devise a formula for sharing the value so created. The problem is rendered complex by the uncertainty surrounding the size of this value, since the licensee's profit must come from eventual buyers of the product. (This chapter has provided several criteria or benchmarks for assessing this value; however approximate they may be, they are much superior to mere guessing.)

What is known to experienced licensing executives, a fact algebraically demonstrated in Appendix A, is that the size of the economic value from a technology transfer is also determined by the nature of the arrangements or the compensation formula devised. Hence, it is not merely a matter of a licensor increasing their share of earnings at the expense of the licensee. More fundamentally, the issue is how the total economic value can be maximized in the first place in the licensee's territory, with the question of sharing the gains as a second-tier issue.

A good licensing arrangement is therefore a long-term, cooperative venture. As we have seen in earlier chapters, transferring a technical or administrative capability from one enterprise to another is not a one-time act; it is, rather, an ongoing process. Only in a few cases is the technology recipient well versed enough to be able to simply take a patent right, or interpret a blueprint or specification, and proceed independently. Trust and coordination are desirable, therefore, to effectuate the transfer and enable the licensee to develop his market to the optimum extent.

APPENDIX A:
The Mathematics of Negotiations

This appendix gives only a summary of principal results but with enough information that the interested reader can reproduce them. The foreign technology-supplying firm has three income types it can earn from a locally incorporated company that is also to be the licensee.

• Return on equity	α is the share of the foreign firm in the local licensee's equity, where $0 \leqslant \alpha \leqslant 1$
• Royalty	r is the royalty rate, based on the local company's revenues, where $r \geqslant 0$
• Markup on traded item	m is the foreign firm's markup on any component supplied, $m \geqslant 0$. (A markup may also be earned by the foreign firm on any purchase of final product back from the licensee. Algebraically, this is not an important variant.)

Let us define k_1 as the marginal cost per unit, incurred locally by the licensee. The licensor, hereafter called Firm 2, manufactures (or buys) a component at marginal cost k_2 per unit and sells it to the licensee at a price $(1 + m)k_2$. The local partner, hereafter called Firm 1, earns a share $(1 - \alpha)$ of the local company's contribution margin (or profit, neglecting fixed costs). This is defined as $\pi_1 = (1 - \alpha) [PQ - rPQ - k_1Q - k_2 (1 + m) Q]$ where $P = a - bQ$ is the final product's demand schedule in the market. (The fact that a linear demand function and constant marginal cost assumption are used here simplifies the algebra—but the results in general and negotiation outcomes remain valid even for alternative assumptions. In any event, the computer can simulate these alternatives.)

Substituting for P, we find the local partner's (not the local enterprise's) contribution margin is

$$\pi_1 = (1 - \alpha) [((1 - r) a - k_1 - k_2(1 + m))Q - (1 - r)bQ^2] \quad (1)$$

The foreign firm's gross margin π_2 has three components:

$$\pi_2 = \alpha \text{ share of profits } + \text{ royalties } + \text{ net margin on components} \quad (2)$$
$$= \alpha [(1 - r)P - k_1 - k_2 (1 + m)]Q + rPQ + mk_2Q$$

Substituting for P, from $P = a - bQ$, we get

$$\pi_2 = \alpha [(1 - r)a - k_1 - k_2 (1 + m)]Q \quad (3)$$
$$- (\alpha(1 - r) + r) bQ^2 + (ra + mk_2)Q$$

Differentiating π_1 and π_2 we get desired optimum quantities for the local and foreign partner respectively.

$$\overline{Q}_1 = \frac{a}{2b} - \frac{k_1 + k_2(1 + m)}{2b(1 - r)} \text{ (local partner's optimum)} \quad (4)$$

$$\overline{Q}_2 = \frac{a}{2b} - \frac{\alpha k_1 + [\alpha - (1 - \alpha)m]k_2}{2b\,[\alpha + (1 - \alpha)r]} \quad \text{(licensor's optimum)} \quad (5)$$

We notice that the licensor's desired optimum Q_2 is larger (and hence the product price lower) than the local partner's. Obviously, both optima cannot exist simultaneously. Here we assume for our example in the paper that the local partner's optimum prevails, since they are the dominant partner holding controlling interest in the licensee company. (Obviously, we can change to Q_2 as an alternative assumption, that the foreign firm dominates, by reprogramming the computer.)

What are the trade-offs between α, r, and m once a target compensation is set for Firm 2 and the consequent behavior of the local partner in attempting to maximize their profit within Firm 2's target as a constraint? Substituting for Q from equation 4, assuming the local partner's optimum prevails, we get

$$
\begin{aligned}
\pi_2 = &\left\{ \left[(\alpha(1 - r) + r)a - \alpha k_1 - (\alpha(1 + m) - m)k_2 \right] \right. \\
&\left. \bullet \left(\frac{a}{2b} - \frac{k_1 + k_2(1 + m)}{2b\,(1 - r)} \right) \right\} \\
&- \left\{ (\alpha(1 - r) + r)b \left(\frac{a}{2b} - \frac{k_1 + k_2(1 + m)}{2b\,(1 - r)} \right)^2 \right\} = A \text{ constant}
\end{aligned}
\quad (6)
$$

which is an expression for a three-dimensional surface in the three negotiation variables α, r, and m, whose general shape was shown in Figure 6. We should remember that π_2 is only temporarily set at a constant value. In the example, we put $\pi_2 = \$25$ million. In preparing for negotiations, each side may eventually try out different values for π_2. Examining equation 6, which is a long expression, does not reveal much about the shape of the three-dimensional surface. Accordingly, in order to discuss negotiation dynamics it is best to use the computer-generated results of several examples of sufficient variety to present a comprehensive picture to the negotiator.

In general, equation 6 may be represented by a family of curves as shown in solid lines in Figure 6 on the $(m; r)$ isoprofit plane, with each level of foreign equity participation α represented by an individual contour line. π_2 is (temporarily) held constant (in the paper π_2 was set at $\$25$ million) so that every α, r, m combination is a matter of indifference to the foreign technology supplier. But not to the local partner, whose margin from substituting for Q becomes

$$\pi_1 = \frac{(1 - \alpha)}{4b(1 - r)} \left[(1 - r)a - k_1 - k_2\,(1 + m) \right]^2 \quad (7)$$

From equation 7 we see that every α, r, m combination represents a different margin π_1 to the local party. This can be depicted by a series of contour lines shown as dashed lines in Figure 6, each representing a certain level of π_1. π_1 increases as r and m decrease in a "southwestward" direction. π_1 is maximized at the origin where:

$$\pi_1 = \frac{(1 - \alpha)(a - k_1 - k_2)^2}{4b} = \$31.25 \text{ million}$$

in our example (solution e) where $r = 0$, $m = 0$; α is at a local maximum:

$$\alpha = \frac{4b\pi_2}{(a - k_1 - k_2)^2} = 0.44$$

in our example (solution e).

Thus, we find that the joint profit of both partners is maximized at the origin. We can define joint profit (actually, contribution margin, ignoring fixed costs) of both parties together as $\pi = \pi_1 + \pi_2$. We find that π is maximum at the origin, where by putting $r = 0$ and $m = 0$,

$$\begin{aligned} \pi &= (a - k_1 - k_2)Q - bQ^2 = \$56.25 \text{ million} \\ &= \pi_1 + \pi_2 = 31.25 + 25.00 \end{aligned} \tag{8}$$

Q is also maximized (and P minimized) at the origin where $r = 0$ and $m = 0$. Hence,

$$\overline{Q}_1 = \overline{Q}_2 = \frac{a}{2b} - \frac{k_1 + k_2}{2b} = 1,500 \text{ machines} \tag{9}$$

Hence $P = \$62,5000$ per machine, a minimum. Therefore, it is only in a pure equity-sharing joint venture context with neither licensing (i.e., $r = 0$) nor a component supply arrangement (i.e., $m = 0$) that the two parties can agree on an appropriate profit-maximizing product price and quantity. In the mixed arrangements of the general case, they cannot agree and for the example we assumed that the local party's optimum $\overline{Q}_1$ was used. This is understandable especially for a minority equity holding when $\alpha < 0.50$. Thus optimum quantity is Q_1 defined in equation 4. (Later of course one may change this assumption to where the foreign firm's optimum $\overline{Q}_2$ prevails and see the consequences on the computer plot.) Since $\overline{Q}_1 < \overline{Q}_2$ except in the pure equity-sharing case, $\overline{P}_2 < \overline{P}_1$, i.e., the optimum price desired by local partner is greater than the price $\overline{P}_2$ the foreign firm will desire to set, which is detrimental to consumers.

APPENDIX B:

BEDFORD PRODUCTS CASE
James D. Goodnow

In January 1983, George Harris, president of Bedford Products, Inc. (Bedford) of Battle Creek, Michigan, was discussing his firm's current and future international marketing plans with John Duncan, international sales director.

Bedford was founded in 1915 by Thomas J. Bedford as a small motor parts manufacturing company. By 1983, the company had expanded its product offerings. The company manufactured small compressors for refrigeration and air-conditioning equipment. The home office and 600,000 square foot modern factory were located on a forty-acre site 4 miles north of downtown Battle Creek. Total employment of the firm was about 700 as of December 13, 1982. (For the firm's 1982 balance sheet and income statement see Tables 50 and 51.)

Bedford compressors were sold to important manufacturers of refrigeration and air-conditioning equipment throughout the United States and Canada. Bedford's small compressors were especially in demand for use in window air-conditioning units and small domestic refrigerators. With annual factory sales of $42 million, Bedford held about 5 percent of the U.S. compressor market.

In 1978, following the lead of its larger competitors, Bedford began to seek export markets actively. Duncan, then a 25-year-old MBA recipient from the University of Michigan, was hired as export manager. Duncan built export sales from $20,000 in 1978 to $2 million in 1982. Much of his success came from locating aggressive distributors in England, Venezuela, Brazil, and Australia. Duncan also made certain that Bedford's late model compressors were patented in major European, Latin American, and Asian markets.

One of the major purchasers of Bedford compressors in Western Europe was Prickett, Ltd.—a large British manufacturer of refrigeration equipment for homes and small industries. Prickett officers were facing a serious cost squeeze. Although they had been well pleased with the quality of the Bedford line, terms of sale, and dependable delivery, Prickett officials became aware of the differences in price between Bedford's line and the prices of German products that could be substituted in Prickett's output for relatively little retooling expenses. However, with the aid of Bedford's British distributor, Duncan had developed a strong sense of personal rapport with some individuals in important decision-making posts at Prickett. Because these Prickett officials recognized that lower labor and materials costs existed in the United Kingdom (see Table 52), they suggested to Duncan that he consider licensing a British firm to manufacture Bedford's patented compressors. The Prickett officials believed that it would take a year or more before they could adequately sample alternative compressor sources and select one with quality and delivery standards competitive with Bedford.

Table 50
Bedford Products, Inc. Consolidated Income Statement
Year Ending December 31, 1982

(Thousands of Dollars)

Income
    Net Sales $40,238

Expenses
    Materials, overhead, etc. $26,860
    Payroll*   7,952
    Depreciation   272
    Total Expenses $35,084

    Profit before taxes $ 5,154
    Federal and state income taxes   3,006
    Net Income $ 2,148

*includes administrative, production and marketing personnel.

Table 51
Bedford Products, Inc. Balance Sheet for Year Ending December 31, 1982
(Thousands of Dollars)

Current assets
    Cash $1,690
    Net accounts receivable $4,506
    Inventories (raw materials,
    work in process, finished goods) $3,380
    Supplies $ 140
    Current assets $9,716

Long-term assets
    Property, plant, equipment
    (after depreciation) $3,942
    Deferred charges $ 142
    TOTAL ASSETS $13,800

Liabilities
    Current liabilities:
        Accounts payable $2,394
        Accrued payrolls,
        taxes, etc. $ 422
        Total current liabilities =
        total liabilities $2,816

Equities
    Capital stock = $2 par value $ 142
    Shares authorized   100,000
    Shares issued   71,000
    Capital surplus $3,662
    Retained earnings $7,180
    Stockholder's equity $10,988
                               $13,800

Duncan telephoned Harris from London to relay the feelings of the Prickett officials. Harris believed that growing European competition might close out other outlets for Bedford products unless action were to be taken soon. He instructed Duncan to explore opportunities for potential licensing partners. Both men agreed that they would feel more at home with a British partner than with a partner outside the English-speaking world.

Duncan visited several British refrigeration parts manufacturers and finally decided that Stock, Ltd. of Stockport, England (a few miles south of Manchester), might make an interesting and compatible partner. Stock's executives were very interested in the opportunity to manufacture compressors on license from Bedford. But Stock's plant was currently operating close to full capacity. Therefore, it would be necessary to build a new plant on a piece of property owned by Stock five miles east of Wexford, Wales (approximately 50 miles southwest of Liverpool and 60 miles southwest of the existing Stock plant). Stock's officials believed that, although cash reserves were substantial as was the firm's borrowing power, an investment in a new plant might bring about a somewhat uncomfortable squeeze on working capital. Nevertheless, the Stock officials recognized the potential profits that might accrue as the result of a licensing venture.

Therefore, Stock officials made two alternative propositions to Duncan. One was that Bedford enter into a licensing agreement; the other was that a sixty–forty joint venture be formed with Bedford as minority partner.

Table 52
Comparison of Unit Costs of Producing and Marketing
(Typical 3 Horsepower Compressor)
United States v. United Kingdom

	U.S.	U.K.	U.K. as % of U.S.
Materials	$67.00	$50.26	75%
Payroll	18.00	9.00	50%*
Total Cost	$85.00	$59.26	70%

Compressors sold in the U.S. for $100.00 each. Similar compressors could be bought from German and French supplies for $65.00 apiece. The U.K. tariff rate applied to both sources of compressors was identical.

*Although the local Welsh wages per man-hour in manufacturing compressor units are projected to be about 56% under U.S. labor costs (i.e., $2.58 per hour in the U.K. versus $6.30 per hour in the U.S.), labor output per hour expended was considered to be 20 percent lower than in the U.S.due to differences in management efficiency, educational preparation, and effort expended by the labor force in the two countries. However, the percentage gap between the U.S. and the U.K. in terms of output per unit of input is considered to be narrowing. The differences in both wages and productivity are taken into account.

Duncan felt that he should have more specifics as to provisions of each agreement. He wanted to know what sales levels might be projected for the proposed partnership, what costs would be borne by each of the partners—both initial and long term—what fees and other earnings might accrue to Bedford, etc. He also recognized the importance of considering production and marketing management capabilities of both Stock and Bedford as well as obstacles and incentives erected by both the British and U.S. governments. Finally, he recognized the importance of looking at the cash and borrowing capabilities of the two firms.

After receiving approval from Harris to conduct necessary inquiries to find answers to the above questions, Duncan gathered a set of facts (contained herein as Tables 53 to 60).

THE PROBLEM

Based on the facts gathered by Duncan, what decision would you make with respect to choosing a licensing arrangement versus the joint-venture? Make a cash flow analysis of each alternative. Then incorporate this with qualitative strategy considerations to make a final choice.

Table 53
Manpower Outlook for the Proposed Agreements

Bedford Products, Inc.—Management and engineering staff is currently being fully utilized. However, the company could afford to release one experienced engineer or the equivalent for about 90 man-days during the coming year. All international sales are currently being coordinated by Mr. Duncan with the assistance of a part-time secretary and a sales trainee (who is spending about half his time in the international sales department). Duncan is on the road about 50 percent of the time. Since he speaks fluent Spanish, he spends much of his time developing sales in Latin America.

It would take Bedford about nine to twelve months to train and develop a technically able salesman for international sales.

Stock, Ltd.—The management and engineering staff is experienced in producing and marketing parts for large refrigeration equipment. It has relatively little experience with equipment for small refrigeration equipment. However, there is a considerable overlap in the O.E.M. outlets for large and small refrigeration parts. Stock now has two multi-lingual salesmen who regularly solicit business in the EEC and EFTA countries. One of these is a national of Switzerland who speaks English, French, Italian and German. The other is a national of West Germany.

Stock has an aggressive vice-president with both a technical and international marketing background who could either become the manager of the proposed plant or who could become president of the proposed joint venture. He is aware of British sources of both production and sales management personnel.

Table 54
Sales Outlook for the Proposed Agreements

The conservative sales estimate would be identical for either alternative selected.

Year	Total Sales in $		U.K. Production		U.S. Production*
1984	$ 200,000	=	$ 0	+	$200,000
1985	1,200,000	=	1,000,000	+	200,000
1986	2,400,000	=	2,400,000	+	0
1987	4,000,000	=	4,000,000	+	0
1988	4,800,000	=	4,800,000	+	0
1989	5,800,000	=	5,800,000	+	0

*Although U.S. production of finished goods falls to zero in 1986, the U.S. will sell components to licensee or joint venture at 90 percent of U.S. price (F.O.B. Factory). This will make component prices competitive with alternative sources of supply. Profit to Bedford before taxes will be about 3 percent of sales of these components.

Projected component sales: (F.O.B. Battle Creek)
```
        1984 - None          1987 - $600,000
        1985 - $150,000      1988 - $720,000
        1986 - $360,000      1989 - $870,000
```

Support for above projections:

1. Stock now holds 10 percent of the U.K. compressor market, has inroads to potential buyers in U.K. and on the European continent.

2. Average annual rate of GNP growth per capita will be about 4% in Western Europe.

3. Electrical consumption in Western Europe growing by nearly 10% annually. This suggests increasing consumption of consumer durables.

4. Less frequent shopping trips by housewives in Europe suggests the need for more refrigeration.

5. Small air-conditioning units made in the U.K. may be exported to Commonwealth countries of Africa and Asia.

6. Refrigerator sales in Western Europe have been growing at about 5% annually.

7. Compressor units made in the U.K. could be sold at a price competitive with French and German producers — about $20 per unit on the average for small compressors.

Table 55
Abilities to Finance a New Plant

Bedford has $1,690,000 in cash, three-fourths of which is needed for working capital purposes. Receivables are also needed for working capital purposes. The company has a line of credit with a Detroit bank with which it can borrow up to $1,200,000 at 12 percent. Bedford has a nearly stable domestic market—since its products are used in equipment which is limited almost exclusively to new residences and replacements. Its average after-tax return on sales has been and will probably continue to be about 6 percent. Average return on total assets has been and is likely to remain about 13 percent. However, these rates of return may decline by as much as one percent per year if imports of refrigerators from Italy are allowed to continue their rapid growth in the U.S. market.

Stock has the equivalent of one million dollars in cash. Slightly under half of this amount is needed for working capital. Receivables are also needed for working capital. Stock can borrow up to $2.4 million from a London bank. It has a growing domestic market and a very rapidly growing export market (especially to the EFTA countries as well as Italy and Germany). Exports now account for 40 percent of annual sales.

Table 56
Government Obstacles and Incentives for Foreign Investment

The U.S. Government's investment controls are nonexistent. Therefore, there will be no difficulty sending money abroad for the proposed Wales venture. Moreover, the U.S. permits companies to deduct taxes paid abroad from corporate income taxes due on royalties, dividends, and other income repatriated from overseas ventures.

The U.K. government has no local ownership or local content requirements on foreign investors. There are no limits on capital repatriation—except for a withholding tax of 15% on dividends repatriated to the U.S. This tax may be deducted from U.S. taxes. The tax does not apply to licensing fees or capital gains. The current U.K. corporate income tax rate is 42 percent on before tax profits up to $140,000 US (£50,000). It ranges from 42 to 52 percent, between $144,000 (£90,000) and $360,000 US (£225,000). It is 52% on profits above $360,000 (£225,000). Depreciation on new investment in plant and equipment may be written off at 79 percent in the first year (less any development grants) and 4 percent each year thereafter. In case trade profits are less than the depreciation allowance in the first year, any excess depreciation can be carried forward to be applied to successive year's taxes.

Wexford, Wales is located in a Development Area. Therefore, the U.K. Government (through the Development Corporation for Wales) provides a 15 percent grant on the cost of new equipment, the plant building, and new permanent fixtures. No grant is given for the purchase of land. The U.K. Government will also help recruit, relocate, and train the labor force.

There is no problem for a U.S. citizen to obtain a work permit for a temporary management post in the U.K.

U.K. import duties on refrigeration components shipped from the U.S. are about 10 percent ad valorem.

Table 56 *(continued)*

If the joint venture route is selected, registration fees will be about $600.

Working capital financing may be obtained by foreign investors in the U.K. Only a limited amount of fixed assets can be financed by British sources if the investing firm is wholly-owned by non-U.K. residents. Local property taxes will be about 50 U.S. cents per square foot in this part of Wales.

Table 57
Proposed Terms: Licensing Agreement

1. Bedford will provide Stock with all present and future patents, trademarks, and know-how for a period of five years.
2. Stock will have right of exclusive distribution of patented Bedford products in the United Kingdom, non-exclusive rights in Western Europe, Africa, Asia and Oceania. North and South American markets are excluded.
3. Products are to be sold under Bedford trademark.
4. Bedford will provide salaries, travel, and living expenses for technical and managerial training up to 90 man-days during start-up period and 10 man-days each year thereafter.
5. Distribution rights will begin upon signing agreement. (Existing distributor of Bedford Products is willing to go along with provision.)
6. Stock will pay $60,000 down payment on signing the contract and an engineering fee of 3 percent of sales (F.O.B. factory). Engineering fee is applicable to all sales of finished goods shipped from the U.S. during the start-up period as well as to all Bedford patented goods made in the U.K.
7. Bedford may convert up to 50 percent of its royalties received from Stock into Stock's voting common stock (cumulative participating preferred as to dividends).
8. Engineering fees not taken in common stock are to be transferred to the U.S. in dollars. Stock will obtain the dollars.
9. Bedford will sell components and finished goods to Stock at the U.S. F.O.B. factory price. However, Stock will pay transportation, insurance, duties, etc.
10. If the British Pound should be temporarily blocked, Stock will owe for back payments of fees and interest at the rate of 12 percent per year.
11. Stock will make a full annual disclosure to Bedford of its accounting and production records pertaining to the products and know-how licensed. In addition, Bedford will have the right to make a quarterly physical check (monthly during start-up period) of production and marketing facilities pertaining to the items licensed. An audit will be performed by a U.K. chartered accounting firm.
12. Stock agrees not to manufacture or sell products competitive with the Bedford line.
13. Stock will hold the transferred technology as confidential and will not sublicense as long as the agreement is in force.
14. Stock will pay transportation, living expenses and $150.00 per man-day for Bedford personnel sent from the U.S. as trainers and remaining in Wales beyond the times specified in number 4 above. The same method will be used by Stock to cover costs of U.K. personnel visiting the U.S. for training purposes.

Table 58
Proposed Terms: Joint Venture Agreement

1. The name of the company will be Stock-Bedford, Ltd.
2. Sixty percent of the equity shares will be held by Stock, which will provide three members for the Board of Directors. Forty percent of the equity shares will be held by Bedford, which will provide two members of the Board of Directors. Each share will carry an equal vote.
3. Stock will supply the land and locate the necessary manpower.
4. Bedford will supply its patents, trademarks, and know-how as well as 90 man-days of technical assistance during the start-up period and 10 man-days each year thereafter. Transportation and living expenses for the technical advisers will also be paid by Bedford.
5. The joint venture will have exclusive distribution rights in the United Kingdom and non-exclusive distribution rights on Bedford-trademarked goods in the rest of Europe, as well as Africa, Asia, Oceania. The markets of North and South America are excluded.
6. A new plant will be built in Wexford, Wales at an initial cost (including fixtures, machinery, and equipment) of $2.2 million dollars (1,452,000 pounds). The British Government will provide $330,000. The new plant will have 60,000 square feet of floor space—including offices.
7. The initial outlay by the partners will be $800,000 (plus the government grant mentioned above). One fourth of this amount will be in cash (the government grant will be entirely cash), the remainder will be a five year note on a London bank at 13 percent interest. These notes will be gotten in January 1985 from the proceeds of the joint venture.
8. The partners will together on an equal basis supply an additional $400,000 for working capital on January 1, 1985. During both 1986 and 1987, the joint venture will supply an additional $100,000 per year from its revenues for plant expansion purposes. Thereafter, the joint venture will allocate $200,000 of its net annual earnings after tax for expansion of working capital. The remainder of the earnings will be split between the partners as dividends in accord with the number of shares owned by each.
9. The two Bedford directors will have the right to veto any new capital expenditures of research and development expenditures for amounts greater than $10,000. Moreover, they will have the right to request an independent audit of the books of the joint venture at their mutual expense.
10. Bedford will supply necessary finished goods or components at 90 percent of the U.S. F.O.B. factory price. However, the joint venture will pay for transportation, insurance, and duties on these goods.
11. In case adequate working capital funds are not available during the start-up period, each of the partners will provide such funds in proportion to their equity shares.
12. It can be assumed that the dollar:pound exchange rate will stay relatively constant over the near term future and that neither the U.S. nor the U.K. will institute exchange controls.

Table 59
Anticipated Costs of Licensing Alternative

---

1. During the first year of the agreement, two representatives of the licensor's top management will visit the licensee to negotiate the agreement and to inspect the plant under construction. The cost of these trips (including travel, the relevant proportion of management salaries, and living expenses) will be about $16,000.
2. A local British attorney will inspect and write the final agreement at a cost of about $1,000.00 to the licensor.
3. Technical assistance (including the relevant portion of engineering salaries, travel and living expenses plus reproductions of drawings, sample products, etc.) will be about $20,000 during the first year and $4,000 each year thereafter.
4. Clerical and secretarial expenses pertaining to the licensing agreement will be about $2,600.00 per year beginning with the second year of the agreement.

Table 60
Anticipated Costs of Joint Venture Alternative

---

1. In addition to expenditures for plant and equipment (including principal and interest on the five-year bank note), the joint venture will have to pay for the following:
   a. cost of goods sold (direct labor and materials) = about 70% of sales
   b. sales, administrative and miscellaneous expenses =
         $100,000 in first year,
         200,000 in each of the 3 succeeding years and 5% of sales each year thereafter.
2. Technical assistance costs to Bedford will be the same as under the licensing alternative.
3. Top management inspection will cost Bedford $16,000 during the first year but only $8,000 each year thereafter since the joint venture will pay travel and expenses of U.S. members of the board of directors. Moreover, the joint venture will probably hire an American expatriate as one of its executive officers (probably in a vice-presidential capacity).

SOLUTION TO THE BEDFORD PRODUCTS CASE

This case has no single solution. An answer depends on additional information and/or assumptions used by the decision maker. For example, let us make the following assumptions.

1. The performance of the proposal license or joint venture will come up to Bedford's quality and sales expectations.
2. Annual sales of the licensee or joint venture will stabilize at $6 million annually beginning in 1990.

3. The rate of increase in the price levels in the United States and the United Kingdom over the next ten years will be about the same.

4. Neither the pound nor the dollar will be revalued or devalued with respect to each other during the coming ten years.

5. There will be no significant changes in local, state, and national property or income tax rates in either the United States or the United Kingdom during the next ten years.

6. There will be no major recession in the U.K. economy that will greatly offset the forecasted sales.

7. Setting up a licensee or joint venture in the United Kingdom will not detract from Bedford's marketing goals in other parts of the world. Moreover, the right of non-exclusive distribution granted the licensee or joint venture will not create a serious competitor for the parent company or its future affiliates and licensees.

8. Bedford's cost of capital over the foreseeable future will remain fixed at 12 percent, which is equal to the borrowing rate of return on total assets (given increasing import competition which is likely to lower the historical return on assets by 1 percent).

9. Bedford will not exchange licensing royalties for equity shares in Stock, Ltd.

10. The proposed method of financing the joint venture will be followed. For example, research might show that leasing a plant would be as expensive as buying in the short run and more expensive in the long run.

11. The proposed licensing down payment and fees will be accepted by both parties.

12. There will be no changes in the requirements for local ownership and/or content which will adversely affect the proposed joint venture.

13. The licensing contract will be renegotiated after five years with essentially no change in its provisions. Therefore, Bedford will not risk the creation of a competitor.

14. The cost predictions for each of the alternatives are about correct. This includes a plan to repay the bank loan in five years (one-fifth of the principal each year plus 13 percent interest on the remaining balance).

Given the above assumptions, we can calculate the expected profits and cash flows resulting from each of the alternatives. We can also calculate the cumulative discounted cash flows for the alternatives.†

As illustrated in Figures 9 and 10, we find that licensing is the more profitable

---

†Once the firm's management has decided on an appropriate cost of capital it can turn to a present value table to find the corresponding discount rate. Because of compound interest, the discount rate (or the present value of a dollar of profits or of cash remaining after taxes) declines through time.

Present value tables are based on this formula:

$$\text{Discount rate} = \frac{1}{(1+r)}^n \text{ where } r = \text{cost of capital } n = \text{number of years}$$

To find the discounted present value of profits for a particular year, you multiply the discount rate corresponding to the appropriate cost of capital and appropriate year by the expected profits. You can add the discounted present value of profits for each successive year to find the cumulative discounted present value of profits.

Normally, firms use the cumulative discounted present value of profits or cash flow to compare investment alternatives. Cash flow = profits + depreciation. Note that depreciation is an accounting term and is not an actual expenditure. Calculations are shown in Tables 61 and 62.

Figure 9
Comparison of Annual Cash Flows (Projected)

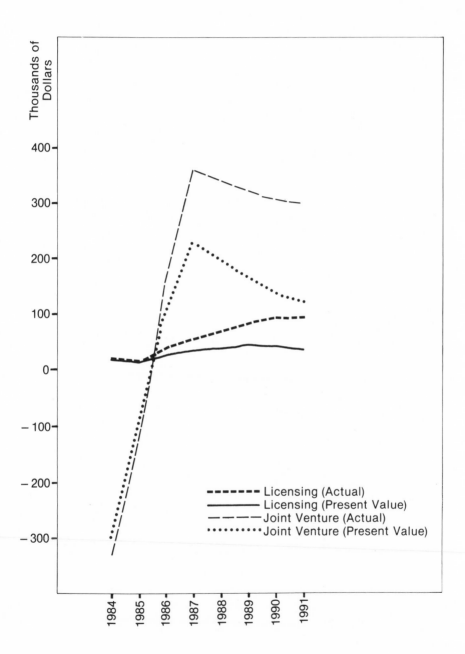

Figure 10
Comparison of Cumulative Cash Flows (Projected)

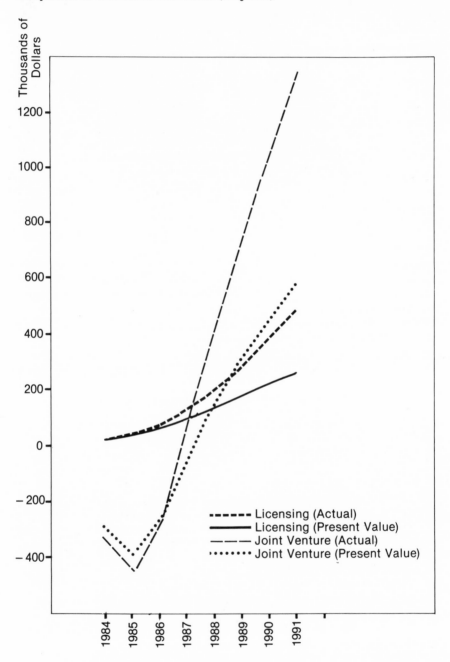

alternative for the first four years (if you look at the actual cumulative cash flows) or five years (if you look at the discounted cumulative cash flows). Thereafter, the joint venture looks more profitable. If any of the assumptions were changed, it would alter the solution of the case. Details of the calculations are shown below.

Therefore, the solution of the case boils down to whether the firm's managers have a long or short time horizon. Moreover, the solution is related to the firm's ability to supply adequate funds to expand licensing or joint venture activities in other countries.

The most common solution would probably be the selection of the licensing route since this will give the firm somewhat greater flexibility to explore the market potential before spending funds on plant and equipment overseas. Li censing will also free funds for the establishment of licensees in other countries.

NOTES

1. Studies show that some 80 percent of international agreements have royalties expressed as a percentage of licensee turnover. Most of these have a fixed percentage. A small minority have a provision whereby the royalty percentage decreases after a certain volume of output is reached. Cases where the royalty percentage increases with production volume beyond a certain point are rare. See Lightman, J., "Compensation Patterns in U.S. Foreign Licensing," *IDEA*, Spring 1970, pp. 1–26. Lovell, E., *Appraising Foreign Licensing Performance* (New York: Conference Board, 1969). Contractor, F., *International Technology Licensing: Compensation, Costs and Negotiation* (Lexington, Mass.: D. C. Heath & Co., 1981).

2. Despite fears of licensees exporting their output to compete with licensors in third nations, what empirical evidence exists suggests a very low propensity of exporting on part of licensees. See, for example, Contractor, *International Technology Licensing*, and Stobaugh, R., *The International Transfer of Technology in the Establishment of Petrochemical Industries in Developing Countries* (New York: United Nations, 1971).

3. For example, see Ways, M., "The Virtues, Dangers and Limits of Negotiation," *Fortune*, January 15, 1979, pp. 86–90.

4. In any event, valuing patents or trademarks, *per se*, is impossible. If they are given a value, this is an arbitrary figure. The point here is that as already created assets, their cost may be treated as sunk, since the focus here is only on incremental costs to the licensor.

5. We may also include here the costs of helping the licensee set up administration and marketing, considering "technology" in its broadest sense as an organization's "total capability."

6. A constant marginal cost (MC) and linear demand function are used in this example. In any event, what this chapter is doing is laying out a negotiation approach. In practice, the negotiator can use whatever *MC* or demand curve is appropriate.

7. The numbers do not add up exactly because of rounding errors.

8. This is akin to focusing on contribution margin instead of profit for making decisions in micro-economic theory, although here the foreign partner's actual contribution is not proportional to their shareholding.

9. Such a solution may appear to only be a theoretical possibility. However, an overly conservative pricing policy of this kind may be actually used by multinational firms in several less-developed countries. See Leff, N., "Multinational Corporate Pricing Strategy in Developing Countries," *Journal of International Business Studies*, Fall 1975, pp. 55–63.

10. Solutions (f) and (g) are therefore not on Figure 7. New graphs would have to be plotted.

11. In Contractor, *International Technology Licensing*, the author examines the actual influence of industry norms, the number of alternate global sellers of technology, exchange of information among recipients, and other factors in a sample of 102 global agreements.

12. A highly oversimplified explanation of the effects of the theory is provided in the example below. Consider a country with an annual inflation rate of 100 percent and a consequent devaluation that halves the value of its currency each year in foreign exchange markets

	This Year	Next Year
Sales of product	1,000 pesos	2,000 pesos
Royalty (at 6%)	60 pesos	120 pesos
$ Value (at 4 pesos/$)	15 dollars	15 dollars (at 8 pesos/$)

Of course, the difficulty is that inflation and the exchange rate are never so perfectly indexed. But in the long run the theory (and evidence) suggest a reasonable correlation. At any rate, in the majority of cases devaluation lags domestic inflation, rather than vice versa; that benefits the licensor.

13. That assumes the availability of a reliable price index for that country. Some nations may not have one. In such a case one solution may be to express royalties in dollars— "per square foot" or "per gallon," etc. This is not an idea that sits well with licensees. Its acceptance depends on how badly the licensee desires the technology. The author has seen agreements where the licensee has not only accepted expressing royalties in dollars, but an escalator clause tying dollar royalties to the U.S. producer price index.

14. See Articles 85 and 86 of the Rome Treaty for the European common market. Among developing countries, the ones with considerable regulatory scrutiny are India, Mexico, Colombia, Peru, Equador, Argentina, Bolivia, Chile, and Venezuela.

15. Contractor, *International Technology Licensing*, p. 109.

Table 61
Comparative Analysis Sheet, Licensing Alternative, Incremental Cash Flows
(Figures Expressed in Constant in 1984 U.S. Dollars)

	1984	1985	1986	1987	1988	1989	1990	1991
Licensee Sales	200,000	1,200,000	2,400,000	4,000,000	4,800,000	5,800,000	6,000,000	6,000,000
Downpayment and Engineering Fees	66,000	50,000	96,000	120,000	144,000	174,000	180,000	180,000
Before Tax Profit on Exports to Licensee	6,000	10,500	10,800	18,000	21,600	26,100	27,000	27,000
Income from Licensing	72,000	60,500	106,800	138,000	165,600	200,100	207,000	207,000
Management Inspection and Travel	16,000	24,000	24,000	24,000	24,000	24,000	24,000	24,000
Technical Assistance & Expenses	20,000	4,000	4,000	4,000	4,000	4,000	4,000	4,000
Legal, Secretarial & Misc.	1,000	2,000	2,000	2,000	2,000	2,000	2,000	2,000
Total Expenses of Licensing	37,000	30,000	30,000	30,000	30,000	30,000	30,000	30,000
Profits Before Tax	39,000	30,500	76,800	108,000	135,600	170,100	177,000	177,000
U.S. Income Tax (48%)	18,720	14,640	36,864	51,840	65,088	81,648	84,960	84,960
Profits After Tax - Cash Flow	20,280	15,860	39,936	56,160	70,512	88,452	92,040	92,040
Cumulative After Tax Profits	20,280	36,140	76,076	132,236	202,748	291,200	383,240	475,280
Discount Factor (12% Rate)	.893	.797	.712	.636	.567	.507	.452	.404
Present Value of After Tax Profits	18,110	12,640	28,434	35,718	39,980	44,845	41,602	37,184
Cumulative Present Value of After Tax Profits	18,110	30,750	59,184	94,902	134,882	179,727	221,329	258,513

Table 62

Comparative Analysis Sheet, Joint Venture Alternative, Incremental Cash Flows
(Figures Expressed in Constant 1984 U.S. Dollars)

	1984	1985	1986	1987	1988	1989	1990	1991
Sales of Joint Venture	200,000	1,200,000	2,400,000	4,000,000	4,800,000	5,800,000	6,000,000	6,000,000
Cost of Goods Sold (Include duties)	200,000	700,000	1,680,000	2,800,000	3,160,000	3,860,000	4,200,000	4,200,000
Depreciation	-0-	108,900	407,920	894,940	416,998	74,800	74,800	18,700
Principal and Interest on Loan	-0-	89,100	82,080	75,060	74,540	61,020	-0-	-0-
Local Taxes	-0-	30,000	30,000	30,000	30,000	30,000	30,000	30,000
Sales Adm. and Misc. Expenses	100,000	200,000	200,000	200,000	240,000	290,000	294,000	294,000
Before Tax Profit	100,000	-0-	-0-	-0-	878,462	1,484,180	1,401,200	1,484,300
Bedford Share: Before Tax J.V. Profit 40%	40,000	-0-	-0-	-0-	351,385	593,672	560,480	593,720
Before Tax Profit on Exports to J.V.	6,000	10,500	10,800	18,000	21,600	26,100	26,100	26,100
Income from J.V. Related Activities	134,000	10,500	10,800	18,000	372,985	619,772	586,580	619,820
Investment Contribution	160,000	160,000	-0-	-0-	-0-	-0-	-0-	-0-
Technical Assistance	20,000	4,000	4,000	4,000	4,000	4,000	4,000	4,000
Management Inspection	16,000	8,000	8,000	8,000	8,000	8,000	8,000	8,000
Before Tax Profit: Bedford	-330,000	-161,500	-1,200	6,000	360,985	607,772	574,580	607,820
U.S. taxes paid in U.K.— 52%	-0-	-0-	-0-	3,120	187,712	316,041	298,781	316,066
After Tax Profit: Bedford	-330,000	-161,500	-1,200	2,880	173,273	291,731	275,799	291,754
Bedford Share Depreciation (40%)[a]	-0-	-43,560	-163,168	-357,976	-166,799	-29,920	-29,920	-7,480
Bedford Annual Cash Flow[b]	-330,000	-117,940	-161,968	360,856	340,072	321,651	305,719	299,234
Discount Factor (12% rate)	.893	.797	.712	.636	.567	.507	.452	.409
Present Value of Annual Cash Flow	294,690	93,998	115,321	229,504	192,821	163,077	138,180	122,387
Cumulative Present Value of Cash Flow	294,690	388,688	273,367	43,863	148,958	312,035	450,215	572,602
Cumulative Cash Flow	330,000	447,940	285,972	74,884	414,956	736,607	1,042,326	1,341,560

Notes: a. Downward adjustment in value of capital stock.

b. Dividends received (or net loss incurred).

9

Government Regulation and Corporate Responses

International transfers of technology are increasingly subject to governmental regulation and scrutiny. Countries that are net "exporters" of technology are concerned about the effects of uncontrolled transfers (that is to say, not under the aegis of a direct investment by a firm headquartered in their own country) on the long-run competitiveness of their economy, on employment, and on balance of payments. In recent years, much attention has also been devoted to the issue of technology transfers to Communist-bloc nations and the effect these may have in enhancing their military and "strategic" industries.[1] But this is a very small part of the overall picture. Observers such as M. Boretsky or J. Abegglen and T. Hout have argued that for the United States, with an overwhelming net outflow of technology, the more critical question is whether American firms are parting with their technologies and diffusing them overseas in nations like Japan for small short-term earnings but with large long-term costs to the international competitive stance of the U.S. economy.[2] This chapter will examine these issues.

However, the main focus, when we discuss government regulation in a global context, has to be on nations as recipients of technology. Why? Because of the fact that today almost all nations are net "importers" of technology. The asymmetry in global technology flows appears startling to new observers. Effective measures of international technology flows are lacking; however, let us take one (imperfect) indicator as an example, royalties and licensing fees. Perhaps only four nations in the world receive more royalties and license fees than they pay to other countries.[3] All other nations have a net deficit on this balance-of-payments account, i.e., they are net licensee countries. The underlying reason, of course, is the less acute, but no less remarkable concentration of innovation, research, and scientific development in a handful of countries. By any criteria such as patent filings, R&D expenditures, or citation ratios for scientific and technical articles, just seven countries—United States, West Germany, Japan, United Kingdom, France, Canada, and Switzerland—account for the great bulk of the global total.[4] Of these, the United States dominates. Its researchers' articles comprise 37 percent of the world's total, U.S. firms receive some 40 percent of all global licensing payments, and so on.[5] The point again is that almost every other nation is a net technology importer, and regulation of technology importation is today more important for strategy in international firms than are the relatively infrequent controls on its exportation.

We will mention in this chapter developing countries' policies more often than their share in international technology flows would justify. Their share in global royalties and fees or direct investment is only between a quarter and a third of the total (although the profitability of ventures and agreements in LDCs is higher than in industrial nations, on average). There are several reasons. Negotiations there are thornier for technology suppliers who need to understand the regulatory mentality to cross that hurdle successfully. Second, scrutiny of licensing and investment proposals is hardly confined to LDCs—some of them only represent an extreme on a spectrum that includes Canada, France, or Japan among industrial, "free market" countries that also examine proposals for congruence with national objectives. Third, some of today's LDCs are rapidly growing markets that can no longer be ignored or written off as in the 1950s or 1960s, when a comfortable technological lead and booming European and North American markets sufficiently occupied executives. In short, there is more regulation in the United States and outside than ever before, and there is a need to sensitize executives to national or societal concerns. Nevertheless, in international investment or licensing today the situation in most countries is not a matter of confrontation; ways can often be found to adapt corporate policies to governmental concerns without sacrificing fundamentals. This is the chapter's purpose.

Readers will find that the tone of the discussion is deliberately iconoclastic toward government regulation of technology transfer. There is a point beyond which regulation is counter-productive and impedes the flow. Moreover, if each technology transfer is a unique situation involving two companies, as we have stressed earlier, then government rules and regulations that perforce have to be somewhat across the board, are ill suited. Like doing surgery with an ax, across-the-board rules (such as a flat 5 percent limit on royalty rates) will sometimes work but at other times kill the patient. A theme that will be developed is that, while the objectives of regulation are usually sensible and perhaps noble, national and corporate objectives are not met without a great deal of sophistication and flexibility on the part of both executives and the bureaucrats, especially when it comes to international technology transfer.

Let us begin with a detailed examination of regulation in technology receiving countries, their national objectives, and the problems in formulating effective policies, especially in the LDCs. Later we will look at the U.S. position as far and away the leading disseminator of technology to the world.

REGULATION IN TECHNOLOGY-IMPORTING COUNTRIES

Government intervention, broadly speaking, seeks to affect three important aspects: (1) the mode of association between the foreign supplier of technology and the local operation; (2) the cost or price of the transfer, directly in terms of balance of payment outflows over the long run or indirectly in terms of restraints upon the local firm and other "negative externalities"; (3) the content of the technology transfer "package."[6]

A great deal has been written about the presumed disadvantageous position of technology receivers, especially the developing nations, in acquiring technology. Most technology being proprietary, it has to be obtained from large, multinational firms who are claimed to have the dominant position in any negotiations over the transfer of their knowledge and patent or trademark rights. While one cannot help but be sympathetic to the idea of a nation endeavoring to obtain technology at the least cost as an ideal, the objective here is to examine critically, in the light of recent theoretical and empirical evidence, certain hallowed assertions and presumptions made by technology-importing government spokesmen. This is followed by a look at some longer-term policies that may be more effective.

There is no comprehensive theory for a nation optimizing technology imports.[7] Rather, we seek to compare government policies regulating the mode, cost, and content of technology transfer into their country with such empirical data as are available, and with relevant economics models.

The Three Parties to the Negotiation and Their Diverse Interests

There are three transactors or negotiating parties presented: the government, the foreign firm, and local investors as either joint venture partners or licensees. The description of technology transfer as usually conveying some specific advantages to the recipient firm over its local competition is a well-received model. Unless the local market for the item finally produced is strongly competitive, which is usually untrue in protectionist or faraway countries like Australia, and unless there is significant international competition between suppliers of the same technology, again true only in a minority of cases, the negotiation between the prospective foreign company and local licensee or joint venture partner can be described as a bilateral monopoly. The two parties have to decide how to share the economic rent as we saw in the last chapter.

What is questioned here is whether the government's interests in intervening in the terms of technology importation with a foreign firm are as T. Agmon and S. Hirsch describe:

Once the government negotiates for the local economic agents—labour, entrepreneurs, owners of natural resources, etc.—the "national interest" is no longer fragmented. The LDC speaks, or at least could speak, with one voice. . . .[8]

While this may be more true for a relatively sophisticated technology-importing nation like Japan, where its Ministry for International Trade and Industry plays a useful role in improving the terms of technology purchased by Japanese firms, one finds in most LDCs the government's participation is sometimes valued, but more often regarded as a nuisance by potential local joint venture partners and licensees.

Not only are the interests of the foreign and local firms noncongruent, but the government's own objectives are usually, though not always, contradictory. Of these, four important ones are: (1) maximizing revenues from tax and tariff collections; (2) minimizing balance-of-payment outflows; (3) maximizing the benefit or value of the technology received by the recipient firm and country; and (4) minimizing the price paid by eventual buyers of product made by the technology. While the value of technology is not easily quantifiable, we did examine quantifiable criteria in the last chapter that did provide a basis, albeit mostly from the technology supplier firm's perspective.[9] In any event, we seek to illustrate the divergence of policy objectives in the next section rather than aim for econometric quantification.

THE MODE OF ASSOCIATION BETWEEN THE TECHNOLOGY SUPPLIER AND RECIPIENT COUNTRY

The mode of association can range from full ownership of the operation by the foreign investor to a purely contractual relationship at the other extreme, with several equity-cum-contractual combinations in between. Royalties as we have seen are usually contractually pegged between 1 and 8 percent of sales. Licensing agreements have a limited legal life, although frequently renewed. By contrast, foreign investments have no limitation on duration or the magnitude of pre-tax dividends. Therefore, it might *prima facie* be surmised that non-equity modes are a "cheaper" method of technology acquisition. Can developing nations follow the example of earlier Japanese policy? Japanese policy, particularly in the period 1950–1975, used licensing, turnkey, and management service contracts as preferred vehicles for technology acquisition, while inhibiting foreign investment. We treat this question first as a simple theoretical model and illustration to show that even under the simplest assumptions there is a divergence of the various objectives. Then we generalize the discussion to examine issues such as the availability of technology from international firms under non-equity arrangements and empirical evidence on the benefits of the technology under alternative arrangements.

Let us suppose as in the last chapter that a joint venture is established with the foreign firm holding a share α in the equity. $0 \leq \alpha \leq 1$, i.e., α ranges from zero, a no-equity or pure licensing deal, to 1, where the local operation is fully foreign owned. As often occurs, the local venture will also sign a technology licensing arrangement with L, an initial lump-sum payment and a running royalty of r per unit sales. Theoretically, the royalty can be any percentage of sales value, i.e., $0 \leq r < 1$, although practically speaking, from studies such as J. Lightman, royalties typically will range up to 10 percent, i.e., $0 < r < 0.1$.[10] When $r = 0$, there is no running license, and the arrangement is a pure equity relationship (i.e., $\alpha > 0$).

Finally, let P = unit selling price for the product made by the venture, Q = quantity sold, v = unit variable cost of production, F = total fixed cost, t_E = the effective tax rate on the local enterprise, and t_F = the effective tax rate faced by the foreign company.[11]

As before, let us state the demand for the local company's final product as simply $P = a - bQ$, where a and b are constants, a condition of weak or monopolistic competition. (For our purpose, no additional insights are derived by alternative configurations of the demand schedule, nor is anything extra gained by generating multiperiod models; so the simplest form is used.)

The objectives of the three parties are as under:

- The foreign firm: profit maximization after all taxes.
- The local firm: profit maximization after local taxes.
- The government: here four important objectives. are—

  •• Tax revenues

  •• Lowering foreign exchange outgo

  •• Lowering the price charged for the product to consumers. For the product market, we have assumed (weak or) monopolistic competition, a fairly ubiquitous condition in LDC industrial and consumer markets, a fact corroborated by studies going back to I. Little, T. Scitovsky, and M. Scott.[12] It is significant that in the literature on technology transfer and foreign investment in LDCs, the cause of the consumer is conspicuously unmentioned, despite the cumulative importance of prices to the economy at large. This overall effect is measured by the calculation for "consumers' surplus" which the government should seek to maximize by inducing the lowest possible price for the product.[13]

  •• Obtaining for the local company (and nation) the largest benefit from the technology transfer. While this is not precisely measurable, many studies, e.g., L. Mytelka, F. Sagasti, or V. Balasubramanyam, confirm that the closer the organizational links and the longer the duration of the association, the greater is the value of the technology received by the local venture.[14] Obviously then, from this perspective alone, majority foreign equity participation is preferable to minority joint ventures, and these in turn are preferable to a pure licensing agreement with no equity participation by the technology seller, *ceteris paribus*.

Four cases are treated: (1) joint equity venture-cum-licensing agreement (with royalties paid to the foreign firm a deductible expense under local tax law); (2) licensing only, an arm's-length agreement, with the venture fully owned by local interests; (3) an equity-sharing joint venture between foreign and local firms with no additional licensing arrangement; and (4) joint equity venture-cum-licensing agreement (but royalties are not a deductible expense under local tax law). These four cases cover most of the types of arrangements found, and by varying the value of α, one can vary the extent of the foreign firm's participation in the equity from zero ($\alpha = 0$) to 100 percent ($\alpha = 1$). By varying the value of r, one can vary the importance of licensing from nil ($r = 0$) to a larger royalty figure.

The purpose is to see what happens to the government's objectives under each of the arrangements above, assuming after-taxes profit-maximizing desires of technology supplier and local investors. We start with algebra, but since this becomes very cumbersome, an arithmetic example is shown later in Table 65 to appreciate implications for government policy best.

Next, by differentiating the above expressions with respect to Q, and substituting P for Q, we arrive at the optimum price for the product desired by each party.

Not surprisingly, there is divergence on the desired price. What is of note is that the foreign technology supplier will desire to set a lower price for the final product than the local investors (in all cases except number 3). This is contrary to the assertion that having a foreign firm in full ownership of a local enterprise will enable it to exact a high price from consumers, and that this can be tempered by policies requiring local participation or contractual relationships, e.g., see R. Newfarmer.[15]

Of course, two prices cannot prevail simultaneously. If the foreign firm has a majority equity portion, its desires will usually prevail. As we get closer to an arm's-length licensing arrangement, the local investors get the dominant say (although it is quite clear from several studies that even an arm's-length licensor continues to wield, in some instances, a large influence on the licensee because of the local firm's technological, trademark, or overseas market access depend-

Table 63
After-Tax Profit Expressions under Different Assumptions

Case	After-Tax Profit*	
	Foreigner	Local Investor
1. Majority foreign joint venture; royalties deductible	$[(PQ - F - vQ - L - PQr)\alpha + (L + PQr)]$ $(1 - t_F)$	$(PQ - F - vQ - L - PQr)$ $(1 - \alpha)(1 - t_E)$
2. Arm's-length licensing (no equity)	$(L + PQr)(1 - t_F)$	$(PQ - F - vQ - L - PQr)$ $(1 - t_E)$
3. Only equity sharing (no licensing)	$(PQ - F - vQ)(\alpha)(1 - t_F)$	$(PQ - F - vQ)(1 - \alpha)$ $(1 - t_E)$
4. Majority foreign joint venture; royalties not deductible	$[(PQ - F - vQ - L - PQr)\alpha + (L + PQr)]$ $(1 - t_F)$	$[(PQ - F - vQ)(1 - t_E)$ $(L + PQr)](1 - \alpha)$

Note: *See note 11 for tax assumption.

Table 64
Optimum Price Desired by Foreign and Local Companies

Case	Optimum Price Desired by	
	Local Partner	**Foreign Firm**
1. General case: licensing-cum-joint venture	$\dfrac{a}{2} + \dfrac{v}{2(1 - r)}$	$a - \dfrac{\alpha(a - v - ar) + ar}{2(\alpha + r - \alpha r)}$
2. Licensing only (arm's-length relationship, $\alpha = 0$)	$\dfrac{a}{2} + \dfrac{v}{2(1 - r)}$	$\dfrac{a}{2}$
3. Equity sharing only, no licensing agreement, $r = 0$	$\dfrac{a + v}{2}$	$\dfrac{a + v}{2}$
4. Licensing-cum-joint venture; royalties not deductible	$\dfrac{a}{2} + \dfrac{v(1 - t_E)}{2(1 - t_E - r)}$	$a - \dfrac{\alpha(a - v - ar) + ar}{2(\alpha + r - \alpha r)}$

encies on the licensor. Thus, the licensor's pricing desires may well prevail in some cases).

Table 65 shows a numerical example working out the implications for government objectives of each of the types of associations between the foreign and local firms. All of the governmental objectives are not met under any one arrangement (which implies the dangers of across-the-board policies favoring a particular mode of association). A pure licensing deal (without equity) is by far the cheapest in terms of foreign exchange outgo, even when the licensor's product price is implemented. But *ceteris paribus* the value of the technology transfer is also less as compared with an equity arrangement; this is elaborated on later. We see also that an independent local licensee will set the highest price for the product. If the foreign licensor influences the licensee's pricing decision, that may be considered an antitrust violation; but where such influence is exerted, the product price is lowest (i.e., we have the highest consumers' surplus), incidentally without the government tax revenues becoming very much lower.

Under joint equity arrangements, product prices are lower than in arm's-length licensing; but there is a significantly higher cost to the economy under the balance-of-payments category, offset only somewhat in the last two cases by increased tax collections. Under our tax assumption, if the government does not allow royalties paid to the foreign firm to be a deductible expense, this of course improves tax collection, but at the expense of the local investor's net income (the more so if *ex ante* this leads the foreign firm to negotiate on an after-tax basis).

We can extend the example in Table 65 with two other cases of government intervention, where the technology buyer is required, in one instance, to pay just one lump-sum amount, i.e., a flat one-time fee; in the other case let us suppose there is a ceiling on royalty rates. Let us examine what happens to the negotiation process as a result of such government intervention.

Table 65

National Objectives under Different Technology Transfer Agreements

Note: Let the demand for the product be $P = 100,000 - 25Q$ with variable cost $v = 30,000$ and fixed cost $F = 10,000,000$, and tax rates $t_E = 0.3$ and $t_F = 0.5$. When applicable, a licensing agreement will involve a lump-sum fee $L = 1,000,000$ and royalty rate of $r = 0.08$ on production value PQ for ten years. The foreign firm pays local tax at the 0.3 rate, credit for which is available against foreign tax t_F. This assumption preserves the foreign firm's after-tax profit even if royalties are not deductible, the local government's higher tax collection coming partially from the local joint venture partner, and partially from the foreign firm's tax liability to their government. The lump-sum is paid in the first year on signing the license.

Case	Desired Price		After-Tax Profit		Government Concerns			
	Foreigner	Local	Foreigner's	Local's	Tax Revenue	Foreign Exchange Outgo	Consumers Surplus*	Technology Transfer Value
				Annual Figures in Millions Local Currency				
Majority foreign equity ($\alpha = .7$) with licensing	64,503	n.a.	14.897 (first year) 14.747 thereafter	6.44 (first year) 6.65 thereafter	9.50	21.345 (first year) 20.645 thereafter	25.20	High
Only licensing arrangement ($\alpha = 0$)	—	66,305	4.075 (first year) 3.575 thereafter	21.548 (first year) 22.248	11.68	5.704 (first year) 5.004 thereafter	22.71	Low
$r = 0.08$	50,000	—	4.50 (first year) 4.00 thereafter	14.70 (first year) 15.40 thereafter	9.00	6.30 (first year) 5.6 thereafter	50.00	Low
Only equity association with $\alpha = .7$, $r = 0$, $L = 0$.	65,000	65,000	13.65	8.19	11.70	19.11	24.50	High
Majority foreign equity ($\alpha = .7$) with licensing fees not deductible	64,503	n.a.	14.897 (first year) 14.747 thereafter	5.69 (first year) 5.99 thereafter	13.89	21.345 (first year) 20.645 thereafter	25.20	High

Note: *"Consumers' Surplus" is the benefit derived by all all buyers who would have been willing or forced to pay more than the price P. It gives a comparative idea of the benefit of lower prices. It is calculated as $\dfrac{(a - P)Q}{2}$

In a pure licensing deal with no royalty and only one lump-sum payment to minimize foreign control on licensee, suppose the licensor's cost of capital is 15 percent. They will demand $1 million plus present value of ten years royalties (at 15 percent) = $36.88 million. This is probably too large a first year burden on the licensee, whereas royalties are at least paid as future sales occur—unless of course the $36.88 million is financed by an additional loan. But this increases fixed cost and the vulnerability of the licensee, whereas royalties are a variable cost.

Similarly, if the government rules prescribe a ceiling of say 5 percent on royalties, the licensor would then demand $36.88 million – present value of 5 percent royalties (at 15 percent) = $36.88 − $22.43 = $14.45 million in lump-sum fees, plus the 5 percent royalty.

Note also that, with a one lump-sum arrangement, the technology-supplying firm has no continuing incentive to transfer manufacturing or managerial capability to the recipient once payment is received. Such arrangements may be useful when the local firm is independently capable and merely requires rights to a patent or trademark via this arrangement. However, as discussed later, only a minority of technology transfers meet this description. The value of a technology transfer under such one-time arrangements can be very low outside of mere patent and trademark agreements.

Finally, for a country to decide on what type of arrangement is "best," we have to return to the fundamental question of what theory and empirical studies say about the value of technology transfer under licensing or equity arrangements. This is closely related to how we view technology. In classical economies, technology is freely transferable information, akin to a free or public good. In this perspective, the free dissemination of technology is said to be hindered by "imperfections" in the international marketplace, such as the patent system, and by the power of a few firms among which technology is concentrated. In this school of thought, technology transfer is viewed mostly as an act of conveying information, formulae, and patent or trademark rights to recipient firms otherwise capable of assimilating this information. P. Buckley and M. Casson and J. Dunning focused on the transactions costs of technology transfer, building on O. Williamson, R. Coase, and J. Schumpeter, and more correctly viewed technology transfer as a long-term relationship between firms.[16] Technology transfer as we saw, is a one-time act only in the minority of cases, where the recipient firm is independently capable and awaits only the legal conferral of a patent or trademark right to proceed on its own. In such a case, a licensing arrangement, if available, is likely to be "cheaper" than equity modes for both the recipient firm and nation as a method for acquiring technology. However, this is an idea pursued with apparent success by only few nations, such as Japan in the period 1950–1975.

Empirical evidence on the above question is significant, if not complete. Besides my own work, Business International related the experience of some Eastern European companies, who, having purchased only the technical documentation and patent rights from Western suppliers in the early 1970s, found themselves unable to convert this into viable production.[17] For the foreign firm, equity participation would have committed them to giving as much technical help as necessary. The Eastern Europeans were forced to enter into auxiliary "technical assistance" agreements for engineers and technical personnel to be sent for extended periods of time from the licensor, confirming this as an instance where the transfer process was costly and arduous. Teece and my 1981 work measured significant technology transfer costs borne by supplier companies over long periods of time.[18] L. Mytelka showed direct equity investment to be more frequent in complex technologies, while Balasubramanyam, examining India, implied that the country was better off allowing foreign equity control in sophisticated processes.[19] My 1981 study of U.S. Commerce Department data, analyzing figures for U.S. licensing revenues from thirty-three countries, a statistical model showed that technology-receiving nations that are more developed and industrialized have a lesser need for technical and managerial services to accompany the conveyance of patent rights.[20] Moreover, the more developed the nation, the larger was the relative share of pure or arm's-length licensing. The regression equation was also robust for the sub-sample of seventeen LDCs, confirming the overall conclusion of the other studies, that all LDCs are not equally capable of going it on their own by receiving technology via pure licensing. Accordingly, policies on this question cannot be identical. The Japanese example can perhaps be successfully followed only by the most advanced of LDCs. The only general conclusion appears to be that across-the-board policies are likely to be sub-optimal. For many nations, more complex arrangements, including equity investment by the technology supplier, may be both necessary and desirable.

Of course, this discussion has thus far begged the crucial question of the availability of technology to LDCs under non-equity arrangements; i.e., are supplier firms willing to give technology under contractual arrangements? J. Baranson, Dunning, and earlier chapters on corporate practices, suggest that, while in high-technology areas several companies may continue to refuse non-equity modes of association in LDCs, in general over the last five years, companies are becoming more receptive to licensing at least some of their processes or products, where before they would have reflexively ruled this out.[21] There is no evidence yet in the aggregate data of a shift away from the traditional direct investment method for doing business abroad. However, there is sufficient circumstantial evidence to have justified the launching of an OECD study.[22]

THE COSTS OF IMPORTING TECHNOLOGY AND GOVERNMENT ATTEMPTS TO LOWER THESE

From government policies seeking to influence the mode of technology acquisition, we now turn to another important type of intervention, namely governments attempting to reduce the direct costs of a technology "package" by restrictions on certain types of payments (e.g., ceilings on royalty rates) and seeking alternative international suppliers for the same technology.[23]

Obviously, the price paid for a technology package is also a function of its contents and the territorial or other restraints placed on the enterprise receiving the foreign technology as we saw in the last chapter. But first, we treat the theoretical underpinnings of this regulatory desire on the part of LDC governments and the claim by some of their spokesmen in international forums that developing countries are being "overcharged" for technology received.

If technology is seen as freely transferable information, akin to a public good, then to maximize global welfare, the noted economist Harry Johnson wrote, "optimality requires that technical knowledge be made available to all potential users without charge."[24] From this theoretical perspective, (1) the cost of transferring technology is zero, or at most, small; (2) any price charged to the technology receiver in excess of this small transfer (or variable) cost is a "monopoly rent" and therefore sub-optimal for global welfare; and (3) the multinational companies are able to do this because of imperfections in the "technology market," such as the patent systems (see S. Lall), internalization of firm-specific information (see Dunning), and the ignorance and weak bargaining position of LDCs.[25] The last point is used by LDC governments to assert in international forums that developing nations are being overcharged for technology, and that justifies regulatory intervention in the technology importation process to improve the terms of purchase.[26]

Recent evidence shows that these perspectives do not all correspond with the facts. Not that such imperfections do not exist. But observers such as Agmon and Hirsch, S. Magee, and others are increasingly coming around to the view that the imperfections in the international technology market are not nearly as serious as the lack of sufficient competition in the national market for the final product in protectionist countries, which produces "rents" for the local firm in the first place.[27] The local licensee or joint venture partner then shares this rent with the foreign technology supplier, a situation akin to a bilateral monopoly.

What empirical evidence do we have on these questions? There is not much. My studies and those by W. Davidson and D. McFetridge provide the first data in examining the above hypotheses.[28] Examining licensor revenues and costs on a sample of over 100 arm's-length agreements, my earlier study presented figures for total revenues received over each agreement life, and what it costs the supplier firm to transfer the technology.[29] These are shown in Table 66. The figures are for totals over each agreement life. Returns include royalties, lump-sum fees, technical fees, net margins and commissions on goods supplied or received, and payment in equity of the licensee, if any. Transfer costs refer only to the direct cost of executing the agreement's obligations, such as cost of technical, managerial and legal personnel, testing, building models, and including travel and other associated overhead. Not included were the research and development costs of the transferred technology or the "opportunity costs" of the licensor in partially or fully vacating the market in favor of the licensee over the duration of the agreement.

Table 66

Means of Licensor Returns, Transfer Costs and the Ratio of Returns over Transfer Costs, from a Sample of 102 Licensing Agreements between U.S. Licensors and Independent Licensees
(Dollars Thousands)

Product Type	Industrialized Market Economies		COMECON and Socialist Countries		Developing Nations	
Consumer goods (not elsewhere stated)	778 76 702	(11.06)	--		1,432 289 1,143	(5.95)
Industrial equipment (not elsewhere stated)	5,188 358 4,830	(42.32)	5,520 750 4,770	(7.36)	12,210 564 11,646	(8.19)
Intermediate industrial components and processes (not elsewhere stated)	4,468 487 4,281	(50.34)	1,800 375 1,425	(8.94)	1,377 221 1,156	(12.59)
Chemicals	2,340 97 2,243	(46.06)	605 124 481	(19.14)	1,067 54 1,013	(13.50)
Pharmaceuticals	6,250 109 6,141	(64.04)	--		450 40 410	(11.25)
Other	94 23 71	(4.08)	--		--	

Notes: Product types are United Nations' Broad Economic Categories.

Cell entries are:

Mean returns
Mean costs
Mean Margin

$(\text{Mean of the ratio multiple}) = \sum_{i=1}^{n} \frac{R_i/C_i}{n}$

Mean of the ratio multiple does not equal (Mean returns)/(Mean costs), since

$$\sum_{i=1}^{n} \frac{R_i/C_i}{n} \neq \frac{\sum_{i=1}^{n} R_i/n}{\sum_{i=1}^{n} C_i/n}$$

where R_i and C_i are totals for returns and transfer costs for the i th agreement over its life.

Source: F. Contractor, _International Technology Licensing: Compensation Costs, and Negotiation_ (Lexington, Mass.: D.C. Heath & Co., 1981)

It is clear that transfer costs are by no means negligible. However, revenues are a very large multiple of transfer costs. There are three aspects of this evidence that pertain to the issue of the terms of importation into LDCs. First, in every industry segment, the value of this multiple is lower in developing nations. *Prima facie* this does not support the contention that LDCs are charged more because of their weaker bargaining position. (A caveat is in order, however; as the study indicated, LDCs appear to be getting more mature and less patented technologies, which may explain the lower value of the ratio.) Second, the ratio or multiple of returns over transfer costs may well be strikingly high, but this is of little interest to the licensor firm, as compared with the difference or margin between the two, which contributes toward R&D and central overheads. This margin, at least in this sample, is modest in the LDC category (except for industrial equipment) when one considers that the figures are over the entire agreement life in each case. Third, even if an ample margin exists, this in itself would not justify the demand of some LDC spokesmen that technologies be sold to them at the transfer cost per agreement, if one holds the Schumpeterian view that the margins are a contribution to central company overheads, such as ongoing research and development, as opposed to the Ricardian conception of such margins as (fortuitous) rents.[30] Whether the Ricardian or Schumpeterian perspective is more appropriate for technology transfer to developing countries is a question elaborated on later.

For the sample as a whole, there were, on average, four alternate suppliers for a technology globally. A caveat is in order here: these data were obtained from the supplier companies' impressions of other companies their licensees could have turned to, in order to get the technology. It is quite likely that LDC governments and firms may not be aware of all the alternatives. Nevertheless, the evidence does show that, with a sufficient search, alternates may be found in the great majority of cases. We are far from a situation of there being an international monopoly on technology—this occurred in only 27 percent of cases in the sample.

Regulatory measures to control payments by bureaucratic fiat proliferated in the early 1970s. These involve restrictions on the convertability of dividends and, more explicitly, in licensing agreements, ceilings on royalty rates, or on *per diem* fees for technicians, etc. Practically speaking, the intent of the government is unenforceable if the local firm, even as an independent licensee, chooses to collude with the foreign technology supplier. Besides royalties and dividends, we saw that there are other commonly used forms of compensation, such as technical fees, commissions on goods and equipment, or margins on components, lump-sum fees, and grantbacks of technical information, which can be used to compensate the technology supplier. Earlier, we discussed two examples of how government rules can and are readily circumvented in conjunction with the numerical exercise in Table 63. The prospective licensor firm had, in each instance, a target present value of receipts expected over the agreement life, a target that it can achieve with higher up front fees if royalty rates are circumscribed. We saw that often the net result of such government intervention is to impose an additional financial burden on the recipient enterprise in the early years when it can least afford it. Even if the entire payment to the licensor is capitalized (in one lump sum) and financed by a bank, this creates a fixed charge. Royalties, on the other hand, are a variable cost, which is not only more convenient to manage financially (since royalties are paid out of earnings as and when accrued), but in a sense they also commit the technology licensor to the local firm's continuing viability. By contrast, in a one-payment contract there is no ongoing obligation or commitment, as we also saw in the Eastern European example above. We can say much the same sort of thing for prescribed ceilings on the duration of agreements and scheduled equity phase-out arrangements.

If one accepts the idea that, with limited competition in sheltered LDC markets, prospective technology buyers will be eager for foreign association and pass on the costs, in turn, to the willing local product purchasers, then one understands why government intervention is considered a nuisance in many LDCs by the very firms such rules are meant to assist. Wisely, of late, bureaucracies are treating their rules, such as prescribed ceilings on royalty rates and agreement duration, as mere points of departure in negotiations. For example, Circular No. 393 of the Central Bank of the Philippines quickly follows its rule, "The royalty/ rental . . . shall not exceed five (5) percent . . . etc.," with a qualifier, "however, in meritorious cases. . . . "

There appears to be no short-cut or across-the-board rules that can be effective in this regard. If the Japanese example teaches anything, it is the very detailed case-by-case approach used by MITI, assessing alternative international sources carefully from a good knowledge of the industry on the part of the bureaucrat and in close consultation with the prospective licensee or joint-venture partner.

THE CONTENT OF THE TECHNOLOGY TRANSFER "PACKAGE"

It is not the intention here to enumerate the various elements that can comprise a technology transfer. Conceptually speaking, we can place them into four categories: (1) information in formulae, specifications, designs, models, and descriptions; (2) services such as testing, instruction, and even plant erection; (3) rights such as territorial prerogatives for use of patents and trademarks or guaranteed buy back of production; and (4) restraints such as prohibited sales territories and purchase or sale through designated agents only.

Regulatory intervention in this regard has two broad aims. First, it seeks to inhibit the transfer of components of the package deemed by the regulators to be unnecessary, such as trademarks. Second, it seeks to enlarge the production and sales of the local firm and local economy by disallowing restraints on exports, for example, or by mandating local content minimums.

Let us first examine the case of foreign trademarks. In developing countries, a foreign brand name often, if not always, increases the marketability of the product over its competition and can be said to increase the economic "rent" accruing to the local enterprise, which, accordingly, craves the trademark right. For example, in 1971 a count of items appearing in 399 licensing agreements in Chile showed trademarks heading the list with 78 percent occurrence, where, by comparison, transfer of rights to patented processes and inventions occurred in 49 percent and 32 percent, respectively. (See note 30.) We saw in Chapter 6 that this was probably an extreme case. Nevertheless, foreign trademarks are scrutinized in some LDCs. Here, the actions of governments, when foreign brand names are inhibited, as notably in Mexico, are taken in the name of protecting consumers. But there are benefits and costs. The consumer benefits from an identification of quality and feature standardization. The trademark owner benefits from goodwill or quasi rent; but this is said to be a social cost to the extent that the foreignness of the trademark inhibits local competition. There is an additional cost if the quasi rent so obtained is expatriated to the foreign trademark owner, rather than at least retained in the nation. S. Patel and D. Chudnovsky make a reasonable theoretical case that, in some LDCs, the costs outweigh the benefits.[31] The matter needs empirical investigation. There is practically no analysis of empirical data; nor have international firms proven even the basic contention that the quality of the product is materially diminished if a local brand name is substituted for the international one, *ceteris paribus*. Of course, a somewhat more persuasive argument companies may make is that, without the privilege of using their well-known brand name, the revenues available from that market would be uninteresting and, therefore, technology accompanying the trademark that is needed by the nation would not be transferred. As Lall puts it,

We find that even very low technology industries go multinational if they can market their products effectively, while in the absence of product differentiation, a high technology industry may well prefer to stay in its home country.[32]

The experience of Mexico since 1973 would appear to disprove this contention; however, there is no concrete evidence.

In our next example involving regulatory measures to increase local value added, we return to the theme that there is no substitute for a case-by-case scrutiny of each proposal's costs and benefits—that across-the-board rules and guidelines will not always work. Let us consider an illustration from the registration of licensing agreements. A number of countries disallow using as royalty basis the imported component of licensee sales volume; royalty may be paid only on finished value less imported parts. A UNIDO study gives the rationale: "This method of calculating royalty is likely to induce the licensor to provide technology for making components."[33] It is easy to show that this is true only under certain conditions. Let us disaggregate the total finished value of the licensee's production, F, into four parts:

$$F = V + B + I_L + IO$$

where V is value added by licensee, B is local ancillary purchases, I_L and I_0 are components imported from the licensor and from general sources, respectively.

The licensor's revenue is

$$R = (F - I_L - I_0) r + I_L m$$
$$= (V + B) r + I_L m$$

where r is the royalty rate and m the rate of margin on components supplied.

From the licensor's perspective, if $m > r$, there is no incentive to provide the licensee technology for making components locally. Even if $m < r$ (which is less likely than the reverse), the licensor still has no incentive in providing technology to substitute V for B.[34] The only unconditionally attractive substitution for the licensor is to reduce I_0.

One might argue that, in any event, lowering the royalty basis can reduce royalty payment. True, but here again, the licensor has other negotiations variables, such as the royalty rate, or duration of the agreement, which can be raised to bring present value of agreement revenues up to target, as we saw in the additional examples following Table 65.

We can generalize this to other restraints, on exports of the local enterprise, for example, or model changes at the behest of the foreign firm. In general, it turns out that LDC joint venture partners or licensees are far less concerned about this than the flat prohibition of these practices in the books of some governments would suggest. Governments flatly prohibiting such restrictive clauses may even put the prospective local licensee at a disadvantage. This is because the technology seller may then demand a higher price, even if such restraints are *de facto* not relevant in many instances. For instance, the actual propensity of independent exporting by LDC licensees is low. Insistence on a larger territorial purview in the agreement may merely increase the price of the technology acquired without materially improving the benefits to the nation from the presumed ability to export.

Wisely, several LDC governments are *de facto* shying away from their earlier flat prohibition of such restraints to an assessment of the costs of such "restrictive practices" versus the benefits of the technology transferred.

EFFECTIVE LONG-TERM POLICIES: DIFFICULTIES IN IMPLEMENTING THEM

We have so far taken a partially iconoclastic view of governmental regulation. This does not suggest that such intervention is entirely futile or unwarranted. This section examines some longer-term policy measures that can be more effective from the point of view of the recipient government.

On theoretical and practical grounds, there are several measures that may eventually lower a country's cost for imported technology, although not in all industries. We began by describing technology transfer as often akin to a bilateral monopoly. By conveying proprietary information, training, and rights to patents or trademarks, i.e., its firm-specific technical assets, an international company shares its "monopolistic" power with the local firm, be it on an equity and/or licensing basis.[35] The local enterprise, armed with this special product or process, will typically command an advantage or economic rent in its product market in turn. This is true particularly when competition from other firms is weak. Profits are shared, in turn, with the international technology supplier by a negotiated arrangement that we detailed in the last chapter.

For the purpose of the following discussion, another model from economics theory is also relevant, that describing the technology seller as a "discriminating monopolist," segmenting buyers from each other by assigning territories, preferably keeping each other ignorant of prices paid for the same technology and charging each what the "traffic will bear." There is not much comprehensive evidence on the actual behavior of companies on this score, except for the observation that firms will try to maximize profit in each country or territory. My earlier study indicated that, for the same technology licensed globally, it is not until the number of licensees exceeds thirty that there is a convergence in price, and that this was true only for certain mature or peripheral processes such as galvanizing of steel or aluminum cans, which did not involve high technology.[36]

The implication of this economics model for government policy is clear: to foster an association between the purchasers of technology. Translating this into specific policy and action is regrettably difficult, and certain regulations can have curious consequences. Following the idea that the discriminating monopolist maximizes total income by segmenting buyers from each other, several LDCs and Socialist-bloc nations prohibit more than one joint venture or license for a particular technology in their country.[37] A priori, there is no reason to believe that this will necessarily improve product consumers' welfare or lower the country's total payment for the technology. Under certain market conditions, one can even make a case that multiple licensing in a nation, increasing competition among producers, would not only lower the market price for the product and thereby the payment made by each licensee, but also the aggregate cost of importing the technology. Enacting (by legislation) only one licensee or joint venture that will import a technology is often tantamount to creating a monopoly. There is no assurance that this firm, so blessed, will not maximize its profits upon hapless local consumers (a familiar story in protectionist LDCs) and not share the technology with other national firms—unless of course it is a government organization or unless such legislation includes a provision for compulsory sub-licensing.

Another policy measure has been a nascent association between developing nations for exchange of technical information, sources of technology, terms of importation, etc., under U.N. auspices.[38] There is no doubt a tremendous value, at least for the smaller or least-industrialized LDCs, in the mere exchange of information. In a large majority of cases, there are likely to be two or more international suppliers for a particular technology, and the simple policy of requiring prospective joint venture partners or licensees to obtain competing proposals does much to improve the final terms obtained from one. Beyond this, however, it is difficult to see how or why a "technological information bank" would work. For one thing, many studies have disabused the naive idea that technology transfer is an act of transferring documentation. The point is, many of the activities involved are person to person and involve long-term learning of technical, managerial, and sometimes marketing skills as well.[39] For another thing, it assumes too much altruism on the part of companies to expect them to share their technologies without precisely the same revenue-maximizing behavior of the technology supplier firms.

Of course, to the extent that technologies in some industries (e.g., pharma-ceuticals, chemicals) are not firm specific or patented and involve documented process specifications or formulae that can be easily assimilated and used suc-cessfully by an LDC firm on its own, the idea of a data bank has merits for the technology buyers. Unfortunately, there is no comprehensive empirical evidence. In Chapter 6 we saw some evidence that the above conditions apply more to the chemicals and pharmaceutical industries than to others. The crucial issue is the extent to which the above two conditions apply in general to all industry types. The answer seems to be "not to a great extent."

There is, therefore, no escaping the necessity, in most nations, of importing technology from corporations where it is held as a proprietary asset. Even where some aspects of a technology are patented, as we saw in Chapter 6, the more crucial elements of production and commercial success are usually not revealed. They may not even be put on paper but merely reside in the collective organi-zational memory.

Thus, if technology is proprietary and unique, the basic conclusion for reg-ulation is that across-the-board rules are often sub-optimal. In some cases, the governmental constraints will be above the privately negotiated terms and there-fore of no relevance. In other cases, regulatory constraints may only serve to increase the overall cost of technology acquisition. In yet other cases, the tech-nology seller may find the compensation that is payable is inadequate, and no transfer would take place. It is easy to point to the example of Japan's Ministry for International Trade and Industry, where an army of highly sophisticated bureaucrats, intimate with their industry specialities and knowing their country's needs, are said to have done an outstanding job. For example Abegglen claims that

Between 1950 and 1980, the Japanese essentially acquired all of the technology in the world that they considered worth having for a small fraction of the current annual U.S. expenditure in research and development.[40]

Whatever the merits of this assertion, the Japanese regulatory apparatus cannot be replicated elsewhere easily and certainly not in developing countries, most of which lack the qualified personnel in government, knowledgeable enough in the details of each technology, alternative global sources, local demand conditions, etc., to be able to make a case-by-case analysis of each proposal.

Lacking this capability, many nations have been forced to enact uniform guidelines and rules as administrative artifacts that unfortunately tend to become embedded in stone in some countries. Wiser governments these days tend to view their rules more as bargaining chips, or as points of departure, in negotiating with foreign technology sellers.

GOVERNMENT SCRUTINY IN SUPPLIER COUNTRIES: IMPLICATIONS FOR THE FUTURE

Since there are less than five net technology-exporting countries in the (non-Communist) world, the main focus of regulation has been on the import side. On the export of technology, the most visible apparatus has been COCOM (acronym for Coordinating Committee), an intergovernmental group of NATO countries and Japan that monitors and regulates exports and technology transfer to the Soviet-bloc and other Communist countries.[41] The objective is to screen out specific equipment and technologies of a military and strategic nature such as computers, numerically controlled machining equipment, aircraft technology, etc., so as to delay their development in Communist nations. Delay is probably a far more realistic objective than stopping their development altogether. For one thing, there is a sophisticated internal capability in many of those countries. Second, the lessons of history show it is impossible to bottle up technology indefinitely.[42] Third, there are an increasing number of international sources of technology both within and outside NATO. (Sometimes, government controls in the U.S. may simply mean that the American firm loses business to a foreign competitor, as described in case studies by G. Bertsch, R. Cupitt, J. McIntyre, and B. Robinson.[43]

In the long run, however, there are perhaps more important issues that policymakers should be concerned with. There have been moves in recent years to make the applicability of international patents more restricted (e.g., see Z. Mijatovic for Yugoslavia's 1981 law).[44] Arguments for whittling away at some of the current practices under the patent convention are summarized by Lall.[45] They return in the ultimate analysis to the desire of technology-importing countries to receive technology at its variable cost, that is to say, at the cost to the supplier firm to transfer the technology (as opposed to the cost of generating the technology in the first place).

Buyers of technology would prefer not to accept the Schumpeterian argument that the excess of revenues over transfer costs (see Table 65) is a necessary contribution to central overheads and R&D at the multinational firm headquarters. Some in the LDCs have rejected this argument on the specific grounds that developing nations, after all, do not figure in either the planning for R&D expenditure decisions or the amortization of R&D expenses. Indeed, there is some evidence that LDCs do not figure in the market purview for projected returns on planned R&D in many companies. The question boils down to this: In a hypothetical world order, if many technology recipients pay at best a little over, or equal to, the variable or transfer cost of technology, what effect would that have on the continued generation of new technologies?

It is this issue that ought to engage the attention of policymakers in the advanced industrial nations, for, whichever way it is addressed, there are potentially serious implications for technology producing firms. For if we answer "yes," lower returns from abroad will constrain future R&D in the industrial countries. The implications are obvious. On the other hand, if we answer "no," then the rate of technological change in the industrial nations is not much affected. However, developing and socialist nations with better information, knowledge of alternative supply sources for technologies, and sharpened bureaucratic skills may not only succeed in lowering repatriated cash flows (which under the scenario is not of great current import) but may increase the degree of local control. Today, these nations do not contribute more than a quarter to a third of overseas profit for U.S. companies. But some among today's developing nations will advance rapidly to the developed affluent market status.[46] Moreover, even among the already developed nation category, there has been a rise in economic nationalism. For international business, this may force a move away from corporate policies which refused, like an IBM, to have any significant arm's-length licensing and toward a greater willingness to share technology with other firms on a contractual basis.

NOTES

1. For a review of this subject see Bertsch, G.; Cupitt, R.; McIntyre, J.; and Robinson, B., "Decision Dynamics of Technology Transfer to the USSR," *Technology in Society*, Vol. 3, 1981, pp. 409–422.

2. Boretsky, M., "Trends in U.S. Technology: A Political Economist's View," in Kuehn, T., and Porter, A. (eds.), *Science, Technology and National Policy* (Ithaca, N.Y.: Cornell University Press, 1981), pp. 161–188. Abegglen, J., and Hout, T., "Facing Up to the Trade Gap with Japan," *Foreign Affairs*, Fall 1978, pp. 146–168.

3. See United Nations (Center on Transnational Corporations), *Transnational Corporations in World Development: A Re-examination* (New York: United Nations, 1978) and updates.

4. See National Science Board, *Science Indicators, 1982* (Washington, D.C.: U.S. Government Printing Office, 1983), Appendix Tables 1-18, 1-1 to 1-6, and 1-12 to 1-14.

5. Ibid., p. 203.

6. The broader question of the "appropriateness" of the imported technology to the developmental objectives of the country is not treated here, although it is important. This book has a firm-level focus.

7. There have been some highly stylized and abstract macro-economic models, however, which may interest the theoretical economist. See, for instance, Brunner, K., and

Meltzer, A., *Optimal Policies, Control Theory and Technology Exports* (New York: North Holland, 1977). Findlay, R., "Some Aspects of Technology Transfer and Direct Foreign Investment," *American Economic Review,* May 1978, pp. 275–279. Krugman, P., "A Model of Innovation, Technology Transfer and the World Distribution of Income," *Journal of Political Economy,* April 1979, pp. 253–266.

8. Agmon, T., and Hirsch, S., "Multinational Corporations and the Developing Economics: Potential Gains in a World of Imperfect Markets and Uncertainty," *Oxford Bulletin of Economics and Statistics,* Vol. 41, 1971, pp. 333–344. The quote is from page 341.

9. Of course such an analysis helps the licensee in the bargaining process.

10. Lightman, J., "Compensation Patterns in U.S. Foreign Licensing," *IDEA*, Spring 1970, pp. 1–26.

11. Throughout the discussion, it is assumed that for the foreign firm, foreign tax credit is usable, $t_E < t_F$. One can introduce tariffs, foreign exchange risk, uncertainty, etc. However, the purpose here is to show that even under the simplest assumptions, there is a divergence of objectives between the parties.

12. Little, I.; Skitovski, T.; and Scott, M., *Industry and Commerce in Some Developing Countries: A Comparative Study* (Oxford, England: Oxford University Press, 1970).

13. "Consumers' surplus" is defined as the benefit (of a lower price) derived by all classes of buyers who would have been willing or forced to pay more than the asking price. For our calculation, we quantify it as $(a - P)Q / 2$ the area bounded by the demand curve, the vertical axis, and the price line $P =$ asking price. Readers unfamiliar with this concept may consult any economics text.

14. Mytelka, L., "Licensing and Technology Dependence in the Andean Group," *World Development*, June 1978, pp. 447–459; Sagasti, F., "National Science and Technology Policies for Development: A Comparative Analysis," in Ramesh, J., and Weiss, C. (eds.), *Mobilizing Technology for World Development* (New York: Praeger, 1979), pp. 162–173; Balasubramanyam, V., *International Transfer of Technology to India* (New York: Praeger, 1973).

15. Newfarmer, R., *The International Market Power of Transnational Corporations* (New York: UNCTAD, 1978).

16. Buckley, P., and Casson, M., *The Future of the Multinational Enterprise* (New York: Holmes & Meier, 1976); Dunning, J., "Non-equity Forms of Foreign Economic Involvement and the Theory of International Production," Working Paper, University of Reading, 1982; Williamson, O., *Markets and Hierarchies: Analysis and Antitrust Implications* (New York: Free Press, 1975); Coase, R., "The Nature of the Firm," *Economica*, November 1937, pp. 386–405; Schumpeter, J., *Capitalism, Socialism and Democracy* (New York: Harper & Bros., 1942).

17. Business International, *Doing Business with Eastern Europe* (Geneva: Business International Corp., 1972).

18. Teece, D., *The Multinational Corporation and the Resource Cost of International Technology Transfer* (Cambridge, Mass.: Ballinger, 1977); Contractor, F., *International Technology Licensing: Compensation, Costs and Negotiation* (Lexington, Mass.: D. C. Heath & Co., 1981).

19. Mytelka, "Licensing and Technology Dependence in the Andean Group"; Balasubramanyam. *International Transfer of Technology to India.*

20. Contractor, F., "The Composition of Licensing Fees and Arrangements as a Function of Economic Development of Technology Recipient Nations," *Journal of International Business Studies*, Winter 1980, pp. 47–62.

21. Baranson, J., *North-South Technology Transfer: Financing and Institution Building* (Mt. Airy, Md.: Lomond, 1981); Dunning, J., "Towards an Eclectic Theory of International Production: Some Empirical Tests," *Journal of International Business Studies*, Spring 1980, pp. 9–31.

22. Oman, C., "Changing International Investment Strategies: The New Forms of Investment in Developing Countries," Working Paper no. 7, OECD Development Center, Paris, 1980.

23. The objective here is not to catalogue all the possible rules and forms of direct government intervention—we have that in several U.N. and other publications. Rather, we wish to assess the effectiveness and implications of the overall attempt.

24. Johnson, H., "The Efficiency and Welfare Implications of the International Corporation," in Kindleberger, C. (ed.), *International Corporations* (Cambridge, Mass.: MIT Press, 1970), pp. 35–56.

25. Lall, S., "The Patent System and the Transfer of Technology to Less-Developed Countries," *Journal of World Trade Law*, January 1976, pp. 1–15; Dunning, "Nonequity Forms of Foreign Economic Involvement."

26. See, for instance, UNIDO, *Guidelines for Evaluation of Transfer of Technology Agreements* (New York: United Nations, 1977, DTTS Series no. 12); UNIDO, *The Technological Self-reliance of Developing Countries: Towards Operational Strategies* (Vienna: UNIDO, 1979, ICIS. 133).

27. Agmon and Hirsch, "Multinational Corporations and the Developing Economics"; Magee, S., "Technology and the Appropriability Theory of the Multinational Corporation," in Bhagvati, J. (ed.), *The New International Economic Order: The North-South Debate* (Cambridge, Mass.: MIT Press, 1977), pp. 317–340.

28. Davidson, W., and McFetridge, D., "International Technology Transactions and the Theory of the Firm," *Journal of Industrial Economics*, March 1984, pp. 253–264.

29. Arm's-length, because otherwise the payment for the technology would be heavily influenced by the international strategy and global tax minimization policies of the technology supplier. The cutoff used was "less than a 25 percent equity stake in the licensee," although influence over a licensee can admittedly be exerted even with no equity participation. For further details see Contractor, *International Technology Licensing*.

30. UNCTAD, *Major Issues in the Transfer of Technology to Developing Countries: A Case Study of Chile* (New York: United Nations, 1974).

31. Patel, S., "Trademarks and the Third World," *World Development* Vol. 7 (7), 1979, pp. 653–662; Chudnovsky, D., "Foreign Trademarks in Developing Countries," *World Development* Vol. 7 (7), 1979, pp. 663–682.

32. Lall, "The Patent System and the Transfer of Technology to Less-Developed Countries."

33. UNIDO, *Guidelines for Evaluation of Transfer of Technology Agreements*, p. 44.

34. Since royalty rates in international agreements average approximately 4 to 5 percent, one can guess that $m > r$ in most cases—particularly if the supplier uses marginal costing for the components.

35. Economists use the term "monopolistic" to describe a situation where the selling firm has some influence on the market. It does not literally mean a monopoly.

36. Contractor, *International Technology Licensing*.

37. For example, see the new Yugoslavia law of June 9, 1981 summarized in Mijatovic, Z., "New Legislation in Yugoslavia," *Les Nouvelles: Journal of the Licensing Executives Society*, December 1981, pp. 331–332.

38. UNIDO, *Industrial and Technological Information Bank* (New York: United Nations, 1980, GEN / ID/ B 241).

39. For examples and detailed cases illustrating this see Baranson, *North-South Technology Transfer*.

40. Abegglen, J., "U.S.-Japanese Technological Exchange in Perspective, 1946–1981," in Uehara, C. (ed.), *Technological Exchange: The U.S.-Japanese Experience* (New York: University Press, 1982), p. 3.

41. For an excellent overview of this subject, see McIntyre, J., and Cupitt, R., "East-West Strategic Trade Control: Crumbling Consensus?" *Survey: A Journal of East–West Studies*, Spring 1980, pp. 81–108.

42. For an example, see Jeremy, D., "Damming the Flood: British Government Efforts to Check the Outflow of Technicians and Machinery 1780–1843," *Business History Review*, Spring 1977, pp. 1–34.

43. Bertsch, et al., "Decision Dynamics of Technology Transfer to the U.S.S.R."

44. Mijatovic, "New Legislation in Yugoslavia."

45. Lall, "The Patent System and the Transfer of Technology."

46. It is safe to say that only "some" LDCs will rapidly become affluent developed markets, though most will continue to have thriving enclaves or pockets, as they do today. After the First World War, some proclaimed Argentina as poised to join the ranks of major industrial powers. Most failed on the other hand to anticipate the speed of development, and technical change, after the Second World War in Japan and other Far-Eastern nations.

Bibliography

Abegglen, J., "U.S.-Japanese Technological Exchange in Perspective, 1946–1981," in
   Uehara, C. (ed.), *Technological Exchange: The U.S.-Japanese Experience* (New
   York: University Press, 1982).

Abegglen, J., and Hout, T., "Facing Up to the Trade Gap with Japan," *Foreign Affairs*,
   Fall 1978, pp. 146–168.

Agmon, T., and Hirsch, S., "Multinational Corporations and the Developing Economics:
   Potential Gains in a World of Imperfect Markets and Uncertainty," *Oxford Bulletin
   of Economics and Statistics*, Vol. 41, 1971, pp. 333–344.

Aharoni, Y., *The Foreign Investment Decision Process* (Boston: Harvard University
   Press, 1966).

Aliber, R. Z., "A Theory of Direct Foreign Investment," in Kindleberger, C. P. (ed.),
   The International Corporation (Cambridge, Mass.: MIT Press, 1970).

Arrow, K., "Economic Welfare and the Allocation of Resources for Invention," in
   National Bureau of Economic Research, *The Rate and Direction of Inventive
   Activity: Economic and Social Factors* (Princeton, N.J.: Princeton University
   Press, 1962), pp. 609–626.

Balasubramanyam, V., *International Transfer of Technology to India* (New York: Praeger, 1973).

Baldwin, R., "Determinants of Trade and Foreign Investment: Further Evidence," *Review
   of Economics and Statistics,* Vol. 61, 1979, pp. 40–48.

Baranson, J., *North-South Technology Transfer: Financing and Institution Building* (Mt.
   Airy, Md.: Lomond, 1981).

————, *Technology and the Multinationals* (Lexington, Mass.: Lexington Books, 1978).

Berg, N., "Strategic Planning in Conglomerate Companies," *Harvard Business Review*,
   May-June 1965, pp. 79–91.

————, "What's Different about Conglomerate Management?" *Harvard Business Review*, November-December 1969, pp. 112–120.

Bergsten, C.; Horst, T.; and Moran, T., *American Multinationals and American Interests*
   (Washington, D.C.: Brookings Institution, 1978).

Bertsch, G.; Cupitt, R.; McIntyre, J.; and Robinson, B., "Decision Dynamics of Technology Transfer to the USSR," *Technology in Society*, Vol. 3, 1981, pp. 409–422.

Berweger, G., and Hoby, J., "Wirtschaftspolitik Gegenuber Auslandscapital," *Bulletin of the Sociological Institute of the University of Zurich*, no. 35, 1978, pp. 20–30.

Billerbeck, K., and Yasugi, Y., *Private Direct Foreign Investment in Developing Countries*, World Bank Staff Working Paper no. 348 (Washington, D.C.: World Bank, 1979).

Blau, P., "A Formal Theory of Differentiation in Organizations," *American Sociological Review*, April 1970, pp. 200–218.

Bleeke, J., and Rahl, J., "The Value of Territorial and Field-of-Use Restrictions in the International Licensing of Unpatented Knowhow: An Empirical Study," *Northwestern Journal of International Law and Business*, Fall 1979, pp. 450–483.

Bloxam, G., *Licensing Rights in Technology: A Legal Guide to Managers in Negotiation* (London: Gower Press, 1972).

Boretsky, M., "Trends in U.S. Technology: A Political Economist's View," in Kuehn, T., and Porter, A. (eds.), *Science, Technology and National Policy* (Ithaca, N.Y.: Cornell University Press, 1981), pp. 161–188.

Brunner, K., and Meltzer, A., *Optimal Policies, Control Theory and Technology Exports* (New York: North Holland, 1977).

Brunsvold, B., and Farabow, F., "The Impact of Antitrust Laws on International Licensing," *Licensing Law and Business Report*, October 1978, pp. 41–52.

Buckley, P., and Casson, M., *The Future of the Multinational Enterprise* (New York: Holmes & Meier, 1976).

Buckley, P., and Davies, H., "The Place of Licensing in the Theory and Practice of Foreign Operations," Discussion Paper no. 47, University of Reading, November 1979.

Business International, *Doing Business with Eastern Europe* (Geneva: Business International Corp., 1972).

———, *International Licensing: Opportunities and Challenges in World-Wide Technology Management* (New York: Business International Corp., 1977).

———*Managing and Evaluating Country Risk* (New York: Business International Corp., 1981).

Calder, K., "Technology Transfers, Promise or Peril?" in *U.S.-Japan Relations in the 1980's: Towards Burden Sharing*, 1981-82 Annual Report of the Program on U.S.-Japan Relations, Center for International Affairs, Harvard University, pp. 49–58.

Casson, M., *Alternatives to the Multinational Enterprise* (New York: Holmes & Meier, 1979).

———, "Introduction: The Conceptual Framework," in Casson, M. (ed.), *The Growth of International Business* (forthcoming), Chapter 1.

Caves, R., "International Corporations: The Industrial Economics of Foreign Investment," *Economica*, February 1971, pp. 1–27.

Caves, R.; Crookell, H.; and Killing, J., "The Imperfect Market for Technology Licenses," *Oxford Bulletin of Economics and Statistics*, August 1983, pp. 249–267.

Chandler, A., and Daems, H., "The United States: Seedbed of Managerial Capitalism," in Chandler, A., and Daems, H. (eds.), *Managerial Hierarchies* (Cambridge, Mass.: Harvard University Press, 1980), Chapter 1.

Child, J., "Predicting and Understanding Organization Structure," *Administrative Science Quarterly*, Vol. 18 (2), 1973, pp. 168–185.

Chudnovsky, D., "Foreign Trademarks in Developing Countries," *World Development*, Vol. 7 (7), 1979, pp. 663–682.

Coase, R., "The Nature of the Firm," *Economica*, November 1937, pp. 386–405.

Conrads, R., "Strategic Partnering: A New Formula to Crack Markets in the '80s," *Electronic Business*, March 1983.

Contractor, F., "The Composition of Licensing Fees and Arrangements as a Function of Economic Development of Technology Recipient Nations," *Journal of International Business Studies*, Winter 1980, pp. 47–62.

———, *International Technology Licensing: Compensation, Costs and Negotiation* (Lexington, Mass.: D. C. Heath & Co., 1981).

———, "The 'Profitability' of Technology Licensing by U.S. Multinationals: A Framework for Analysis and an Empirical Study," *Journal of International Business Studies*, Fall 1980, pp. 40–63.

———, "The Role of Licensing in International Strategy," Columbia *Journal of World Business*, Winter 1981, pp. 73–81.

Davidson, W., "Location of Foreign Direct Investment Activity: Country Characteristics and Experience Effects," *Journal of International Business Studies*, Fall 1980, pp. 9–22.

Davidson, W., and McFetridge, D., "International Technology Transactions and the Theory of the Firm," *The Journal of Industrial Economics*, March 1984, pp. 253–264.

Davies, H., "Technology Transfer through Commercial Transactions," *Journal of Industrial Economics*, December 1977, pp. 161–191.

Delgado, J., "Comment on Mexico's Amended Law," *Les Nouvelles: Journal of the Licensing Executives Society*, September 1982, pp. 202–203.

Dunning, J., "Alternative Channels and Modes of International Resource Transmission," a paper presented at the NSF Conference on Technology Transfer Control Systems in Philadelphia, February 1979.

———, "Non-equity Forms of Foreign Economic Involvement and the Theory of International Production," Working Paper, University of Reading, 1982.

———, "Towards an Eclectic Theory of International Production: Some Empirical Tests," *Journal of International Business Studies*, Spring 1980, pp. 9–31.

Findlay, R., "Some Aspects of Technology Transfer and Direct Foreign Investment," *American Economic Review*, May 1978, pp. 275–279.

Finnegan, M., and McCarthy, R., "U.S. Tax Considerations in International Technology Transfers," *Licensing Law and Business Report*, April 1979, pp. 101–112, and May 1979, pp. 113–119.

Ford, D., and Ryan, C., "Taking Technology to Market," *Harvard Business Review*, March-April 1981, pp. 117–126.

French, W., and Henning, D., "The Authority-Influence Role of the Functional Specialist in Management," *Academy of Management Journal*, September 1966, pp. 187–203.

Goodnow, J., and Hansz, J., "Environmental Determinants of Overseas Market Entry Strategies," *Journal of International Business Studies*, Spring 1972, pp. 33–50.

Green, R., and Cunningham, W., "The Determinants of U.S. Foreign Investment: An Empirical Examination," *Management International Review*, Vol. 15 (2–3), 1975, pp. 113–120.

Hayden, E., *Technology Transfer to East Europe: U.S. Corporate Experience* (New York: Praeger, 1976).

Hull, C., et al., *Statistical Package for the Social Sciences* (Chicago: SPSS Inc., 1981).

Hymer, S., "The International Operations of National Firms: A Study of Direct Investment," Ph.D. dissertation, Massachusetts Institute of Technology, 1960.

Jeremy, D., "Damming the Flood: British Government Efforts to Check the Outflow of Technicians and Machinery, 1780–1843," *Business History Review*, Spring 1977, pp. 1–34.

Johanson, J., and Vahlne, J., "The Internationalization Process of the Firm—A Model of Knowledge Development and Increasing Foreign Market Commitments," *Journal of International Business Studies*, Spring/Summer 1977, pp. 23–32.

Johnson, H., "The Efficiency and Welfare Implications of the International Corporation," in Kindleberger, C. (ed.), *International Corporations* (Cambridge, Mass.: MIT Press, 1970), pp. 35–56.

Khandwala, P., "Viable and Effective Organizational Designs of Firms," *Academy of Management Journal*, September 1973, pp. 481–495.

Killing, P., "Technology Acquisition: License Agreement or Joint Venture," *Columbia Journal of World Business*, Fall 1980, pp. 38–46.

Kobrin, S., "The Environmental Determinants of Foreign Direct Manufacturing Investment: An Ex-Post Empirical Analysis," *Journal of International Business Studies*, Fall 1976, pp. 29–42.

Kopits, G., "Intra-firm Royalties Crossing Frontiers and Transfer-Pricing Behavior," *The Economic Journal*, December 1976, pp. 791–803.

Krugman, P., "A Model of Innovation, Technology Transfer and the World Distribution of Income," *Journal of Political Economy*, April 1979, pp. 253–266.

Lall, S., "The International Allocation of Research Activity by U.S. Multinationals," *Oxford Bulletin of Economics and Statistics*, November 1979, pp. 313–331.

———,"The Patent System and the Transfer of Technology to Less-Developed Countries," *Journal of World Trade Law*, January 1976, pp. 1–15.

Leff, N., "Multinational Corporate Pricing Strategy in Developing Countries," *Journal of International Business Studies*, Fall 1975, pp. 55–63.

Lightman, J., "Compensation Patterns in U.S. Foreign Licensing," *IDEA*, Spring 1970, pp. 1–26.

Little, I.; Scitovski, T.; and Scott, M., *Industry and Commerce in Some Developing Countries: A Comparative Study* (Oxford, England: Oxford University Press, 1970).

Lovell, E., *Appraising Foreign Licensing Performance* (New York: Conference Board, 1969).

Lynn, L., "Technology Transfer to Japan: What We Know, What We Need to Know, and What We Know That May Not Be So," paper presented to the Social Science Research Council, Subcommittee on Science and Technology Indicators, New York, June 2–3, 1983.

McIntyre, J., and Cupitt, R., "East-West Strategic Trade Control: Crumbling Consensus?'' *Survey: A Journal of East-West Studies*, Spring 1980, pp. 81–108.

MacMillan, K., and Farmer, D., "Redefining the Boundaries of the Firm," *The Journal of Industrial Economics*, March 1979, pp. 277–285.

McNamee, B., "A Primer on Patent, Trademark and Knowhow Licensing," *MSU Business Topics*, Summer 1970, pp. 14–22.

Magee, S., "Technology and the Appropriability Theory of the Multinational Corporation," in Bhagwati, J. (ed.), *The New International Economic Order: The North-South Debate* (Cambridge, Mass.: MIT Press, 1977), pp. 317–340.

Mandros, P., "WIPO Conference on the Revision of the Paris Convention," *Les Nouvelles: Journal of the Licensing Executives Society,* December 1981, pp. 6–7.

Mexico, Government of, "Law on the Control and Registration of Transfer of Technology and the Use and Exploitation of Patents and Trademarks of December 29th, 1981," *Diario Oficial*, January 11, 1982.

Mijatovic, Z., "New Legislation in Yugoslavia," *Les Nouvelles: Journal of the Licensing Executives Society*, December 1981, pp. 331–332.

Mirus, R., "A Note on the Choice between Licensing and Direct Foreign Investment," *Journal of International Business Studies*, Spring 1980, pp. 86–91.

Mytelka, L., "Licensing and Technology Dependence in the Andean Group," *World Development*, June 1978, pp. 447–459.

National Science Board, *Science Indicators 1980* (Washington, D.C.: National Science Board, 1981).

——, *Science Indicators 1982* (Washington, D.C.: U.S. Government Printing Office, 1983).

Newbould, G.; Thurwell, J.; and Buckley, P., *Going International: The Experience of Smaller Companies Overseas* (New York: Wiley, 1978).

Newfarmer, R., *The International Market Power of Transnational Corporations*, (New York: UNCTAD, 1978).

Oman, C., "Changing International Investment Strategies: The New Forms of Investment in Developing Countries," Working Paper no. 7, OECD Development Center, Paris, 1980.

——,"New Forms of International Investment," Working Paper, OECD Development Center, 1982.

Ozawa, T., *Japan's Technological Challenge to the West, 1950–1974: Motivation and Accomplishment* (Cambridge, Mass.: MIT Press, 1974).

——,"Technology Transfer and Control Systems: The Japanese Experience," a paper delivered at the NSF Conference on Technology Transfer Control Systems in Seattle, April 1979.

Patel, S., "Trademarks and the Third World," *World Development*, Vol. 7 (7), 1979, pp. 653–662.

Perlmutter, H., "The Tortuous Evolution of the Multinational Corporation," *Columbia Journal of World Business*, January 1969, pp. 9–18.

Pugel, T., "The Determinants of Foreign Direct Investment: An Analysis of U.S. Manufacturing Industries," *Managerial and Decision Economics*, December 1981, pp. 220–228.

Robinson, R. D., *National Control of Foreign Business Entry* (New York: Praeger, 1976).

Ronstadt, R., *Research and Development Abroad by U.S. Multinationals* (New York: Praeger, 1977).

Root, F., *Foreign Market Entry Strategies* (New York: AMACOM, 1982).

Root, F., and Ahmed, A., "Empirical Determinants of Manufacturing Direct Foreign Investment in Developing Countries," *Economic Development and Cultural Change*, July 1979, pp. 751–767.

Root, F., and Contractor, F., "Negotiating Compensation in International Licensing Agreements," *Sloan Management Review*, Winter 1981, pp. 23–32.

Rugman, A., "A New Theory of the Multinational Enterprise: Internationalization versus Internalization," *Columbia Journal of World Business*, Spring 1980, pp. 23–29.

Sagasti, F., "National Science and Technology Policies for Development: A Comparative Analysis," in Ramesh, J., and Weiss, C. (eds.), *Mobilizing Technology for World Development* (New York: Praeger, 1979), pp. 162–173.

————, *Technology, Planning and Self-reliant Development: A Latin American View* (New York: Praeger, 1979).

Sato, M., and Bird, R., "International Aspects of the Taxation of Corporations and Shareholders," IMF Staff Paper no. 22, July 1975.

Schollhammer, H., "Organization Structures of Multinational Corporations," *Academy of Management Journal*, September 1971, pp. 345–365.

Schumpeter, J., *Socialism, Capitalism and Democracy*, (New York: Harper & Bros., 1942).

Singh, R., "A View Favoring Collective Bargaining," paper presented at the UNIDO/ LES Symposium on Licensing and the Proposed New International Economic Order, in New York, 1976.

Smith, A., *An Inquiry into the Nature and Causes of the Wealth of Nations*, Cannan, E., (ed.) (Chicago: University of Chicago Press, 1976). Reprint of 1776 edition.

Stobaugh, R., "How to Analyze Foreign Investment Climates," *Harvard Business Review*, September-October 1969, pp. 100–108.

————, *The International Transfer of Technology in the Establishment of Petrochemical Industries in Developing Countries* (New York: United Nations, 1971).

Stoneman, P., "Patenting Activity: A Re-evaluation of the Influence of Demand Pressures," *The Journal of Industrial Economics*, June 1979, pp. 385–401.

Stopford, J., and Wells, L., *Managing the Multinational Enterprise* (New York: Basic Books, 1972).

Taylor, F., *The Principles of Scientific Management* (New York: Norton & Co., 1967).

Teece, D., "The Market for Knowhow and the Efficient International Transfer of Technology," *Annals of the Academy of American Political and Social Sciences*, November 1981, pp. 81–96.

————, *The Multinational Corporation and the Resource Cost of International Technology Transfer* (Cambridge, Mass.: Ballinger, 1977).

Teece, D., and Romeo, A., "Overseas Research and Development by U.S.-Based Firms," *Economica*, May 1979, pp. 187–196.

Telesio, P., "Foreign Licensing Policy in Multinational Enterprises," DBA dissertation, Harvard University, 1977.

UNCTAD, *Major Issues in the Transfer of Technology to Developing Countries: A Case Study of Chile* (New York: United Nations, 1974).

UNIDO, *Guidelines for Evaluation of Transfer of Technology Agreements* (New York: United Nations, 1977, DTTS Series no. 12).

————, *Industrial and Technological Information Bank* (New York: United Nations, 1980, GEN/ID/B/241).

————, *National Approaches to the Acquisition of Technology* (New York: United Nations, 1977).

————,"Systems Affecting Technology," *Les Nouvelles: Journal of the Licensing Executives Society*, March 1982, June 1982, and December 1982.

————, *The Technological Self-reliance of Developing Countries: Towards Operational Strategies* (Vienna: UNIDO, 1979, ICIS. 133).

United Nations, *National Legislation and Regulations Relating to Transnational Corporations* (New York: United Nations, 1977).

United Nations (Center on Transnational Corporations), *Transnational Corporations in World Development: A Re-examination* (New York: United Nations, 1978).

U.S. Department of Commerce, *U.S. Direct Investment Abroad, 1977* (Washington, D.C.: U.S. Government Printing Office, 1981).

U.S. Department of Justice, *Anti-Trust Guide for International Operations* (Washington, D.C.: U.S. Government Printing Office, 1977).

Vancil, R., "What Kind of Management Control Do You Need?," *Harvard Business Review*, March 1973, pp. 75–86.

Wallender, H., "Developing Country Orientations toward Foreign Technology in the Eighties: Implications for New Negotiation Approaches," *Columbia Journal of World Business*, Summer 1980, pp. 21–28.

Ways, M., "The Virtues, Dangers and Limits of Negotiation," *Fortune*, January 15, 1979, pp. 86–90.

Williamson, O., *Markets and Hierarchies: Analysis and Antitrust Implications* (New York: Free Press, 1975).

Wilson, R., "The Effect of Technological Environment and Product Rivalry on R&D Effort and Licensing of Inventions," *Review of Economics and Statistics*, May 1977, pp. 171–178.

Zinberg, D., "Training Foreign Nationals: An Examination of Science/Engineering Education as an Export Commodity," paper presented to the Social Science Research Council, Subcommittee on Science and Technology Indicators, in New York, June 2–3, 1983.

Index

ABOUT THE AUTHOR

Farok J. Contractor is Associate Professor of International Business at the Graduate School of Management, Rutgers University. He is the author of *International Technology Licensing: Compensation, Costs and Negotiations*, and more than twenty scholarly papers on licensing, joint-ventures, and technology transfer.